WWII AIR WAR
The Men · The Machines · The Missions

From the Publisher of

Foreword By Walter J. Boyne

THE NATIONAL HISTORICAL SOCIETY

Cowles Enthusiast Media/History Group
Roger L. Vance - Editorial Director
Carl von Wodtke - Managing Editor
Nan Siegel - Senior Editor
Gregory Lalire - Senior Editor
Ann Thompson - Copy Editor
Alan Webber - Copy Editor
Barbara Sutliff - Creative Director
Gina B. McNeely - Photo and Art Researcher
Bernadette McCarron-Kincheloe - Photo and Art Research Assistant

Thomas G. O'Keefe - History Group Vice President
Gail Ehresmann-Dryer - Associate Group Publisher
John Stanchak - Editorial Director of New Product Development

Cowles Enthusiast Media/Creative Publishing
Elroy Balgaard - Senior Art Director
Cincy Owens - Senior Project Manager

COWLES Enthusiast Media

Library of Congress Cataloging-in-Publication Data
World War II airwars: the men, the machines, the missions.p. cm.
ISBN 0-86573-858-0 1. World War, 1939-1945--Aerial operations.
2. Air Warfare. 3. Aeronautics, Military. I. Cowles Creative Publishing.
D785.W65 1996   940.54'42--dc21   96-47007 CIP

To order additional copies of this book, call
(800) 358-6327.
To subscribe to *Aviation History* or *World War II* Magazines, call
(800) 829-3340 or outside U.S. (904) 446-6914.

Contents

Foreword...5

Introduction..7

THE MEN

I.   Guts and Glory in the RAF
     By William B. Allmon............................10

II. Flying Circus Over the Pacific
     By John Stanaway..................................18

III. Air War's Top Ace
     By Wil Deac..28

IV. Butch O'Hare: "Friendly Fire" Victim?
     By John G. Leyden................................38

V.   Wolfpack at War
     By Don Hollway....................................46

VI. Battling the Zeros Over New Guinea
     First Person by Richard J. Vodra...........56

THE MACHINES

VII. Zero: Flimsy Killer
     By Bruce Crawford...............................68

VIII. Eagle Flies a Mustang
     By John Stanaway.................................74

IX. Avenger!
     By Jerry Scutts.....................................82

X.   Buzz Bomb Blasts Britain
     By David Alan Johnson.........................94

XI. The Bomb That Ended World War II
     By C.V. Glines....................................104

THE MISSIONS

XII. First Strike Against Japan
     By C.V. Glines....................................116

XIII. The Cactus Air Force: A Thorn in Japan's Side
     By Don Hollway.................................126

XIV. Whose Kill Was It?
     By C.V. Glines....................................136

XV. Ruhr Dam Raids
     By Daniel Wyatt.................................148

XVI. Luftwaffe's Intruders of the Night
     By Timothy J. Kutta...........................158

XVII. The Surrender Flight That Almost Failed
     By Robert C. Mikesh..........................166

Photo and art credits 176

The 50th anniversary of the end of World War II was celebrated with pageantry and pomp around the Allied world amidst a tidal wave of books that recapped everything from global warfare to individual skirmishes. As the year of celebration drew to a close, publishers nodded sagely at one another and said, "Well, that's that for World War II—what's next on the agenda?"

They could not have been more wrong. Public interest in the greatest of all conflicts has been sustained at a high level for a variety of reasons. On the one hand, the Korean and Vietnam wars were so unsatisfactory in their outcome and in their political conduct that many people do not wish to be reminded of them. On the other hand, the Gulf War was so brief, and so technologically one-sided, that it does not command a sufficient audience.

Yet the scope of World War II explains only part of the continuing fascination rivaling that focused in the United States on the Civil War. This compendium of stories is the real reason: People are interested in World War II because its events, desperate as they were, represent the best responses of individuals of all nations under pressure. The interest is apolitical; we can as readily applaud the steadfastness and bravery of the enemy as we can that of our own troops. Here each case—fighter against fighter, long-distance raids, the introduction of new tactics—always boils down to individuals doing their superb best under adverse circumstances.

And we know that it goes deeper than the pilot in the cockpit. We know he would not have been there if a grunting mechanic had not spent a night breaking his knuckles to get the aircraft airborne. Going further back, the battle would not have taken place if individual factory workers had not built the aircraft well or if individual engineers had not designed it for its job.

This is the paradox and the fascination of World War II. It raged from continent to continent, from ocean to ocean, in skies in every corner of the world. Resources were spent by the billions, troops were mustered by the millions, but in the end, each contest boiled down to how well individuals did at every level—and in them, we like to see ourselves.

If there is any glory in warfare—and only an inveterate pessimist would say that there is not—it comes from the individual human effort so well represented in this excellent selection of stories. Let us all hope there is never another world war, even as we hope that the individual effort involved in World War II will always be with us.

Walter J. Boyne
Ashburn, Virginia

Introduction

Pilots, man your planes!

...for a flight into adventure above the quagmire of muddy shell holes, above the pitching decks—above everything except those "other planes" that come up to try to send you down in flames. This is World War II in the air, the battle on high to help resolve the conflict on the ground.

It is the story of *The Men, The Machines* and *The Missions* brought to life in words and pictures by those who were there and those who dug out the details to take you there, in fighters and bombers, over Europe and the Pacific, but always in a heady environment of noise, anxiety, suspense—and surprise. You are in the cockpit as Cowles History Group brings you these stories specially selected to bring aerial combat to life, and to give you insight into the rapid development of air war technology spurred by that conflict.

The basic principles of aerial warfare were already in place and evolving during the interwar years of the 1920s and '30s, but the Allies needed newer, better aircraft and flight techniques quickly to catch up with aggressive belligerents and to overpower them. Follow the design of aircraft from highly maneuverable but slow biplanes into sleek, all-metal monoplanes that climbed higher and flew faster than could have been imagined by even the shrewdest air tacticians at the beginning of the war.

At the outset of World War II, fighter pilots took off after enemy aircraft directed by rudimentary ground radar—to find them with what was referred to as the Mark I "eyeball," and to pump lead into them with traditional machine guns. By the end of the war, on-board radar enabled aviators to find air and ground targets in the day, at night, and in poor weather and to down enemy aircraft with rockets—or destroy cities with a single atomic bomb.

Read in these pages how the once-invincible Japanese "Zero" fighter was tamed in "Zero: Flimsy Killer" and how North American B-25 bombers under the command of Jimmy Doolittle retaliated for the surprise Japanese attack on Pearl Harbor in "First Strike Against Japan." Recall the heroism of Britain's famous leg-less ace Douglas Bader in "Guts and Glory in the RAF" and learn about American P-38 pilots Dick Bong and Tom Lynch's exploits in "Flying Circus Over the Pacific." Taste the glory of *Luftwaffe* pilot Erich Hartmann's more than 350 air victories in "Air War's Top Ace" and experience the tragic loss of one of our own greatest aces in "Butch O'Hare: 'Friendly Fire' Victim?" These are but a few of the several accounts that bring to life the famous words of then British Prime Minister Winston Churchill when he referred to war as "blood, toil, tears and sweat."

These stories of World War II reflect the range of articles found in regular issues of *Aviation History* magazine, which has been bringing the technology and personalities of aviation's rich heritage to readers for nearly seven years. It continues to be the sole U.S. magazine devoted exclusively to the presentation of aviation history, reflecting all of the "ages" of aviation around the world. The collection you will read in these pages focuses on the World War II air conflict. However, regular issues of *Aviation History* continue to provide a balanced mix of civil and military subjects, covering the various stages of aviation from the first balloon flights in the late 1700s to the advent of the jet age.

We hope you enjoy reading this collection of accounts about aviation during World War II as much as we enjoyed putting the anthology together. Special thanks go to the employees of Cowles History Group and Cowles Creative Publishing, who burned the midnight oil to select the best stories, photographs and artwork, and who researched, edited, proofread, managed and designed this book. The finished product you have before you is a reflection of their combined efforts.

So, in the affected casualness of the combat pilot preparing to take off on a mission from which he may or may not return, let's "kick the tires, light the fires and go!" Shove the throttles into full power and take off with us into the fury, the thrill and the moments of terror that define aerial combat.

Enjoy the adventure...and Happy Landings!

Arthur H. Sanfelici
Editor, *Aviation History*

THE MEN

I

GUTS AND GLORY IN THE RAF

Cocky, capable—and legless—Douglas Bader was a pain to RAF bosses and German pilots alike.

By William B. Allmon

F ew men become legends in their lifetime. Douglas Bader was one of these men. *Enfant terrible*, fighter ace, international sportsman, inveterate rule-breaker and incorrigible escaper, he spread exasperation and irritation wherever he went. Yet his courage and determination in the face of crippling injuries continue to inspire people all over the world to this day.

Douglas Robert Steuart Bader was born on February 10, 1910, in London, England, son of Frederick Roberts Bader and Jessie Bader. From the start, his life followed no placid pattern. When Douglas was a few months old, his family returned to India, where his father worked as a civil engineer. Young Douglas was left behind because his family thought him too young for India's harsh climate. He did not rejoin them until he was 2 years old, beginning a long life as a loner.

The Bader family returned to England in 1913. The following year, when World War I began, Frederick Bader went with the British army into France. It was the last time Douglas saw his father, who died in France of complications from a shrapnel wound in 1922 and was buried near the town of St. Omer. Twenty-one years later, his son would be held prisoner in a hospital not far from where his father was buried.

Jessie Bader later married a mild Yorkshire clergyman, Reverend William Hobbs, who was swiftly and rudely awakened to his intransigent new family. Douglas and his younger brother Derick routinely robbed family prayers of their reverence by scuffles and giggles.

Throughout his early years, Douglas showed a fierce spirit of independence and nonconformity. He excelled in sports such as rugby football; when he was captain of the rugby team, his natural leadership abilities became apparent. He later became captain of the cricket team at St. Edwards School, Oxford, at age 15 and won every senior race he entered.

In 1923, Douglas stayed with his aunt Hazel Bader and her husband, Flight Lieutenant Cyril Burge, who at the time was adjutant at the Royal Air Force (RAF) college in Cranwell.

"Seeing airplanes at close quarters for the first time excited him greatly," Paul Brickhill, Bader's biographer, later wrote, "and he stood for hours in Burge's garden watching the cadets jockey the quivering wood and fabric biplanes round the circuit." Nevertheless, at that time young Douglas was more interested in the sporting life at the college than in flying.

In 1927, Douglas tried to figure out what he wanted to become. He decided against attending Oxford University but remained unsure about what he wanted to do until an RAF cadet visited St. Edwards. As a result, Douglas decided he wanted to fly in the RAF.

His mother told him that she did not like flying and that she and his stepfather could not afford the annual fee of 150 pounds

Returning from intercepting a German attack on Britain in late August 1940, Squadron Leader Douglas Bader, leader of No. 242 Squadron, RAF, brings his Hawker Hurricane I in for a landing, in Descent to Duxford, *by Charles J. Thompson.*

at Cranwell. The only route open to Douglas was to try for one of six free cadetships offered each year; they drew hundreds of applicants even though there was a very stiff entrance examination.

Encouraged by his housemaster, Bader studied for months, working hardest at improving his weakest subject—math.

In the summer of 1928 he took the written exam, which he found fairly straightforward. He scored 235 points out of a possible 250. Bader soon received word from the Air Ministry that he had placed fifth in the examination and had won his cadetship.

Bader reported to Cranwell in September 1928, and his flight training went satisfactorily. He soloed after 6½ hours of dual instruction. Standing a muscular 5 feet 10 inches, Bader had, in the words of his biographer, "the athlete's coordination of eye, mind and muscle that makes the deftest airman."

Not all of his flying was regulation. Sometimes on solo flights Bader would climb out of the rear cockpit in midair, straddle the fuselage and tie a handkerchief around the control stick in the front cockpit, all without a parachute.

To his fellow cadets, Bader was a super youth, but his superiors did not like his rebellious nature. Halfway through the two-year course, when the cadets took progress exams, Bader came out 18th out of 21 cadets. Cranwell's commandant, Air Vice Marshal Halahan, warned him: "You're young, I can understand your trouble, but the air force won't go on understanding. They want men here, not school boys."

Bader emerged from Halahan's tirade considerably shaken, knowing the commandant was right. He studied harder, and his flying became better than ever.

Bader missed being awarded the sword of honor, which was given to the top graduating cadet, but he came in a close second. After graduating from Cranwell in 1930, Bader was commissioned a pilot officer and posted to No. 23 Squadron at Kenley Airfield, flying tubby Gloster Gamecock biplane fighters. He settled effortlessly into squadron life, earning a reputation as an athlete, teetotaler and superb acrobatic pilot.

Soon afterward, 23 Squadron was re-equipped with Bristol Bulldog fighters. The Bulldogs were faster than the Gamecocks but heavier and liable to loose height rapidly in low-altitude maneuvers.

On Monday, December 14, 1931, Douglas Bader flew from Kenley to Woodley airfield along with two other pilots from his squadron. In the Woodley clubhouse a young pilot was discussing acrobatics with Bader, the Hendon star, and suggested that he give a demonstration of low flying. Bader refused, citing his inexperience flying acrobatics in a Bulldog. The matter was dropped until Bader and the other pilots were leaving. Another pilot suggested it again, Bader refused, and someone dared him to do it.

In some agitation Bader took off, then turned back toward the field. Flying low and fast across the field, Bader began a slow roll, but in his inexperience with the Bulldog he flew too low. The Bulldog's left wing struck the ground, and the plane cartwheeled quickly into a tangle of wreckage. Both of Bader's legs were crushed, his left leg under the seat, his right torn by the rudder pedal.

Bader was pulled from the Bulldog's wreckage by shocked onlookers and taken immediately to the Royal Berkshire Hospital, where he was placed in the care of Dr. Leonard Joyce, one of England's best surgeons. Joyce immediately amputated Bader's right leg above the smashed knee, which did not take long–it was almost off already.

For a time, there was hope that Bader's left leg could be saved. Then, several days later, gangrene set in. With no choice, Joyce amputated the leg six inches below the knee.

After his second amputation, Bader's condition worsened. None of the doctors expected the 21-year-old pilot to live. Then he overheard one nurse warning another to be quiet, "There's a boy dying in there."

That was intolerable to him. Bader rallied and began to recover. He was never to fear dying again.

After a long, painful recovery, Bader was transferred to the RAF Hospital in Uxbridge in 1932. While there, he became acquainted with the Dessoutter brothers. Marcel Dessoutter had been an aircraft designer until he, too, lost a leg in an air crash. Afterward he started a firm that made artificial legs of light metal alloys like aluminum. Douglas Bader was the first customer to require two artificial legs.

Despite the physical impediment, Bader began to remake his life both physically and mentally. After several months of agonizing and determined effort, Bader learned to walk on both "tin" legs. He refused to use a walking stick, saying, "I'm going to start the way I mean to go on."

He soon began driving a car again, with the pedals modified to accommodate his tin legs. Bader's thoughts then returned to flying. After a weekend spent with the Under-secretary of State for Air, Sir Phillip Sasson, in June 1932, Bader's desire to fly reached fever pitch. His host, who lived near Lympe airfield, arranged a flight for him in an Avro 504 trainer.

Bader's handling of the Avro left nothing to be desired. Later, an RAF medical board found him fit for restricted flying duties.

Soon afterward, in April 1933, Bader was informed by the air force that he was to be retired on grounds of ill health, which left him feeling shocked and numb. Within weeks, Bader left the RAF on a total disability pension.

For six years following his retirement from the RAF, Bader worked at a desk job with the Asiatic (now Shell) Petroleum company. His future, at least at the beginning, looked bleak, but he was lucky in his marriage to Thelma Edwards, whom he met while at Uxbridge when she was working as a waitress at a pub called the Pantiles. They married in 1935, and she was devoted to him for 37 years. Once asked how he survived, Bader replied, "I wouldn't have stuck it out without Thelma."

Bader's defiant spirit, which made no concessions to his disability, found expression in a return to sports. He took up tennis and squash and became interested in golf. (Years later, he had reduced his golf handicap to two.) Despite his new life, however, Bader longed to fly again.

In September 1939, after the start of World War II, Bader again applied to the RAF for flight duties and was helped in his quest by an old squadron friend, Geoffrey Stephenson, who was posted to the Air Ministry. He attended a selection board headed by his old Cranwell commanding officer, Air Vice Marshal Halahan. "I have known this officer since he was a cadet at Cranwell under my command," Halahan wrote. "If he is fit, apart from his legs, I suggest you give him A1B (flying duties) category and leave it to the Central Flying School to assess his flying abilities."

Bader walked out of the Air Ministry "feeling that the wasted

Supermarine Spitfires of No. 610 Auxiliary Squadron set out to take on German fighters during the Battle of Britain. The unit became part of Bader's Tangmere Wing in March 1941.

years were canceled" and that he was picking up life again from the moment he had crashed. Bader's acceptance was conditional on his passing a flying test at the RAF's Central Flying School (CFS) in Upavon.

On November 27, 1939, eight years after his accident, Douglas Bader flew solo again at the controls of Avro Tudor K-3242. Once airborne, he could not resist the temptation to turn the Tudor biplane upside down at 600 feet inside the circuit area. The chief flight instructor reported the stunt to Rupert Leigh, an instructor at CFS and another classmate of Bader's. "I know who it was," the chief instructor said coldly. "Be good enough to ask him not to break *all* the flying regulations straight away."

Bader soon moved up into the Fairey Battle, a single-engine, two-seater day bomber, then to the Miles Master, the last step an RAF pilot took before going on to Supermarine Spitfires and Hawker

Two Hurricanes of No. 501 Squadron take off to intercept enemy bombers during the Battle of Britain. The one on the left is flown by Flying Officer K.N.T. Lee, who scored six victories.

Hurricanes. Two weeks after flying the Master, Bader was delighted to get his chance inside the cockpit of a Hurricane. From the start he felt a part of the Hurricane, which was the most responsive aircraft he had yet flown; after 20 minutes in the air, he made a smooth landing.

In February 1940, Bader joined No. 19 Squadron at Duxford. At age 29 he was older than most of the other pilots in the squadron. Two months later he was appointed flight commander in 222 Squadron, another Duxford-based unit, re-equipping from Blenheim bombers to Spitfires.

Before he took up the appointment, Bader carelessly took off with his section with his Spitfire's propeller set to coarse pitch (used for low rpm cruise) instead of fine pitch that gave high rpm for takeoff power, and he crashed. Bader was uninjured, except for bent legs and a badly dented ego. Shocked by his stupidity, Bader freely admitted his mistake to 12 Group's commander, Air Vice Marshal Trafford Leigh Mallory, who saw it as a one-time mistake

and did not cancel Bader's appointment to 222 Squadron as flight commander, or his promotion to flight lieutenant.

Bader immediately began training his 222 flight pilots in his own style of fighting, quick to see that the standard Fighter Command tactics were a waste of time. Afterward came hours of dogfighting practice and convoy patrols.

Yet nothing happened at Duxford for 222 Squadron until June 1940. The squadron was sent, along with other RAF squadrons, to cover the British and French evacuation from Dunkirk. On one mission over Dunkirk, while leading his flight after some fleeing Messerschmitt Me-110s, Bader sighted four Me-109s approaching his flight.

Bader went after the German fighters. "A 109 shot up in front; his thumb jabbed the firing button and the guns in the wings squirted with a shocking noise," wrote Brickhill. The 109 burst into flames and spun into the ground—Bader's first kill.

In June 1940, Bader was given command of 242 Squadron. A Canadian unit, the only one in the RAF at the time, 242 had been badly mauled in France, and its morale was low. When Bader first arrived at the squadron's headquarters at Coltishall airfield, most of the squadron's pilots were skeptical of their new legless squadron leader, who they thought would lead them from his desk. Bader quickly dispelled the idea by taking one of 242's Hurricane fighters and performing acrobatics over Coltishall for a half hour, deeply impressing 242's pilots.

Bader quickly transformed 242 into a tight, tough squadron through his courage, leadership and uncompromising attitude toward his pilots, ground crews and the RAF high command, with whom he soon had a major brush.

After taking charge of 242 Squadron, Bader soon discovered that the unit did not have the spare parts or tools to keep its 18 Hurricane fighters operational.

After trying to sort out the problem through official channels, Bader signaled 12th Group Headquarters: "242 Squadron operational as regards pilots but nonoperational as regards equipment." And he refused to announce his squadron as operational until its lack of tools and spares was rectified. It took a direct meeting between Squadron Leader Bader and Fighter Command's comman-

Jumped by Adolf Galland, wing commander of Jagdgeschwader 26, Bader escapes by outmaneuvering him, in Duel of Eagles, painted by Robert Taylor with the consultation of both aces.

der, Air Chief Marshal Sir Hugh Dowding, to correct the mess. Within 24 hours, 242 Squadron had all the tools and spares it needed, and Bader signaled 12th Group: "242 Squadron now fully operational."

The squadron, however, took little part in the early stages of the Battle of Britain, flying only convoy patrols and going after occasional high-flying Dornier bombers. Bader shot down one of these on July 11 during a rainstorm that prevented him from getting a section of fighters off the ground. Bader took off alone in a Hurricane, found the Dornier despite the bad weather, and attacked it. He killed its tail gunner and saw it disappear into a cloud. Certain it had gotten away, Bader returned to base. Five minutes after he landed, Bader was informed that a ground observer had seen the Dornier crash into the sea.

On August 30, 242 Squadron intercepted a group of 30 German

bombers and fighters attacking North Weald airfield. Bader shot down an Me-110, and the rest of his squadron claimed 11 kills. It was a respectable total, but Bader believed that if they had had three or more squadrons attacking the huge German formation, all of the attacking planes would have been shot down.

Thus, the "Big Wing" concept was born. Supported by Leigh Mallory, Bader was convinced that launching a large number of fighter squadrons against the *Luftwaffe* armadas was essential for the RAF's success in the battle. Leigh Mallory decided to try Bader's wing in action. He grouped 242 with two other fighter squadrons—19 Squadron and the Czech 310 Squadron—at Duxford. Bader led the wing into action for the first time on September 7, 1940, against a large German formation heading for London.

"We had been greatly looking forward to our first formation of 36 fighters going into action together," Bader wrote years later, "but we were unlucky." Having been scrambled late, the wing was underneath the bombers and their fighter escorts when they intercepted them north of the Thames. All 242 and 310 could do was attack as best they could while 19 Squadron's Spitfires tried to hold off the attacking Me-109s.

The wing managed to destroy 11 aircraft, with only two Hurricanes shot down. Bader himself got a cockpit full of bullets and the right aileron shot off his Hurricane.

After several sorties with three squadrons, two more—the Polish 302 Hurricane Squadron and Auxiliary 601 Spitfire Squadron—were added to the so-called Duxford Wing, giving it five squadrons and 60 fighters. "We thus had three Hurricane Squadrons which flew together at the lower level (20,000 feet if we were called in time) with the Spitfires protecting us 5,000 feet higher," Bader said. "It worked like a charm once or twice, and the arrival of this large formation in support of hard-pressed 11 Group squadrons was highly satisfactory." The tactic really paid off on September 15, 1940, when Bader's Duxford Wing helped 11 Group to break up a massed *Luftwaffe* attack on London.

When the Battle of Britain ended, Bader was awarded the Distinguished Flying Cross (DFC) and Distinguished Service Order (DSO) for gallantry and leadership of the highest order and became commander of the Duxford Wing, which was later credited with destroying 152 German aircraft with the loss of 30 pilots. The Big Wing's effectiveness became controversial—but not Douglas Bader's leadership of it.

In March 1941, Bader, now a wing commander, left 242 Squadron and took over the "Tangmere Wing." Consisting of three Spitfire Squadrons—145, 610 and 616—plus a Beaufighter squadron, the wing began a series of air attacks against targets in northern France and the Low Countries.

While commanding the wing, Bader introduced the so-called "finger four" formation, where the two pairs of fighters flew beside each other, scrapping forever the unwieldy three-aircraft section. Based on the *Luftwaffe's Schwarm* formation, the finger four later became standard throughout both the British and American air forces.

Bader really came into his own commanding the Tangmere Wing. His teamwork with Wing Commander A.G. Woodhall, the ground controller during the wing's raids, was exceptional. Receiving the broad picture from the ground controller, Bader handled his three squadrons with remarkable dexterity, seemingly able to foresee the critical points in an upcoming engagement. He was able to keep track of events around him to a remarkable degree. "Dogsbody" (the call sign for Bader's wing) became an unwelcome and frequent visitor to the other side of the English Channel.

Often, coming back across the Channel after a mission, Bader would flip back the canopy of his Spitfire, unclip his oxygen mask and, while holding the stick between his good knee and his tin knee, light up his pipe. Pilots flying alongside Spitfire DB would sheer off, half in jest and half in earnest, in case Bader's plane blew up.

For his brilliant and inspiring leadership of the Tangmere Wing—which he christened "The Bee Line Bus Service. The prompt and regular service. Return tickets only"—Bader was awarded a bar to his DSO.

Bader seemed invincible—but he was not. While leading his wing over France on August 9, 1941, he was downed by a Messerschmitt Me-109 and captured by the Germans. He would spend most of the war in captivity, including time at the castle-prison Colditz.

Finally, in the spring of 1945, the American First Army took Colditz, liberating its prisoners, including Bader. Once released, he rushed to Paris demanding a Spitfire for one last fling before the war ended. Permission was refused; Bader's personal tally would stand at 22½ German aircraft destroyed.

Bader returned to England and took command of the Fighter Leader School at Tangmere, where he was promoted to group captain. Later that year he commanded the Essex sector of 11th Group at North Weald, and on September 15, he personally led the victory flypast of 300 RAF planes over London.

The RAF offered him the rank and seniority he would have enjoyed if he had not been shot down, but Bader felt the peacetime

Bader (fourth from right) with the predominantly Canadian flying personnel of No. 242 Squadron. He quickly dispelled suspicions that he planned to lead the squadron from behind a desk.

air force would be anticlimactic after his wartime experiences.

Shell Oil Company offered him a job in its aviation department, with his own airplane. Bader thought about it for four months, then resigned from the Royal Air Force for the last time. Sir James Robb, chief of Fighter Command, wrote Bader, "All I can say is that you are leaving behind an example which as the years go by will become a legend."

After leaving the RAF in late February 1946, Bader flew all over the world, often with Thelma, touring Europe, Africa and America. He spent many hours visiting veterans hospitals.

In 1976 Bader was knighted by Queen Elizabeth for his services to amputees, "so many of whom he had helped and inspired by his example and character."

After Thelma's death, he married Joan Murray, who shared his interest in public work for the disabled. His workload would have been exhausting for anyone, let alone a legless man with a worsening heart condition, but iron willpower drove him on until August 1982, when he suffered a mild heart attack after a golf tour-

nament in Ayrshire. Three weeks later, on September 5, 1982, after serving as guest speaker at a London Guildhall dinner honoring the 90th birthday of the Marshal of the Royal Air Force, Sir Arthur "Bomber" Harris, Douglas Bader died of a heart attack. He was 72 years old.

"He became a legend at first in the personification of RAF heroism during the Second World War," the *London Times* obituary said. "And in the years that followed a shining example of that defiant courage that overcomes disablement and refuses to accept that anything is impossible."

Bader's brother-in-law, Wing Commander P.B. "Laddie" Lucas, himself a distinguished RAF pilot, said of Bader, "One thing is certain; historians will never find another like him."

II

FLYING CIRCUS OVER THE PACIFIC

Dick Bong and Tom Lynch teamed up in their P-38s to terrorize the Japanese air force.

By John Stanaway

January 1944 was something of a dividing point in the progress of World War II Allied air operations. In Europe, the U.S. Eighth Air Force was mounting its strategic bombing campaign against German industry, and a faltering *Luftwaffe* was about to receive crushing blows that would hasten its decline throughout the spring and summer.

Similarly, the Japanese encroachment in the Southwest Pacific was being rolled back in New Guinea. Saidor, the first base west of the Huon Gulf to fall, was invaded in January. By the end of April, the last major Japanese base, Hollandia, had fallen, clearing the northern New Guinea coast below the Vogelkop Peninsula.

The fighter battles that spearheaded this progress in the air war produced some extraordinary comradeship between individual pilots. Earlier in the war, there was the unlikely pairing of the Royal Air Force's Irish fighter ace Brendan "Paddy" Finucane and the Australian Keith "Bluey" Truscott. Later, over Europe, Americans Don Gentile and John Godfrey achieved remarkable records in their North American P-51 Mustangs during March and April 1944.

Among the pilots who flew together in the Pacific, at least two symbolized growing Allied strength in the air. One of these was Dick Bong, an agreeable youngster who would eventually become the top-ranking American fighter ace of all time. The other was Tom Lynch, also a popular young pilot who displayed great potential and leadership in the air. He had commanded the 39th Fighter Squadron in mid-1943 and had seen it emerge as the top-scoring outfit in the entire Fifth Air Force.

Bong, especially, would emerge as a local icon. Everyone from bomber commanders to PT-boat crewmen claimed they could pick out his Lockheed P-38 Lightning flying overhead, and they would be cheered by the myth of his invincibility. (One bomber commander claimed that other P-38s would tend to disappear after initial contact with the Japanese over the hot target of Rabaul, New Britain, but that Bong was always evident, his distinctive P-38 darting in and out of the formations under attack.)

Lynch and Bong were much alike in their devotion to combat missions. Both men had been assigned to the 39th Fighter Squadron when it began operating the twin-engine P-38 fighter over eastern New Guinea. Lynch already had claimed three Japanese aircraft shot down while flying Bell P-39 Airacobras, and he became an ace on December 27, 1942, during the first significant P-38 mission in the theater. Bong scored his first kill during the same mission and had become an ace by January 8, 1943.

One major difference between the two men probably contributed greatly to Bong's becoming the foremost American ace. Aside from being a dedicated combat pilot, Lynch was a born engineer with a mathematical approach to problem-solving. While

Captain Richard I. Bong and Lt. Col. Thomas J. Lynch battle Japanese Kawasaki Ki.61 Hiens, in Mission to Tadji, *by Jack Fellows. Lynch shot down one of the* Hiens, *known to the Americans as "Tonys," during the March 3, 1944, fight.*

Bong was a naturally excellent pilot with the innate ability to master the art of flying, Lynch focused on the technical matters of airmanship. When Bong flew in one of Lynch's formations, he took Lynch's after-mission critiques to heart.

Most of the 39th Squadron pilots who flew with Lynch accepted him as their sometime mentor. He understood the science of air fighting and methodically passed on its principles to his squadron mates. Bong not only accepted Lynch's tutelage but also came to consider him his closest friend.

Lynch ended his first combat tour and handed over command of the 39th Fighter Squadron to Captain Charles King—another ace and respected leader of the unit—late in September 1943. It had been a rugged 16 months for Lynch. Japanese bullets had obliged him to exit his P-38 over the sea, and he broke his arm while bailing out. The P-38 had exploded when it hit the water. Lynch had been picked up by a native boat soon afterward. He had neglected to inflate his brand-new life vest, choosing to swim to the boat with the broken arm because of the stories of sharks he had heard.

Other factors, such as bouts with dengue fever and the natural wearing down of his youthful energy on prolonged operations, dictated a rest, and Lynch was home by the beginning of October. He was hailed in his hometown of Catasauqua, Pa., as one of the top aces of the day, with 16 credited kills. He shared the honor with Bong and Captain George Welch, who also flew in New Guinea and had claimed four of his victories during the Pearl Harbor attack.

By now Lynch was 26 years old and a major in the U.S. Army Air Forces (USAAF). He capped his moment of glory by marrying his Seton Hall College sweetheart, Rosemary Fullen, on October 23, 1943. They had become engaged before Lynch left the University of Pittsburgh to go to war, and now he was returning as a hero to rejoin his sweetheart in the most romantic tradition.

The newlyweds' pleasant interlude lasted until Lynch's personal leave ended on November 15 and he reported back to Washington for assignment conferences prior to his return to the Pacific. At approximately the same time, Bong also returned a hero—to his hometown of Poplar, Wis. While Lynch was arguing persua-sively for his second tour in a combat area, Bong arrived home just in time for the deer-hunting season.

During their respective leaves, both Bong and Lynch were permitted by the Army to express their views to the press. Even viewed through the veil of perpetual censorship exercised by the wartime military, one can get some idea of the genuine feelings of these two fighter aces.

Lynch, as was noted before, was the technician. He lived by probabilities and the law of averages. Flying, to him, was a matter of eliminating uncertainties in taking off, controlling the aircraft in flight, and successfully making a good landing. Fighting was simply seeing the enemy first and destroying him with superior firepower. When he was asked what he would do if he saw a Zero in his rearview mirror, Lynch answered that it was too late for anything if a capable enemy got that close.

Fear in combat was something that Lynch readily admitted. He was able to translate that fear into an edge of excitement, as have many other successful fighter pilots. Always aggressive in battle, he also had a reputation for amazing clarity in his observations and deadly precision in his judgment. Two of his earliest kills were confirmed by an Australian patrol that found the wrecks lying close together in the New Guinea bush exactly where Lynch said he had seen them going down.

Part of Lynch's confidence in combat was enhanced by the P-38's performance. "[The P-38] is some ship—no fooling," he said. "The Zeros might have outmaneuvered us, but we had the speed, the firepower and the protection; we went to town."

Dick Bong was back in Wisconsin because of a promise by Fifth Air Force Commander General George Kenney to send him home on leave when he got more than 20 kills to his credit. Like the exuberant youth he was, Bong had scheduled his 20th—and 21st—kill in time to return for the deer-hunting season in his home state. He despised the adulation and hero worship that he knew were waiting for him, but he naturally wanted to be there.

Bong was in the United States at the same time Lynch was there, but apparently their paths did not cross. Bong was free until he also reported to Washington in the middle of December. Of course, since he was acknowledged as the top U.S. Army fighter

ace, he was besieged by the press for his opinions. He repeated the views expressed by Lynch that the P-38 was his favorite airplane, that the Japanese pilot standards were declining, but that they were still formidable.

It was not until he had been sent back to the Pacific that Bong mailed a letter home to his mother about his younger brother, who intended to join the USAAF. In a letter dated April 10, 1944, he offered this advice: "He must not get contemptuous of any airplane, no matter how simple and easy it may be to fly....Don't just get in and fly it, but know what makes it tick....If he forgets, why, any airplane in the world can kill him if he isn't its complete master."

By the first week of January 1944, Lynch was back in the Pacific, and Bong followed within a few weeks. Major Lynch was now the

Bong's P-38J-15, in April 1944—before Bong added an enlarged photo of his fiancee, Marjorie Vattendahl, to the port gun bay door on its nacelle. Bong and Lynch were among the first pilots to receive uncamouflaged P-38s.

operations officer for V Fighter Command, and Bong was assigned directly to his office.

Captain Richard Bong's flight record form (referred to as the Form 5) lists his first combat mission after his return to New Guinea as a 1¾-hour flight to Nubia, about midway between Alexishafen and Wewak. That probably was one of the first of the Bong and Lynch two-plane missions. In writing home, both pilots dismissed the danger of the missions as something like "having fun without risking [our] neck[s]."

Soon the flights became known as "the Flying Circus," partly because Bong and Lynch would tag along with any unit or formation that was likely to see action. Young P-38 pilots would feel a bit more secure with the talent that had hitched onto their flight, and would expect to witness quite a show if enemy aircraft were encountered.

Another reason for the appellation was that, because of their special duties and assignment, the two pilots had their pick of new and not-yet-camouflaged P-38J-15-LO models coming into the theater late in January. Bong selected one (J-15, serial no. 42-103993) and painted distinctive red nose and tail markings on it. He had met his future wife, Marge Vattendahl, during his leave and was so smitten with her that he later had a photo of her enlarged and hand-tinted to be mounted on the port gun bay door of his fighter. Lynch used a simpler white-and-dark-striped motif on the spinners and tail of his P-38J-15, serial no. 42-103987.

The first real combat that the two pilots experienced together was during a fighter sweep over Tadji, northwest of Wewak, on February 10, 1944. They took off a few minutes after 2 p.m. from their base at Nadzab. Patrolling over Tadji airstrip for just a few minutes at 15,000 feet, they noticed six single-engine fighters taking off in one direction while a twin-engine airplane was just becoming airborne from a different runway.

Lynch decided that the lone twin-engine plane was the logical target. He called for Bong to follow him down, and both planes released the long-range external tanks attached beneath their inboard wings. The diving P-38s came down and caught the hapless Japanese just a few hundred feet off the ground and only one-quarter mile from the Tadji strip. Only one burst was required for Lynch to set the right wing aflame. Bong witnessed the burning plane plunge straight into the ground.

Fifth Air Force leaders were aware of the boost in morale that the Flying Circus potentially offered and bent over backward to not impede it. Lynch was his own boss, and Bong's chief responsibility was counting new fighters coming into V Fighter Command, a job that hardly consumed every waking minute.

It was Bong's turn to perform the next time the pair engaged the enemy. A major U.S. air raid against Kavieng, New Ireland, took off on the morning of February 15, 1944. Every available fighter was needed to escort a mixed force of Consolidated B-24 Liberators, North American B-25 Mitchells and Douglas A-20 Havoc light bombers. Bong and Lynch jumped at the chance and were in the air by 7:30 a.m.

There was no interception over Kavieng Harbor itself, and the Flying Circus had to content itself with covering the A-20s. Anti-aircraft fire was generally ineffective against the high-flying B-24s, but did score some success against the B-25s and A-20s. After the last American raider cleared the harbor, Bong and Lynch left for home. Approximately 10 miles north of Cape Hoskins, in the Kimbe Bay region, the two Americans sighted a lone Kawasaki Ki.61 "Tony" fighter, whose pilot apparently had no idea that enemy fighters were in the area, flying placidly toward Rabaul.

Bong took the initiative and dived quickly and gracefully onto the tail of the Tony—sleek, silvery and with a distinctive pointed nose. A deadly burst of fire from close range caused the fighter to explode, and this time Lynch watched it spin all the way to the water below.

Air-to-air victories were the stuff aces were made of, and most American air units operating against the Japanese did not bother to count enemy aircraft destroyed on the ground, even though, in the case of the Fifth Air Force, ground kills may well have represented as much as half the total. Bong got at least one ground kill while he and Lynch flew together. A Japanese radio message was intercepted late in the afternoon of February 28, almost too late for anything to be done about it, revealing that some Japanese staff officers were en route from Rabaul to Wewak. Bong and Lynch were in the air almost as soon as they got the word at 4:30 p.m.

They arrived over Wewak a few minutes after 6 and sighted a twin-engine bomber just landing. Both P-38s came down from 9,000 feet and started a pass as the Japanese plane—it looked like a Mitsubishi G4M "Betty" in the transport mode with all guns removed—taxied to a stop. Lynch made the first attack; between 60 and 70 people who were gathered to meet the plane scattered like ants.

The only visible result of Lynch's pass was to make the people

Pilots of the 39th Fighter Squadron in 1943. Left to right, front row: Charles Sullivan, Tom Lynch and Ken Sparks; back row: Richard Suehr, John Lane and Stanley Andrews.

in the open take cover. But Bong was right behind. The transport's propellers had just ceased turning over when bullets from Bong's P-38 ripped into the wings and fuselage, causing the aircraft to erupt into flame.

For several seconds the two Americans circled the flaming wreckage, amid ineffective anti-aircraft bursts, to verify that no one had left the Betty before or after the attack. Closing weather on the route home prevented completion of a planned mission to Tadji, but the Flying Circus had gotten what it came for and even strafed some trucks near Awar and a barge in Hansa Bay on the way back to Nadzab.

On March 3, 1944, Lynch—by then promoted to Lieutenant Colonel—scored his 19th victory; Bong was still the top U.S. Army pilot with 24. A public relations ploy developed around breaking Eddie Rickenbacker's traditional World War I score of 26 aerial victories—a score that he, in fact, never claimed but which was ascribed to him in later years by converting all partial claims to whole ones.

By the beginning of 1944, two U.S. Marine pilots—Gregory Boyington and Joe Foss—had been credited with scores equal to Rickenbacker's record, but no one had yet officially broken it. American fighter pilots in Europe were credited with as many as 20 air victories, and the publicity regarding the perceived contest was heating up.

The consensus in the Pacific was that either Bong or Lynch would break the record if Colonel Neel Kearby, formerly of the 348th Fighter Group and head of the 309th Bomb Wing by late February 1944, did not claim the honor. Kearby was an extraordinarily gifted fighter pilot who was now operating with much the same freedom of movement enjoyed by Bong and Lynch with their Flying Circus.

Perhaps Kearby was also somewhat more determined to break the record than either Bong or Lynch. He had had a frustrating time trying to sell the Republic P-47 Thunderbolt fighter to the pilots and commanders of the Fifth Air Force. The long-ranging P-38 had won a central berth in the livery of the Fifth Air Force that even the impressive record of the Thunderbolt-equipped 348th Fighter Group—including a Medal of Honor for Kearby—failed to dislodge. Breaking the record could win the P-38 acceptance as well as add some crowning prestige to Kearby's combat career.

For Bong and Lynch, Rickenbacker's record had little attraction. If one of them did happen to surpass the magic number, then both of them would certainly be sent back home for good. Neither pilot relished the thought of facing Stateside public attention again. On the other hand, neither coveted the prospect of independent combat operations; every pilot in the theater at some point realized that the law of averages did not favor long careers in combat. Even the bravest of pilots welcomed the order that finally sent him home.

Bong was a natural fighter pilot, but he learned a lot about the technical aspects of airmanship and tactics from Lynch.

On March 3, 1944, Lynch reported over the radio that he and Bong had accounted for four more Japanese aircraft. When Lynch landed, his boss, General Paul "Squeeze" Wurtsmith, greeted him and congratulated him on the kills—and then mentioned in an offhand, anti-climactic way that he had just been promoted to lieutenant colonel.

March 5, 1944, was a busy day for the Japanese Army Air Force's fighter regiments around the Wewak area. Nine Nakajima Ki.43

"Oscar" fighters of the 77th *Sentai* (fighter regiment), with some additional Oscars of the 33rd *Sentai,* were patrolling the But-Wewak sector in the morning. Most of the flight was running low on fuel when the formation vice-commander, Captain Kuwahara, ordered a return to base except for 1st Lt. Miyamoto and Warrant Officer Mitoma, who had enough fuel to remain with him on patrol.

Meanwhile, the Flying Circus had taken off from Nadzab with Lynch leading, for a fighter sweep to Tadji. The two P-38s had actually reached Tadji and were returning at 17,000 feet when they noticed three Oscars flying in the direction of Dagua from Wewak. Dagua is just east of But, in the complex of airfields and villages around Wewak. From a comparison of Japanese and American reports, it would seem that Bong and Lynch had happened on Kuwahara's detachment just as it separated from the other six Oscars.

Lynch immediately released tanks and led Bong down on the three unwary Japanese fighters. Lynch fired at the trailing Oscar, piloted by Lieutenant Miyamoto, at an altitude of 3,000 feet, and the plane burst into flames at once. Bong witnessed it crashing into the water.

Bong had a terrible day. He completely missed Kuwahara's Oscar and sprayed bullets into Mitoma's fighter without apparent effect. His combat report states that he followed one Oscar below the clouds where Lynch could not see him and set fire to the enemy plane, which must have crashed. Since translated Japanese accounts of the event state that Miyamoto's Oscar crashed into the sea east of But and that the other two Oscars were damaged, Bong either encountered another Oscar in the area or the Japanese understated the damage to Mitoma's fighter.

Unfortunately, Bong's gun camera did not function, so the most he could claim was a probable Oscar shot down. The Japanese account states that Miyamoto was killed and that Kuwahara landed safely. No mention is made of Mitoma, who may have crash-landed and returned by foot. Whatever the case, the two Americans sighted six more Oscars heading their way and decided to break off the engagement.

The 77th *Sentai* sent up five more Oscars later in the day to intercept an intruding flight of P-47s. Two of the P-47s were claimed shot down, and one Oscar was reported to be heavily damaged (no mention was made of its return). The American flight, from the 348th Fighter Group, claimed three bombers and a fighter shot down for the loss of one P-47 and its pilot—Colonel Neel Kearby.

News of the death of Colonel Kearby did nothing to lessen the tension of combat for Bong and Lynch. Both men respected Kearby's reputation and interpreted his loss as a reminder of their own mortality. Although Bong had written home in February that he and Lynch were shooting down Japanese "without sticking our necks out," that bit of bravado for the home folk was not in evidence now.

The sky was overcast during the sweep to Tadji on March 8, 1944. Bong and Lynch had taken off from Nadzab at 10:35 in the morning and were over the target area an hour later. There was not much going on at the airdrome below, and it seemed that this mission would be strictly routine. However, a few miles to the north in Aitape Harbor, three fishing luggers and three barges were visible. Perhaps something could be salvaged from this mission after all.

Both P-38s went into a dive and pulled out just above the water. They selected the same lugger, and both P-38s bored in so low that the wash from their propellers churned the water. Together, they fired all eight .50-caliber guns and two 20mm cannons in a murderous fusillade, roared by in a flash, then looked back to see smoke drifting up from the lugger.

Lynch quickly circled for another pass, with Bong some distance behind. As well as Bong could follow the action, Lynch went in for a second pass just above the water; his P-38 was hit by small-arms fire (no explosive shells were seen), and he pulled up in a climbing left-hand turn to 2,500 feet. The right engine was on fire, and pieces of the P-38 were drifting back into the slipstream as if the fuselage were disintegrating.

Lynch was now flying inland and was nearly a mile from the shore when he called Bong on the radio. Bong warned Lynch that his right engine was on fire and that he should bail out. The doomed P-38 was descending quickly toward the jungle, flames pouring from its right side.

Within minutes Lynch was within 200 feet of the ground, struggling desperately to free the left canopy window. Too late, the entire canopy came free, and Lynch tumbled out of the cockpit just as the P-38 exploded below him. His parachute began to open

Major Lynch was operations officer for V Fighter Command when Bong was assigned to his office in January 1944—to form a two-man "Flying Circus."

just as he plummeted into the green sea of the jungle.

Stunned, Bong recovered enough to circle the piece of forest where his friend had vanished. It was a hopeless search that Bong would recount in only the briefest and most despairing terms. His own P-38 was shot up so badly that he had to feather the right engine near the base of Gusap on the way back to Nadzab. No gun positions had been seen on the boats during their first pass, suggesting that at least one of the vessels was a covert flak ship with concealed anti-aircraft weapons.

According to the mission report, Lynch was flying a new P-38J-15 (serial no. 42-104004) on this, his last, flight. His own airplane must have been undergoing maintenance, because his usual P-38,

Bong's fully decorated P-38L. Even before Marge's picture was added, Bong's plane was widely recognizable by its red spinners, wingtips and vertical stabilizer tips.

It was probably Bong himself who talked his way back into action shortly afterward. He was close enough to breaking the 26-kill record, he may have argued, to justify taking risks, and he may have wanted to erase the morale damage done by the sudden demise of the Flying Circus.

By April 1, Bong had returned to action. Without the able comradeship of Tom Lynch, he was left with the option of joining formations likely to engage Japanese aircraft. In early April that meant he had to fly with either the 475th Fighter Group or the 80th Fighter Squadron—the only Fifth Air Force combat units operating the P-38 at the time.

The P-38 that Bong regularly flew now was J-15, serial no. 42-104380, with red spinners, wingtips and tailtips. On one mission he made an exception when he borrowed an 80th Fighter Squadron P-38 to fly a routine operation. Two days later, he went along with the 432nd Fighter Squadron, 475th Fighter Group, and shot down another Oscar in flames for his 25th confirmed victory. Another mission was scheduled to Hollandia on April 12, and he tagged along with the 80th Fighter Squadron.

This time Bong managed to get two more Oscars and another probable, to break Rickenbacker's record. One of the pilots in the flight to which Bong attached himself watched the record-breaking kill and vaguely remembers that Bong was flying a P-38 with red spinners, suggesting that he was using 104380 that day.

This time there was no argument, and Bong was sent home, to be hailed as the top-ranking American ace of the war. Amid the public acclaim, which he detested, Bong was pleased to meet other great fighter pilots from the European theater on war bond drives. He was introduced to Don Gentile, the highest-scoring North American P-51 Mustang ace at the time, who had been touted by the Eighth Air Force as the first pilot to surpass Rickenbacker's record. Bong was then introduced to Bob Johnson, who was also being called the first Eighth Air Force pilot to be credited with more than 26 victories in aerial combat.

Gentile had gotten all his kills by early April 1944. But some of them were ground victories, which left his air total at 21.84. Johnson had originally been credited with 27, gained by early May 1944. Some enthusiastic public relations officer in Europe got John-

serial no. 42-103987, was listed in USAAF loss logs as being written off on the next day, March 9, 1944.

Bong's own plane, serial no. 42-103993, was lost in an unusual manner later in March with another pilot at the controls. Captain Tom Malone of the 421st Night Fighter Squadron took off from Nadzab in Bong's P-38 on a weather mission on March 24, 1944. Somewhere along the way, Malone was forced to bail out and walk back home. Bong was not using his P-38 during this period; his flight record lists his duty as chiefly noncombat copilot of a B-25.

Speculation suggests that it was intended that Bong be gradually removed from the combat arena. The double loss of Kearby and Lynch was enough of a blow to pilot morale; the death of Dick Bong in combat at this point would have been devastating.

son's victory list reviewed and found that a German Messerschmitt Me-110 claimed as a probable by Johnson in November 1943 could be interpreted as confirmed by current kill credit rules. That would give Johnson 26 aerial kills by April 13—very close to the day that Bong got his 27th—and a grand total of 28 aerial victories.

The head of the Fifth Air Force, General George Kenney, had been driving his Southwest Pacific campaign despite the frustratingly low priority accorded it by Washington. He took a personal interest in the welfare of his pilots, but he also appreciated what Bong's accomplishment meant to the Fifth Air Force effort in terms of morale—and publicity.

Hollandia had been captured by this time, and Kenney immediately arranged for a diver from the Allied Technical Air Unit to explore the waters of Tannemara Bay, where Bong had claimed his probable Oscar. A Japanese fighter with damage similar to that described in Bong's report was found, and the order was issued to credit Bong for his 28th kill. It couldn't have mattered less to either Bong or Johnson, who enjoyed each other's company along the ponderous war rally tour.

Bong was promoted to major as of his final combat of April 12. Somehow, he managed to get himself back into the Southwest Pacific in time for the invasion of the Philippines and scored 12 more victories to earn the Medal of Honor. Oddly enough, Bong died in much the same way as Lynch. The jet fighter Bong was testing on August 6, 1945, flamed out on takeoff, too low for him to survive the bailout attempt.

III

AIR WAR'S TOP ACE

Messerschmitt pilot Erich Hartmann's 352 aerial victories,
scored during WWII, may never be equaled.

By Wil Deac

Five times, the Me-109G fighter thundered low over the 9th Squadron's airstrip on the Moldavian plain of northeastern Romania—once for every victory scored during the preceding 50 minutes of aerial combat. Each time—his 1,475-hp engine drowning out the cheering, waving men on the ground— the 22-year-old pilot wagged the plane's black-crossed wings.

Officers and enlisted men swarmed forward as the mottled gray Messerschmitt finally taxied in and shivered to a stop at the squadron leader's parking spot. Moments later, a flower and fern wreath around his neck, the proud flaxen-haired ace was perched on his comrades' shoulders to receive boisterous congratulations. He accepted a glass of unchilled champagne from the radio operator who had monitored the entire air battle.

It was Thursday, August 24, 1944. *Oberleutnant* (1st Lieutenant) Erich Alfred Hartmann had just become the first pilot in history to down 300 enemy aircraft.

That weekend, at his *Führer's* summons, Hartmann flew northwestward to East Prussia to receive a special honor. Once inside the "Wolf's Lair," headquarters of Adolf Hitler, he was asked by an SS officer to surrender his holstered pistol. Security had been tightened after a nearly successful assassination attempt against the Nazi dictator the preceding month. "Please tell the *Führer* that I don't want to receive the Diamonds if he has no faith in his front-line officers," coolly responded the young first lieutenant.

It was a pale SS security man who left to consult with Hitler's air force aide. The latter, a tall *Luftwaffe* colonel, appeared and sighed, "Hartmann, you can wear your pistol if you insist. Now please come in and get your Diamonds." Shortly, a stooped, ailing dictator shook the straight-backed pilot's hand and handed him Germany's then highest decoration: the Swords, Oak Leaves and Diamonds of the Knight's Cross. He was the 18th of 27 to receive the coveted award.

Born on April 19, 1922, in Germany's southwestern Württemberg republic, Erich Hartmann was a toddler when his doctor father moved his family to China to escape his country's post-World War I chaos. Four years later, it was the revolutionary violence shaking China that drove the Hartmanns back home. They settled in bucolic Weil im Schönbuch. Erich most probably would have followed in his father's footsteps but for two factors—his love of flying and World War II. A dynamic woman, Erich's mother took up sport flying and often piloted her two sons high above the southern German hills. In 1936, with aviation actively promoted by the Third Reich, she formed a glider club. Her elder son's later fame had its roots in the silent soaring that, as Hartmann later said, "gave

Temporarily commanding I Gruppe of JG 53, Hauptmann Hartmann prepares to attack Yak-9s escorting Petlyakov Pe-2s near Veszprem, Hungary, on February 2, 1945, in The Blond Knight, *by Jerry Crandall. Hartmann downed one Yak for his 337th victory.*

[him] a wonderful feeling for the air." He was a licensed glider pilot at the age of 14.

An average scholar, Erich was a born leader and sportsman. His single-mindedness was displayed when, at 17, he fell in love with 15-year-old Ursula Paetsch. His first and only love, she would later have her nickname "Ursel" displayed on the arrow-pierced bleeding-heart emblem painted beneath the cockpit of Hartmann's record-breaking Messerschmitt.

The slender German's graduation from high school coincided with the 1940 Nazi invasion of Scandinavia. That year he joined the air force. His disdain for traditional military life, which was to act as an anchor throughout his career, was more than compensated for by the freedom of flying. With the military bureaucracy still confident of victory, pilot training proceeded at an unaccelerated pace.

The young Württemberger progressed from five months of basic military instruction to 7½ months of flight schooling at Berlin's Gatow airfield and 3½ months of pre-fighter instruction before entering gunnery training during the summer of 1942. There, he displayed a remarkable aptitude for aerial marksmanship. Graduation brought orders to report to the celebrated *Jagdgeschwader* (JG) 52 (52nd Fighter Wing) at the southern end of the battle zone most feared by German soldiers, the Eastern Front.

Arriving by rail at the *Luftwaffe's* supply and transfer center at Kraków in southern Poland, Hartmann and three other neophyte second lieutenants were informed that the quickest way for them to join their units was to fly replacement Junkers Ju-87 Stuka dive bombers to a base near their destination. With the cockiness of their breed, the fighter-pilot quartet squeezed into four of the lumbering two-seaters. Hartmann was the last to taxi out. As he applied the left brake to maneuver onto the runway past a controller's small shack, Hartmann was startled to find it would not respond. What followed resembled a scene from a slapstick comedy. The Stuka's three-bladed propeller buzz-sawed into the shack, sending up "a blizzard of shredded paper and wood splinters." Fortunately, no one was hurt.

Cutting the engine, Hartmann jumped from the Junkers' inverted gull wing to the ground. The red-faced and shaken junior officer may well have wondered if he had any future in military aviation. Two months earlier, while at gunnery school, he had been arrested, grounded and fined for putting on an impromptu airshow. Luck, however, was on his side that time. While Hartmann was confined to his barracks, his roommate flew the training mission that was supposed to be Hartmann's; engine trouble caused a fatal crash. Now, as the livid base commander stamped over, one of the Ju-87s that had lifted off earlier returned with a sputtering, smoking motor. What could the commander do but throw up his hands and send these "baby pilots" on their way as passengers in a cargo plane?

Hartmann reported to the 7th Squadron, 3rd Group, of JG 52 in mid-October 1942. The squadron was housed in a tent city adjoining a grass airstrip northeast of Soldaskaya, a village in the fruit- and sunflower-growing plains north of twin-peaked Mount Elbrus, Europe's highest elevation in Russia's Caucus Mountains. Rank was subordinated to experience, and the newcomer was assigned as wingman to a master sergeant, Eduard Rossmann. The latter and crew chief Sergeant Heinz Mertens were two pillars beneath Hartmann's later success, one as a teacher, the second as the ensurer of a reliable aircraft.

The new officer's first combat mission, when included with his earlier grounding and Ju-87 mishap, lent truth to the old saying about never two without three. In an attack on Soviet aircraft that were harassing German ground troops, Hartmann "violated virtually every established rule of aerial tactics." After succumbing to "buck fever," wild with excitement to the detriment of accurate shooting, he ended up fleeing from his leader, whom he mistook for the enemy, and crash-landed his Me-109G when it ran out of fuel. At this low point there seemed only one way to go—up. Hartmann, a fast learner, was to do so with a vengeance.

Flying in a four-ship formation on November 5, the keen-eyed lieutenant sighted an escorted group of red-starred Ilyushin Il-2 *Shturmovik* ground-attack planes. The Messerschmitts split into two-plane elements and screamed earthward. Hartmann slashed through the escorting Soviet fighters and leveled out perhaps 50 yards from the ground. Thumb and fingers moving his control column, he triggered the nose-mounted 20mm cannon and twin

A rare in-flight photograph of Hartmann in the Me-109G-6 "White 1" that he flew as leader of 7./JG 52. He later removed his black "petal" marking from the nose when Russians began avoiding him.

13mm machine guns. To his dismay, the projectiles caromed off the heavily armored *Shturmovik*. He recalled what he had been told about the Il-2s and made another run, this time arcing up beneath the target. His shooting this time was rewarded with an eruption of smoke and flame from the dark-green bomber's oil cooler. Still new at the game, Hartmann continued after his dying victim instead of breaking off. A sudden explosion sent debris streaming back into his Me-109. Another belly landing, but the German pilot, unscathed, had chalked up his first victory.

Between acting as wingman covering his leader, changing bases to keep pace with the Nazi retreat, and putting up with the winter weather, Hartmann was unable to score his next victory (a MiG-1 fighter) until January 27, 1943. His next element leader, the irrepressible new 7th Squadron commander 1st Lt. Walter Krupinski, gave him the nickname of *Bubi* (or boy, because of his boyish appearance) and completed Hartmann's initial combat education. If Rossman taught him the advantage of surprise attack, then Krupinski showed him the value of short-range shooting. "One must wait until the enemy fills the entire windscreen," Hartmann said later, "and not a single shot will miss."

Hartmann's early lessons supported his belief that it is what the fighter pilot "is shown first that helps him survive, and later equips him to bring his new comrades through." It was no coincidence that not one of his own wingmen was killed while flying with him. In March, Hartmann earned the Iron Cross, 2nd Class, by shooting down his fifth Russian. Another five and, by *Luftwaffe* standards, he would be an ace. By late April, he had eight kills to his credit and was advanced to element leader. He was now free to pursue his own tactics, which were not unlike those of the top ace of World War I, Manfred von Richthofen.

The vertical victory bars painted behind the swastika on the rudder of his Messerschmitt began to mount up. There was a kill on April 28. Two days later, he scored twice in one day for the first time, bagging a pair of LaGG-3 fighters in an 84-minute sortie. There were six more shoot-downs in May. Then, on the morning

Landing at Veszprem on February 4, 1945, Hartmann alights from his snow-camouflaged and chevron-marked Me-109G-6.

of May 25, while climbing sunward after an attack on one plane, he collided with a Soviet fighter. Only his flying skill enabled him to crash-land safely within his own lines. The unnerving experience convinced him to take a month's home leave. In addition to visiting family and friends, and hearing firsthand reports of mounting Allied air raids on Germany, Hartmann made a side trip to the idyllic Alpsee resort in the Bavarian mountains to become engaged to his beloved Ursula.

On July 5, 1943, the blue-eyed ace, whose shy smile and slow drawl belied his aerial killing ability, racked up his best one-day score to date—three mid-engine, American-built Bell P-39 Airacobras and one Russian-built La-5, a fighter that was faster than the Me-109 below 20,000 feet. He bettered that achievement two

days later by swatting down seven Il-2s and La-5s in three energy-sapping sorties between 3:06 a.m. and 6:05 p.m. It was the kind of demanding combat—living in makeshift quarters and flying from rough fields even as the Slavic juggernaut ground the Teutonic invasion back onto itself—that enabled Hitler's aces to chalk up the world's most impressive scores. The cost, however, was high. The day of Hartmann's four-in-one-day triumph, his squadron lost a third of its strength.

August 20 was a day that would bring the now battle-hardened lieutenant close to death and would tax his mettle—and luck—to the maximum. Before dawn that Friday, the 7th Squadron pilots were routed from their cots at Kuteynikovo, in western Russia's mineral-rich Donets River basin, for an emergency scramble. The artillery fire that had disturbed the airmen's sleep throughout the night marked a Soviet effort, part of its first successful summer offensive, to break the Axis front in the Ukraine. The squadron's orders were to keep Russian tactical bombers off the *Wehrmacht* ground forces' backs and to cover the Germans' own bombers, a force that was spearheaded by the die-hard Nazi tank-busting ace, Captain Hans-Ulrich Rudel.

Assisted by his trusty Sergeant Mertens, Hartmann slipped into the Messerschmitt's narrow cockpit and completed his pre-flight check. Two mechanics took turns hand-cranking the high-whining inertia starter. The engine burst into life with chugging and puffs of exhaust smoke. After checking his instrument panel gauges, the tense ace taxied to the runway. He signaled thanks to his crew chief, tightened his seat belt, pulled back the throttle (unlike the controls in U.S. aircraft, the Messerschmitt throttle is pulled back to increase power and pushed forward to reduce it) and released the brakes. The sleek, 29-foot-long fighter jiggled ever faster across the field and lifted gracefully into its element. Not 10 minutes away to the northeast, where black smoke columns fingered toward the blood-red sunrise, lay the battlefield.

The eight Me-109s howled down on an estimated 40 *Shturmoviks* pounding their comrades on the ground. Streaking past the LaGG and Yak fighter cover, Hartmann hit an Il-2 with a short burst from about 200 feet. Then came an explosion, and a red-starred wing broke off. Grimly, the lieutenant roared after a second enemy, who

Ground crewmen converge on Hartmann's plane to perform vital maintenance for his next mission.

was too busy strafing to notice the death machine closing on his tail. Nearer than the first time, Hartmann again depressed the trigger buttons. Flames flashed below as the German pulled up to overfly his doomed prey. Suddenly, disaster! A banging on the underside of the fuselage, an engine cover swishing by into the slipstream, and blue smoke swirling into the cockpit. Determined not to land in enemy territory, he completed a turn. Throttle closed, ignition and fuel switches off, Hartmann babied the crippled Messerschmitt toward a field high with sunflowers. A metallic clatter filled his ears as the stricken aircraft sent severed plants and dirt spraying before coming to a relatively smooth stop. The shaken aviator unbuckled his parachute and safety belt. He was removing the precision clock from the instrument panel according to standing orders when he saw movement through his dusty windshield. Relief—it was a German truck.

Reality hit with a shock. The two soldiers who jumped from the truck's open back had Asian faces and wore Russian uniforms. Thinking quickly, Hartmann pretended to be unconscious as the

infantrymen climbed onto the plane's left wing. One tried to pull him out. Feigning injury, the German screamed and groaned. The ruse worked. With a "War over, Hitler kaput," Hartmann's captors transferred him on an improvised stretcher to the back of their captured truck.

The ace's convincing act continued for another two hours as he was taken to a doctor in a nearby hamlet. Mentally groping for a way to escape as the truck trundled ever deeper into the Russian-held countryside, Hartmann was given his chance by the providential overflight of some low-flying Stukas. He slammed the distracted lone soldier guarding him against the truck cab and leaped to the ground. Brakes screeched as he dashed into a sunflower field. Shots cracked through the tall flower stalks. The German ran, gasping for breath, until he reached a stream-crossed valley, "which looked to have come right out of a fairy tale."

A first attempt to walk westward convinced Hartmann he could never make it unseen in the daylight. After sunset, having wisely returned to his "fairy tale" valley to sleep during the daylight hours, the downed pilot traversed sunflower fields and low hills toward the flares, tracers and shell bursts marking the front. He plodded on, frequently pausing to rest, ignoring his hunger and at one point following a Soviet patrol. Finally, at still another slope, the shout "*Halten!*" was followed by a rifle shot. A slug tore through his pants leg. "Good God, don't shoot at your own people!" Hartmann cried out. Through self-discipline and luck, he had reached the German lines.

As August faded into September, Hartmann, with 295 missions and 90 victories behind him, was named commander of JG 52 Group 3's 9th Squadron. On October 29, his 150th victory won him the Knight's Cross of the Iron Cross. It also won him notoriety on the other side. Hartmann was known to the Russians first as *Karaya* (Sweetheart) One, his radio call sign, then as *Cherniye Chórni* (Black Devil) because of a black, tulip petal–shaped design on the nose of his Me-109, and they placed a price of 10,000 rubles on his head. When he realized that his kills were declining because Russian aviators were avoiding him, Hartmann had Mertens remove the distinctive aircraft nose marking.

The ace's score stood at 159 by the end of 1943. During the first two months of the new year, he averaged about two kills for each day of flying. Hartmann sharpened his natural talents and refined his aerial tactics, using minimal ammunition during his attacks. Unlike most pilots, he avoided dogfights. Instead, exploiting the fact that surprise is the dominant factor in air warfare, he relied on the hit-and-run technique to both increase his score and keep himself alive. He piloted his Me-109, painted white in winter and camouflage-speckled the rest of the time, against great odds while remaining relatively untouched.

On March 2, 1944, Hartmann secured an incredible 10 victories in one day, giving him a total of 202. With three other aces from JG 52, he was soon aboard a train bound for Saltzburg en route to Berchtesgaden, where Hitler was to award him the Oak Leaves to his Knight's Cross. What was more natural for young pilots, temporarily rid of the tension of unending combat, than to have a few drinks, and then a few more? At the railroad station, the *Führer's* aide picked up three pickled pilots (one did not drink). He resourcefully drove them up to Hitler's alpine Eagle's Nest in a Mercedes convertible with the top down. At their destination, the aide had them walk around in the 25 degrees Fahrenheit air before being ushered in to see the teetotaling dictator. Immediately before the momentous meeting, the still-tipsy, barely 22-year-old Hartmann clowned around with a military cap he spotted on a nearby stand. It was Hitler's hat. Fortunately, the ceremony proceeded with no further complications. After a two-week home leave, Hartmann rejoined his squadron in the western Ukraine, where he learned of his promotion to *Oberleutnant*.

The base-hopping continued as Germany's armies fell farther back. In April, JG 52 was covering the crumbling positions on the Crimean Peninsula. Here the fliers could vividly see the change in the Third Reich's fortunes. The Red Air Force now dominated the sky, while the *Luftwaffe* was sending experienced men to fight the Americans and British in the west and replacing them in the east with barely trained youngsters. One hectic day in May, Hartmann landed long enough after making his 223rd kill to refuel and squeeze two mechanics into the pencil-thin rear fuselage of his Me-109. They flew out just ahead of the oncoming enemy. Assigned to northeastern Romania, 9th Squadron next challenged American aircraft flying out of Italy to pound Balkan targets.

In late June, Hartmann had his first encounter with the North American P-51 Mustang. U.S. Army Air Forces Boeing B-17 Flying Fortresses were rumbling through black anti-aircraft bursts near the vital Ploesti oil fields when, leading two four-plane *Schwarm*, Hartmann arrived to protect JG 52 Messerschmitts intercepting the bombers. Spying four Mustangs from his 25,500-foot perch, Hartmann ordered an attack. Diving, he swiftly selected a target for himself. A two-second burst chewed chunks from the surprised P-51, then blew it to pieces. He flamed a second while his comrades downed two more Mustangs.

The following days were less successful. Aircraft on both sides were damaged, but there were no kills, as the alerted Americans kept the Germans away from the bombers. On his fifth midday

Hartmann climbs from the cockpit of his Me-109G-6 after returning from a mission in October 1944.

sortie against U.S. aircraft, Hartmann knocked off two more P-51s before his wingman radioed a frantic "Bubi, behind you! Break!" This time the young ace found himself sandwiched between eight Mustangs. Twisting to and fro, he avoided the enemy's .50-caliber bullets. Then, perhaps a half-dozen miles from the base, the Me-109's fuel warning light flashed red. With canopy jettisoned and safety belt unhooked, Hartmann bailed out. As the sweat-drenched German parachuted to earth, a Mustang roared past, its pilot waving a salute before leaving with the others.

On July 1, after some 20 months of combat flying, Hartmann attained his 250th victory, a *Shturmovik*. Later that month, the young squadron leader was summoned to meet his commander in chief, this time to receive Germany's second-highest award. Hartmann, at attention with cap in hand in the wood-paneled conference room at the Wolf's Lair in East Prussia, was shocked by Hitler's appearance. The *Führer*, having survived Lt. Col. Claus von Stauffenberg's bomb four days earlier, could only offer his left hand to shake and was "a shadow of the man" the ace had met in March.

After just over a month back at the front, having become history's top-scoring ace, Hartmann returned again to the Wolf's Lair, this time to receive his Diamonds. During home leave in September, he married his fiancée at the Fighter Pilots' Home in the mountains south of Munich. Then, becoming restive at the gloomy war news, he cut short his honeymoon to return to his squadron.

Now a captain and commander of JG 52's 1st Group, he added 39 more to his kill total before flying back to Germany in March for transition training in the Messerschmitt Me-262 jet fighter-bomber. General Adolf Galland asked him to join his elite JV 44 all-jet "Squadron of Experts" (aces) and fly on the Western Front. The young officer chose instead to stay with the men he had been leading and fighting with. It was a decision he was soon to regret.

In a painting by Harley Copic, Erich Hartmann *of* Jagdgeschwader *52 sets out on a mission in his Me-109G-10 in April 1945.*

His air war during the spring of 1945, now in the skies over Czechoslovakia, was like none he had ever experienced. On an April 1945 mission, for example, he led a four-plane *Schwarm* against a Soviet bombing raid on Prague, only to see a flight of U.S. P-51s come between the Me-109s and the Russians. Hartmann and his wingman swooped down. The ace picked off two Mustangs and slashed through the Red fighter escort to damage an American-built Lend-Lease Douglas A-20. By the time the second two-plane German element had completed its run and rejoined Hartmann, the thoroughly confused pilots of the Russian Yaks and Airacobras were attacking the Americans.

Hartmann's final sortie, on the morning of May 8, was a reconnaissance mission to pinpoint the head of the Red advance. He found it at Brno, just east of JG 52's makeshift base. Then, underlining his truism that "the pilot who sees the other first already has half the victory," he struck an unwary formation of Yak-7s. He had batted one out of the air when, sighting a dozen approaching American fighters, he decided to opt for discretion over valor. The Yak was his 352nd—and last—victory. With U.S. Third Army patrols to the west and the Russians to the east, he knew his fighting days were over. Hartmann, along with the JG 52 commander, disregarded an order to fly to Germany; they would stay with their comrades.

The 25 Messerschmitts on the field, including the lead ace's, were destroyed in fiery blasts, along with the remaining fuel and munitions. Soon afterward, at the head of a ragged column of some 2,000 military and civilian men, women and children, Hartmann surrendered to a tank officer of the U.S. 16th Armored Division. He quickly found himself enmeshed in the controversial political decisions that had deeded eastern Europe and the Germans fighting there to the Soviets. A week later, he and his fellow fugitives became Russian prisoners.

For a decade and nearly five months, Hartmann was illegally held captive at numerous camps. His jailers tried to convert him (as they did the JG 52 commander), then break him. They failed, even after a kangaroo court convicted him of being a war criminal and sentenced him to 25 years at hard labor. Just as political conditions had delivered him into Soviet hands, so now political expediency worked to set him free. A "normalization" of relations between West Germany and the Soviet Union resulted in a release of prisoners of war held by Moscow since 1945. The Bonn government had specifically asked that Hartmann be one of those granted amnesty.

In mid-October 1955, pale, disoriented and down to 100 pounds, the now 33-year-old Württemberger returned home at last. Deciding it was too late to start a new career, Hartmann joined the resurrected German air force in late 1956. His directness, strong values and apolitical attitude impeded his career development. He nevertheless contributed to the new *Luftwaffe's* direction, and he rose from major to colonel.

Refresher training under American tutelage proved Hartmann had lost none of his flair for flying. In 1957, operating out of the ironically named Kraut Field annex at Luke Air Force Base, Ariz., Hartmann flew Lockheed T-33 and Republic F-84F jets in advanced fighter and gunnery training over the Yuma target range. In Germany again, Hartmann founded and trained his country's first postwar, all-jet fighter wing. The JG 71 Richthofen Unit's F-86s were given the same tulip-petal nose design that had adorned its commander's Me-109 during World War II. Hartmann retired in the fall of 1970 as the most decorated officer in West Germany's armed forces.

Erich Hartmann flew 1,425 missions in just over 2½ years and participated in more than 800 aerial battles during the war. He had to parachute to safety once and crashed-landed 15 times, but he was never wounded. While America's top ace scored 40 kills, Britain's 38 and Russia's 62, Hartmann downed 261 single-engine and 91 twin-engine aircraft, making him the most successful air ace of all time.

Hartmann's flying expertise contributed to his impressive record, of course, but these were other factors. The enemy he faced over the Eastern Front was initially wanting in training, tactics and quality of equipment. Other German aces, when fighting in the west, had a harder time scoring victories. And unlike Allied pilots, who were rotated, German aviators served almost continuously, with only short leave time to unwind from the tension of combat flying. Anyway you look at it, however, downing a record number of aircraft and living to tell about it rates as a great accomplishment. And given the nature of modern air warfare, Hartmann's 352 shoot-downs will probably never be equaled.

IV

BUTCH O'HARE: 'FRIENDLY FIRE' VICTIM?

The Navy's first ace of World War II disappeared mysteriously
one night during the Tarawa campaign.

By John G. Leyden

Navy Lieutenant junior grade Edward H. "Butch" O'Hare first experienced the often deadly phenomenon known as "friendly fire" right after he shot down five Japanese bombers in less than five minutes on February 20, 1942, to become the Navy's first fighter ace of World War II. Coming in for a landing on the aircraft carrier *Lexington,* which he had just saved from possible destruction, O'Hare came under fire from a nervous machine-gunner on the ship's catwalk. He survived unscathed because the young sailor's aim was no better than his judgment.

But O'Hare's luck would run out 21 months later during the bloody Tarawa campaign in the Central Pacific. He disappeared without a trace during an experimental night-fighter operation on November 27, 1943 (November 26 in the United States). Many naval historians—including Clark Reynolds, author of *The Fast Carriers,* and Edward P. Stafford, author of *The Big E*—believe he was the victim of friendly fire from another Navy aircraft.

The mystery of O'Hare's death is similar in many ways to that surrounding the murder of his father in November 1939. The senior O'Hare died in a hail of gunfire on a Chicago street. Some believe his death was retribution for informing on Al Capone and helping the federal government send him to prison for tax fraud. But the case was never solved, nor were the killers ever identified.

The Navy's official announcement of O'Hare's February 20, 1942, triumph over the five bombers was made on March 3, and he was erroneously credited with six victories. Numbers aside, it was just about the best war news the demoralized American public had heard since the disaster at Pearl Harbor three months earlier. In a scant five minutes of action, the St. Louis native had destroyed the growing myth of Japanese invincibility and restored the nation's confidence in its fighting men.

No slouch when it came to shaping public opinion, President Franklin D. Roosevelt made the most of this opportunity to boost morale. When *Lexington* returned to Hawaii, he had the nation's newest hero flown to Washington so he personally could present him with the Medal of Honor at White House ceremonies. Flashing the famous FDR grin, the commander in chief also informed O'Hare that he had been jumped two ranks to lieutenant commander. The citation for the medal credited O'Hare with saving *Lexington* from serious damage by single-handedly taking on nine twin-engine Japanese bombers, shooting down five of them and

In a painting by Michael P. Hagel, a Grumman F4F-3 Wildcat flown by Butch O'Hare *dives on a formation of Mitsubishi G4M1 "Betty" bombers en route to attack his aircraft carrier,* Lexington, *on February 20, 1942.*

severely damaging a sixth through "extremely skillful marksmanship." Sparing no superlatives, it called the aerial battle "one of the most daring, if not the most daring single action in the history of combat aviation."

O'Hare's own description of the battle was somewhat more prosaic. He told reporters: "We had 10 planes in the air. The first crowd of our fellows was working the first bunch of Japs to come over, and we had the second bunch all to ourselves. I was leading a second section of two planes and my wingman had gun trouble for about five minutes, and by the time he got his guns fixed it was all over."

After the Washington ceremony, O'Hare made a series of public appearances around the country to boost home-front spirits and inspire war-plant workers to even greater efforts. His first stop was the Grumman plant in Bethpage, N.Y., which made the F4F-3 Wildcat he had used to score his five victories. Then it was on to St. Louis, where he was given a triumphant parade through the center of the city and hailed by the mayor as "Eddie O'Hare, the St. Louis boy who has come home to the rolling thunder of worldwide applause."

The handsome 28-year-old Naval Academy graduate wore the victor's laurels well, if somewhat uneasily. Syndicated columnist Inez Robb noted that O'Hare was the "model hero—modest, inarticulate, humorous, terribly nice and more than a little embarrassed by the whole thing."

Out of respect, perhaps, no one mentioned O'Hare's father, who had been the president of Chicago's Sportsman's Park racetrack and a close associate of Al Capone. The elder O'Hare's exact role in the Capone syndicate has long been a matter of dispute. Some called him a fringe player who restricted himself to legitimate racing activities; others depicted him as a "one-man brain trust in the mob."

It is not clear how much Butch O'Hare knew about his father's shady business connections. Probably it was not a great deal, since his parents had separated when he was still a boy, and later divorced. Moreover, when his father moved to Chicago, the young O'Hare remained with his mother and two sisters in St. Louis until he left home to attend military prep school in Alton, Ill. But he remained the apple of his father's eye, and the two were extremely close. In fact, young Eddie may have been the reason the senior

O'Hare decided to turn on Capone and help the government build its case against the Chicago crime czar.

According to one popular version of this classic double-cross, the senior O'Hare wanted to "square" himself with the government in order to improve his son's chances of acceptance at the Naval Academy. It makes a nice story. And, if true, it means that the Bureau of Internal Revenue got Capone while the Navy got Butch O'Hare as part of a package deal.

Fortunately, none of the father's sins rubbed off on his son. Young Eddie O'Hare grew up to be the proverbial straight arrow. He prepped at Western Military Academy, where he consistently earned good grades. He played guard on the football team and was captain of the rifle team. One of O'Hare's friends was another young man who also would make a name for himself in World War II—Paul Tibbets, who piloted *Enola Gay,* the Boeing B-29 Superfortress that dropped the first atomic bomb on Japan.

In 1933, O'Hare realized a long-cherished dream by winning an appointment to the U.S. Naval Academy in Annapolis, Md. Some writers have suggested that Frank Wilson, who directed the federal investigation of Capone, pulled strings to have him accepted. But Wilson, who became chief of the Secret Service in 1936, never made any such claim in his writings. Indeed, O'Hare failed on his first try for the academy and had to return to school in St. Louis in order to improve his math skills.

O'Hare graduated from the academy with the Class of 1937 after a more or less routine four years, during which he picked up two nicknames—"Butch," which stuck, and "Nero," which did not. His yearbook noted that he had the traits of a good officer and future leader: "a winning personality...no trouble in making lasting friendships...always ready with a pat on the back when you need it most."

O'Hare set his sights on a career in naval aviation following graduation, but he first was required to serve two years in the fleet. In June 1939, after a tour on USS *New Mexico,* he was reassigned to the Pensacola Naval Air Station in Florida for flight training; he earned his gold Navy wings a year later. He then was sent to Fighting Squadron 3 (VF-3) under the legendary John S. "Jimmy" Thach, who developed the team fighting tactic (the "Thach

Weave") that allowed the slow but sturdy F4F Wildcats to hold their own against the more nimble Mitsubishi A6M "Zeros."

Admiral Thach later recalled in an interview that O'Hare had all the attributes of a true fighter pilot. In addition to being a fine athlete, he had "a sense of timing and relative motion that he may have been born with." Even more important perhaps, he possessed "that competitive spirit" that quickly separates winners from losers in the air. O'Hare flew like a veteran right from the start. "He just picked it up much faster than anyone else I've ever seen," Thach said. "He got the most out of his airplane. He didn't try to horse it around."

He did particularly well in practice dogfights with the squadron's "humiliation team." These were exercises designed to deflate the egos of newly arrived pilots, but the tactic did not work with O'Hare. He usually came out on top, and even defeated Thach. "It wasn't long after that," Thach continued, "that we made him a member of the humiliation team, because he had passed the graduation test so quickly."

The squadron got its first taste of action in February 1942 in a planned carrier strike against the Japanese-held port of Rabaul on the South Pacific island of New Britain. It was intended as a surprise attack, but the carrier task force was sighted by Japanese patrol planes before reaching the launch point and soon became the target of land-based bombers.

The first wave of nine twin-engine Mitsubishi G4M1 "Betty" bombers was picked up by *Lexington's* radar in midafternoon on February 20. The six Wildcats of VF-3 flying combat air patrol ripped through the formation, bringing down three Japanese planes on the first pass. Other VF-3 Wildcats then joined the fray, and the Japanese ended up losing eight of their nine aircraft without scoring a single bomb hit on the task force. The lone bomber to escape was shot down on the way home during a running fight with a Douglas SBD Dauntless dive bomber.

Meanwhile, a very frustrated Butch O'Hare was flying cover over the fleet with his wingman, Lieutenant Marion W. Dufilho. Then *Lexington's* radar picked up a second wave of Bettys flying in a large V formation composed of three smaller V's and closing fast on the task force from the east. With the other Wildcat pilots still pursuing the remnants of the Japanese first wave, O'Hare and Dufilho

After receiving the Medal of Honor from FDR, Lt. Cmdr. Edward H. O'Hare was described as "modest, inarticulate, humorous, terribly nice and more than a little embarrassed by the whole thing."

were all that stood between the incoming bombers and the American carrier.

O'Hare and Dufilho met the enemy formation some 12–15 miles out from the task force, flying at an altitude of 11,000 feet. They

O'Hare (left) is congratulated by his commander and mentor, Lt. Cmdr. John S. "Jimmy" Thach, who downed 1½ Japanese Betty bombers in the same fight.

the formation. He then realized for the first time that his wingman was not with him. Dufilho had dropped out of the fight when his guns jammed. Unperturbed, O'Hare moved up the line, shooting down two more airplanes. Then, on his third pass, he went after the lead bomber with the master bombardier on board and sent it down in flames. He also damaged a sixth aircraft, but ran out of ammunition before he could claim another victory.

This traditional account of the engagement is somewhat disputed, however, by John B. Lundstrom's book *The First Team,* a well-documented history of the Pacific campaign from Pearl Harbor to Midway. Drawing on material from Japanese sources, Lundstrom asserts that the second wave of bombers included only eight aircraft and that one of the planes shot out of formation by O'Hare actually managed to limp back to Rabaul. O'Hare was still officially credited with five victories that day, which made him the Navy's first ace of World War II. Afterward, with characteristic modesty, he made it all sound like a simple training exercise. "It seems as if all you need to do is to put some of these .50-caliber slugs into the Jap engines and they come all apart and tear themselves right out of the ships," he said.

Lexington's crew cheered as the Japanese bombers fell from the sky. Those belowdecks heard a play-by-play account over the ship's loudspeaker system, being broadcast by a United Press reporter. Fellow pilots later marveled at O'Hare's gunnery, noting that he used only about 60 rounds to shoot down each bomber.

The strike against Rabaul had to be canceled because the element of surprise had been lost, but it was a great day for naval aviation. The Navy claimed that 16 of the 18 attacking aircraft had been "splashed," along with two four-engine patrol planes. U.S. forces lost two F4Fs but only one pilot, and the task force was undamaged. For his part, O'Hare didn't seem to mind that he had been the target of a jumpy Navy machine-gunner as he returned to the carrier. According to Thach, he walked over to the trigger-happy sailor and said gently, "Son, if you don't stop shooting at me when I've got my wheels down, I'm going to have to report you to the gunnery officer." Later, O'Hare expressed a certain degree of annoyance about the incident. "I don't mind him shooting at me when I don't have my wheels down," he said, "but it might

flew straight at the lead section, climbing above the formation and then rolling their Wildcats for a rear attack on the trailing aircraft on the right side of the V.

Ignoring heavy fire from the well-armed Bettys, O'Hare closed to 100 yards and sighted his guns on the starboard engines of the last two aircraft. Two quick bursts, and both engines seemed literally to jump out of their mountings. O'Hare pulled up, dodging debris from the stricken aircraft, and crossed to the other side of make me have to take a wave-off, and I don't like to take wave-offs."

It would be more than a year before anyone—friend or foe—would shoot at O'Hare again. By returning to Washington for the decoration ceremonies, he missed both the Battle of the Coral Sea in early May, during which *Lexington* was sunk, and the pivotal Battle of Midway one month later.

In June, with his public relations assignment completed, O'Hare was given command of his old squadron (redesignated VF-6). But by then most of his old squadron mates were gone, and his job was training new pilots rather than fighting the enemy.

As a training officer, "O'Hare preached the Bible according to Thach," Barrett Tillman wrote in *Hellcat.* "Teamwork and marksmanship were the virtues he stressed." And, like Thach, he was all business where flying was concerned. Once, when several squadron pilots wanted to try out some Army Curtiss P-40s at a nearby airfield in Hawaii, he hauled them over the coals, saying it was more important to gain experience in the new Grumman F6F-3 Hellcats that were replacing their Wildcats.

Finally, in late August 1943, O'Hare's squadron took part in an assault by the new generation of fast carriers against Marcus Island in the Central Pacific. The American raiders achieved such complete surprise that no Japanese planes even got off the ground. O'Hare was awarded a Distinguished Flying Cross (DFC) for disregarding "tremendous anti-aircraft fire" in leading his squadron "in persistent and vigorous strafing raids against hostile establishments on the island."

The squadron took part in a carrier raid on Wake Island five weeks later. The Hellcat pilots finally got to test their machines against the legendary Zero. O'Hare shot down one, his first kill since he bagged five in one day in February 1942. On the way home, he spotted a Betty and also sent that crashing into the sea for his seventh victory. His day's work earned him a Gold Star in lieu of a second DFC.

Next came the campaign against the Gilbert Islands and the bloody Marine invasion of Tarawa. By now, O'Hare was an air group commander assigned to *Enterprise.* Edward P. Stafford, who wrote the ship's history, *The Big E,* noted: "O'Hare was unchallengeably the best shot and the best pilot in his command. His men stood in awe of him for the hero he was. They respected him

Photographed from Lexington, *Lt. Cmdr. Takuzo Ito's G4M1, its left engine shot away by O'Hare, makes a last attempt to reach its target before crashing into the sea.*

for his repeatedly demonstrated professional competence and they loved him for his warmth, his enthusiasm and his courage."

Enterprise was part of Task Group 50.2, which also included two light carriers, *Belleau Wood* and *Monterey,* three fast battleships and six destroyers. The group's mission was to secure the airspace over Makin Atoll at the northern end of the Gilberts, destroy the island's defense installations, support invasion forces on November 20, and then stand by to repel any Japanese counterstrike.

Resistance on both Makin and Tarawa had been crushed by November 23 (with the Marines taking more than 3,000 casualties on Tarawa). But the American Fifth Fleet of Vice Adm. Raymond Spruance was coming under increasing attack from Japanese land-based torpedo planes and submarines. On the morning of November 25, the escort carrier *Liscome Bay* was sunk by Japanese

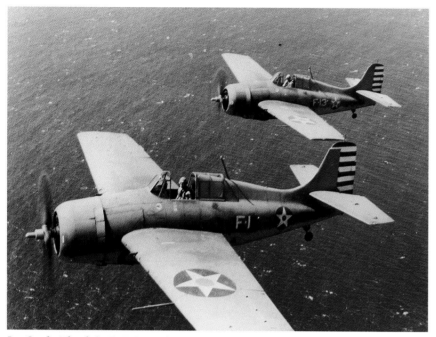

Lt. Cmdr. Thach in F4F-3 F-1 (serial no. 3976) and O'Hare in F-13 (serial no. 3986) near Naval Air Station Kaneohe on April 10, 1942. O'Hare was flying Wildcat No. 4031 on February 20.

submarine *I-175*, 20 miles southwest of Makin, with the loss of some 650 crew members. That night, a Japanese two-engine bomber, looking for a target, crossed the deck of *Enterprise* at an altitude of approximately 400 feet but never saw the ship.

Now O'Hare's top priority was to stop the Japanese torpedo planes that appeared on the ship's radar just after sunset, dropping parachute flares and searching for targets. "The Japs can't attack us by day and make it profitable anymore," he told a writer for the *Saturday Evening Post*. "Our Hellcats and AA [anti-aircraft] guns are too much for them....The Japs have got the word....The only time to sock their fish home is at night when they can avoid our fighters."

O'Hare and other senior pilots had developed a novel night-fighting tactic. They teamed two F6F Hellcats with a radar-equipped Grumman TBF Avenger torpedo-bomber and sent them out on search-and-destroy missions. First, the ship's radar would vector the team toward the enemy. Then the TBF radar would lock onto a target and lead the Hellcats in close enough for the pilots to see the exhaust from the enemy planes' engines and to begin shooting. Up to that point in the war, few, if any, actual combat operations had been attempted in the hours of darkness because of the difficulty of finding the enemy. If approved, O'Hare's plan would be a naval aviation first.

Still, O'Hare was uneasy about landing his team of fighters on *Enterprise* after dark. He wanted an alternative. So on November 26, he flew his Hellcat to the newly captured airfield on Tarawa. The field still was pitted with bomb craters, but he decided that using the runway there might be safer than landing on a pitching carrier in the dead of night. He returned to the ship more determined than ever to try his experiment.

But first O'Hare led a flight of four Hellcats off the deck of the carrier at 3 a.m. on November 27 to see if they could find the enemy without the help of airborne radar. The pilots returned after dawn with nothing to show for their efforts. One pilot later described the experience as "the longest 5½ hours I've ever put in in my life."

O'Hare had made his point and was given permission to run the night-fighter operation later that day. Since it was primarily his idea, he characteristically decided to fly the first mission himself with a volunteer, Ensign Warren "Andy" Skon, as his wingman. They took off from the carrier just before sunset, and then were vectored "on a number of courses in search of bogies," but night overtook them before they could make any contact. They then turned their attention to joining up with the TBF-1C Avenger, flown by Lt. Cmdr. John L. Phillips, commander of VT-6, that had followed them off the carrier.

The join-up proved difficult in darkness despite guidance from *Enterprise's* radar controllers. There also were numerous Japanese aircraft buzzing around unseen in the night sky, but the Avenger pilot shot down two of them with the help of his onboard radar. Finally, after more than 30 minutes of searching, the rendezvous was made. The three aircraft turned on low-intensity running lights to avoid losing contact again. O'Hare flew to the starboard and slightly astern of the Avenger, while Skon took up a similar position on the port side.

In an official statement made after the engagement, Skon estimated that O'Hare was about 200 feet to the right of him when the TBF's turret gunner suddenly opened fire with his .50-caliber machine gun. Skon thought the tracers passed between the two Hellcats, but a few seconds after the first shots, "O'Hare slid out of formation," and Skon could not tell whether "he was making a run, or was out of control and skidding." Skon started to follow him down, but O'Hare was moving too fast and "disappeared from sight." Radio calls to the missing pilot went unanswered. The TBF gunner later stated that he saw a "fourth plane closing in on us," and was given permission to open fire as soon as it was in range. Although it was very dark and he was blinded by his own tracer fire, he thought he hit his target but could not say if he "shot down the Jap." The radar officer supported the gunner's story about a fourth aircraft but said nothing about having another target on his scope.

The report filed by the TBF commander raised further doubts about the accuracy of the gunner's observations. It noted that the "turret gunner was blinded by his own and enemy tracers and had great difficulty in seeing the target." In addition, he said, "the field of vision through the electrical turret sight was very limited," and he recommended the use of "auxiliary sights in future night work."

Ensign Skon, perhaps the only impartial observer, had his own version of O'Hare's fate. "I at no time sighted a second plane to the starboard and astern of the TBF," he said. Nor did he "observe a plane pass over the TBF after Lt. Cmdr. O'Hare slid out of formation." He also stated that he "saw no gunfire other than the TBF turret gunner's." To this day, the question of what really happened to Butch O'Hare remains unanswered.

O'Hare was awarded the Navy Cross for his final action. One year later, he was officially declared dead, although his accomplishments continued to serve as an inspiration for Navy fliers throughout the war. In September 1949, the city of Chicago made sure that his heroism would never be forgotten. The name of the city's airport was changed from Orchard Field to O'Hare Airport.

On February 20, 1992, Butch O'Hare's Medal of Honor was presented to the city of Chicago by his daughter and two sisters during

Hugh Polder's 1st Chutai Meets Butch O'Hare *is one of many paintings based on the February 20, 1942, fight. O'Hare's later exploits have had no such pictorial coverage.*

a commemorative ceremony. The event marked the 50th anniversary of O'Hare's monumental feat. His Medal of Honor is now part of the O'Hare memorial exhibit at the airport that bears his name.

V

WOLFPACK AT WAR

After 'Hub' Zemke whipped them into shape, the P-47 pilots of the
56th Fighter Group went on to score 992½ confirmed kills.

By Don Hollway

As the survivors of the 56th Fighter Group straggled back in over the British field, their commanding officer came down out of the control tower to meet them. Lieutenant Colonel Hubert "Hub" Zemke had listened helplessly to the radio chatter as his men met the enemy over German-occupied Holland for the first time. It was April 1943, and the *Luftwaffe* was still a formidable fighting force; from the confused radio traffic Zemke could tell the combat had not gone well. Missing from the running commentary was the voice of Major Dave Schilling, the 62nd Squadron commander to whom Zemke had entrusted the mission. Now, as Schilling's plane put down, Zemke took a jeep over to find out what had gone wrong.

The major's fighter, *Hairless Joe,* had taken some hits. But the radio, Schilling explained, had gone out before the group ever reached the Dutch coast. Rather than abort, the dashing but impetuous Schilling had retained command and, upon sighting a pair of bandits, had led the 62nd's attack. Scoreless, ambushed by Messerschmitt Me-109s and Focke Wulf Fw-190s, they and the group's two remaining squadrons, the 61st and 63rd, belatedly escaped back over the English Channel. Many of the missing pilots, their aircraft running low on fuel, had simply set down at the first English airfields they came across, but two did not return. It had been, as Zemke later recalled, "an ignominious combat debut."

Another commander might have taken it as an indictment of his own leadership skills. Zemke had joined the 56th only the previous year, a 28-year-old lieutenant with experience only as a combat observer in Great Britain and as a fighter pilot instructor in Russia. Zemke's uncle had died flying for Germany in 1916, and two cousins were killed on the Russian Front while Zemke was in Moscow. In the rapidly expanding U.S. Army Air Forces, however, promotion came easily, and he had risen quickly to captain, then major, and ultimately, as a lieutenant colonel, was placed in command of the group. That the 56th had lost 18 men even before shipping for England he attributed to the combination of inexperienced, gung-ho flyboys and a brand-new, trouble-prone fighter—Republic's P-47B Thunderbolt, the "Jug."

"The pilots were all eager young fellows who thought the Thunderbolt was a terrific fighter simply because they had flown nothing else," said Zemke. Above 20,000 feet the P-47

In Calm Before the Storm, *by Jim Laurier, ground crewmen perform maintenance on Captain Francis S. Gabreski's Republic P-47D Thunderbolt of the 61st Squadron of Colonel Hubert A. Zemke's 56th Fighter Group, better known as "Zemke's Wolfpack."*

© Jim Laurier 1992

In Hunter Becomes the Hunted, *by William S. Phillips, Zemke catches a Focke Wulf Fw-190A-7 in the act of attacking a formation of Boeing B-17s over Holland on March 6, 1944. The German, 1st Lt. Wolfgang Kretschmer of II Gruppe, Jagdgeschwader 1, bailed out and later met Zemke in 1990.*

was capable of speeds of up to 400 mph and had the quickest roll rate of any fighter in the U.S. inventory. But even with a turbosupercharged Pratt & Whitney R-2800 Double Wasp radial engine capable (in later models) of 2,800 hp, the plane required almost a half-mile run just to get 50 feet off the ground. Zemke noted that the aircraft "accelerated poorly and climbed not too much better from a slow airspeed" and that "overall the P-47 was a big disappointment."

In England, the 56th took over an ex-RAF (Royal Air Force) grass strip at Horsham Saint Faith, Norfolk County. (When he was turning over the airstrip to Zemke, Schilling, and pilots Goldstein, Shiltz and Altschuler, the Royal Air Force station chief grinned, saying, "Sounds like I'm handing over to the *Luftwaffe!*")

Equipped with new P-47Cs, they joined the 4th Fighter Group

on a couple of "rodeos"—fighter sweeps intended to lure the *Luftwaffe* into combat—but Zemke had to abort because of an oxygen system malfunction. And on the group's first "ramrod"—a bomber escort mission for which the P-47, with its blunt, high-drag nose and resultant short range, had never been designed—his own radio went out. (Because of faulty ignition systems, early model P-47s suffered from inordinate radio static.) His men bounced some bogeys over Walcheren Island and knocked one down—realizing too late the fighters were British.

In all fairness, the RAF had strayed from its assigned area, and in the heat of combat even experienced pilots sometimes failed at aircraft recognition. But in view of his group's dismal record (and aware that his two aborts could be construed as a failure of nerve rather than equipment) Zemke, upon his promotion to bird (full) colonel, suspected he would be bumped upstairs to make room for a more capable group commander.

Finally, on June 12, the 56th flew another rodeo, 20,000 feet above Pas de Calais. German *Jagdgeschwader* (Fighter Wing) 26 had made these skies so much its own that its pilots were known to Allied airmen as "the Abbeville Boys," named after the town where they were based. By flying 10,000 feet lower than usual, the group caught JG 26 by surprise. Over Ypres, Belgium, Schilling led the 62nd Squadron's Blue Flight down after a *Staffel* (squadron) of Fw-190s, but as the Jerries scattered, a *Schwarm* (flight of four) moved around into kill position on Blue Flight's tail.

Still "upsun," Captain Walter Cook saw the trap and led Yellow Flight down to the rescue. He opened fire on the trailing Focke Wulf from 300 yards. "Suddenly a big ball of fire appeared on his left wing and then black smoke poured out," recalled Cook. "He rolled to the left, went over on his back in a gentle roll, and then went into a violent spin, with smoke pouring out from the fuselage and wing. At no time did the pilot take evasive action, and I believe he was killed."

The next day, again over Ypres, Zemke led the 61st Squadron down behind a *Schwarm* of Focke Wulfs, pulling to within 200 yards of the fourth aircraft. Zemke remembered that a split second after he fired at the plane, "the fuselage burst into flames and pieces of the right wing came off." The third enemy plane twisted away with only minor hits on the starboard wingtip, but the number two plane "sat in the gunsight as one would imagine for the ideal shot. Again, when the trigger was pulled this aircraft exploded with a long sheet of flame and smoke."

Meanwhile, the 61st's Lieutenant Bob Johnson, an aggressive Oklahoman chafing in the "Tail-End Charlie" slot of his flight, left formation to make a solo attack—on no less than the enemy leader. "I didn't think that this was a Focke Wulf," Johnson recalled, "or

Zemke checks his guns. With eight .50-caliber machine guns, the P-47 boasted the heaviest armament of any single-engine fighter.

that the man inside was a German, or that if he managed to whirl that black-crossed airplane around, then four cannon and two heavy guns would be hurling steel and explosives at me."

Johnson flamed the Fw-190 with his first burst. For abandoning formation, however, he was chewed out by his flight leader, Lieutenant Jerry Johnson (no relation); his squadron leader, Major Francis "Gabby" Gabreski; and finally by Zemke himself, whose leadership style had not been softened by his own double kill. "I doubt

I endeared Bob to his group commander," Zemke later reflected. "Privately, it was good to know I had pilots of such aggressive caliber."

As it turned out, all four men were to race each other in downing German aircraft. For the time being, Bob Johnson swore, "The Krauts are going to have to shoot me out of formation."

Two weeks later he made good on his promise. His P-47, *Half Pint,* was again bringing up the rear when Johnson spotted 16 more fighters above and behind—Focke Wulfs, the Abbeville Boys, diving in for the kill. He called out a warning to the rest of the group, but for a fateful second nobody moved. Johnson held position, a perfect target, as the Germans raked him with fire—and then his P-47 was spinning downward, out of control, with the canopy jammed shut, trapping him in a cockpit full of fire.

The speed of his dive blew out the flames. Johnson managed to coast his crippled mount toward the Channel. Just when he thought he had made good his escape, a lone Fw-190 joined up behind him. Unable to dogfight but unwilling to just sit there and take it, Johnson used his lack of speed to force the Focke Wulf into an overshoot so that he could turn the tables. Easily evading Johnson's fire, the German circled back to shoot him up twice more. Still *Half Pint* refused to go down; finally, the German gave up, rocked his wings in grudging salute and turned back. With 21 cannon hits and more than 100 bullet holes in his Jug, Johnson made it across the Channel to a no-flaps, no-brakes landing at an RAF base near Dover, ground-looping to a stop between two parked Hawker Typhoons. That day the 56th scored two kills—including one by Kentucky quail hunter Jerry Johnson—but lost four of its own.

In July, when a bomber group took over Horsham Saint Faith, Zemke's men relocated to a half-built base at Halesworth Suffolk. Upset with the second-rate treatment his command seemed to be experiencing, Zemke joined a group of Eighth Air Force bomber commanders in a gripe session. The 4th Bomb Wing's Colonel Curtis LeMay (chief of the postwar Strategic Air Command) complained that the only fighters he had seen so far "all had black and white crosses on them," but declared his bombers would carry on "with or without fighter escort." Later, in the officers' club, another bomber general stated he "wouldn't pay a dime a dozen for any fighter pilots."

Zemke hurled his pocket change at the man's feet: "Here, General, this is all I have handy at the moment," he responded. "Any time you have a couple dozen fighter pilots handy send them my way. We can sure use them." Then he jumped in his Jug and buzzed the place.

The bomber crews had good reason to be edgy. They were about to depart on one of their bloodiest missions, the first Schweinfurt–Regensburg raid. After escorting the B-17 Flying Fortresses partway to Schweinfurt, the 56th returned to Halesworth and took on 200-gallon pressed-paper ferry tanks converted for combat use. These upset the Jugs' handling and did not feed well in the low air pressure above 20,000 feet, but they gave the Thunderbolts enough range to meet the bombers over Germany.

The Thunderbolts proceeded to teach a *Staffel* of twin-engine Messerschmitt Me-110 night fighters not to venture out in daylight. "The 61st Squadron came screaming down from the front and caught an Me-110 right over the last box of bombers," Zemke recalled. "Two P-47s shot at this guy at the same time—16 guns firing—and both of them hit him simultaneously. That Me-110 blew up as I've never seen anything blow up and fell, on fire, directly through the bomber formation…without hitting one of them."

One of the Me-110 shooters was Jerry Johnson, who downed two more Germans in quick succession—the 56th's first triple kill, except that he had to split credit for the Messerschmitt. (Two days later, Johnson got an Me-109, which could have made him the 56th's first ace. Instead, his score stood at 4½.)

Zemke, having gotten an Me-110 himself, estimated the combat at no more than seven minutes long, but at that distance from base, fuel was already running low and he ordered a return home. From well to the north, however, Captain Bud Mahurin called back, "We've got 'em cornered. There's plenty for everyone. Come on up this way."

Soon after Zemke's run-in with Bomber Command, Mahurin had gotten a little too close to one of the new Consolidated B-24 Liberators in formation and his Thunderbolt's tail had been sucked into the bomber's props; the four-engine B-24 had straggled home, but Mahurin had barely escaped from his falling Jug. Now he saw his chance to make amends—he had spotted a Focke Wulf above

Lieutenant Cameron M. Hart warms up at Boxted in September 1944. Hart, whose plane's nose art was based on the 63rd Squadron's emblem, finished the war with six victories.

the bombers, preparing to turn down into them. Mahurin recalled, "I sneaked up behind it and started to fire from about 300 yards, closing to 200 yards. It blew up."

Mahurin and his wingman circled up through the bomber stream onto the tail of a second Fw-190. "We followed him until he started to make a turn into the front end of the bombers," said Mahurin, "when I took a deflection [angled] shot at him and watched him blow up."

Not one to hold a grudge, Zemke recommended Mahurin for the Distinguished Flying Cross. Later it turned out one of his kills was none other than the commander of II *Gruppe* JG 26, *Oberstleutnant* (Lt. Col.) Wilhelm "Wutz" Galland, brother of the famous *Luftwaffe* General of Fighters Adolf Galland and himself a 55-victory *Experte* (ace). His body was found in his aircraft two months later, driven by the force of impact 12 feet into the ground.

Bomber Command lost 60 of the 375 bombers on the mission. But the 56th, scoring 17 confirmed, one probable and nine dam-

aged, prevented even more slaughter. "We had certainly broken up several German attacks," Zemke said.

In August 1943, the 56th's top guns began to distinguish themselves. Gabreski scored his first kill, Bob Johnson scored his second, and Zemke his fourth. In September, Zemke led the group on its longest mission yet, a 250-mile ramrod to Emden, Germany. (The P-47s had received new 75-gallon underwing tanks made of metal and pressurized to feed at all altitudes.) Spotting a lone Focke Wulf stalking a straggling B-17 several thousand feet below, Zemke dived and fired from 500 yards: "Immediately strikes were registered all over the aircraft," he reported. "Surprisingly, the Focke Wulf flew on in a straight line. Another burst brought smoke and flame, and a third caused the left undercarriage leg to drop. Only then did the stricken plane fall away in a vertical dive. As no evasive action had been observed, I concluded the first burst had killed the pilot."

That made Zemke the 56th's first ace, by a narrow margin. Schilling, who had not scored a victory in 52 missions, got two that same day and three more by October 10, when Bob and Jerry Johnson each got their fifth. With four of the five American aces in the European theater of operations (ETO), the 56th never looked back, scoring its 100th kill, a Messerschmitt Me-210, on November 5 (at this time Major Eugene Roberts of the 78th Fighter Group claimed eight kills). On November 26, during a ramrod to Bremen, "Zemke's Wolfpack" (the nickname given to the 56th) scored an ETO record: 23 confirmed, three probable and nine damaged, including two for Gabreski.

A second-generation Pole who had flown a Curtiss P-40 Tomahawk during the Pearl Harbor attack and a Supermarine Spitfire Mk. IX with the Free Poles in RAF service, Gabreski barreled down on a pair of Me-110s that dived away—always a mistake against the fast-diving Jug. "I closed in rapidly behind them and opened fire on one at about 700 yards range…suddenly I was right on top of the 110. I just barely had time to push the control stick forward and duck below the burning German fighter." Regaining height, Gabreski dived after a second Me-110. "This time I slowed my approach slightly, though we were still traveling at about 420 mph when I opened fire from 600 yards. The 110 took solid hits in its wing root and rolled over into a death fall at 14,000 feet."

Kills four and five were racked up by Gabreski; Schilling and Cook also scored doubles (Cook likewise achieving ace status), and Mahurin got three more Me-110s to become the ETO's first double ace. By March 1944, with 20 kills, he ranked as its highest scorer, with Bob and Jerry Johnson right behind him. The 61st Squadron became the first in the ETO with 100 victories to its credit; the group's tally stood at 300. That month the *Luftwaffe* lost 22 percent of its pilots, a blow from which it never really recovered, and the 56th flew a ramrod all the way to Berlin and back without meeting a single enemy fighter.

Then, on March 27, while shooting down a Dornier Do-217 bomber south of Chartres, Mahurin was hit by its rear gunner: "I could see the shadow of my airplane with a great long trail of black smoke following me," Mahurin recalled. He bailed out and was last seen running for a tree line. And Jerry Johnson, with 18 kills to his credit, was hit by groundfire while strafing a truck convoy and taken prisoner after bellying in. Mahurin made it back to England via the French underground and an RAF rescue plane, but he was not permitted to risk capture—which might mean having to reveal the secrets of his escape route—again. Transferred to the Pacific theater, Mahurin scored another kill before the war's end, as well as 3½ MiGs in the Korean War, before being shot down again and captured by the North Koreans.

So the mantle of high scorer passed to Bob Johnson. By early May 1944, near the end of his combat tour, Johnson led the ETO with 25 victories, just one less than World War I ace Eddie Rickenbacker. Returning from his last mission, an uneventful ramrod to Berlin on May 8, he rolled onto the tail of a passing Me-109. The Jerry banked left, but Johnson rolled inside his turn. "We were real close," Johnson recalled. "Close enough that I could see the pilot look back over his shoulder as I opened fire. He went into a dive but I kept right on his tail pouring fire into him. Suddenly his left wing came off and the fighter spun in. That made 26!" When his numbers three and four chased a flight of Focke Wulfs into a cloud, only to re-emerge with the Germans on their tails, Johnson scared off the lead Fw-190 with a few bursts. "I swung my nose to bear on the second plane. Hits! All over the wings and wing roots, and there it was. Number 27…my last mission couldn't have been more perfect."

By now the Wolfpack, flying out of Boxted, Essex—and accounting for more than 400 kills—had developed P-47 tactics to a high art, diving to the attack and zooming back up to safety. From that strategy evolved group tactics: a lead squadron flying low, covered by the second at medium altitude, with the third high up in reserve. Spreading out ahead of the bombers to sweep the skies clean of German fighters, the "Zemke Fan"—the 56th Fighter Group—presented an awesome array of aerial firepower.

On June 27 Gabreski downed an Me-109 to match Bob Johnson's score, and on July 5 he shot down another Messerschmitt near Evreux. So Gabreski had 28 aerial kills (and 2½ on the ground) and the ETO had a new high scorer. But like Johnson before him, "Gabby" was nearing the end of his tour. On his last day, July 20, he took time off from a ramrod to Frankfurt to strafe Bassinheim Airfield and set a parked Heinkel bomber afire. "At that time our policy was to make one pass on an airdrome and get out," he recalled, "because the flak gunners were always ready and waiting if you tried to come back for more. But I figured the flak had been so light that I could get away with another pass."

Coming back in right down on the deck, Gabreski saw his tracers pass over another He-111. Without thinking, he dropped the nose—and the P-47's big paddle prop clipped the ground. With no hope of returning to England, Gabreski bellied into a wheat field and was captured. (He went on to fly North American F-86 Sabre jets over Korea—as Mahurin's commanding officer—downing 6½ MiGs.)

Of the 56th's original aces, only Zemke and Schilling remained. Offered command of the 479th Fighter Group—Lockheed P-38 Lightnings—Schilling refused ("Hell no, not P-38s") and was stunned when Zemke took it instead. "There was only one group Dave wanted...and deserved to command," said Zemke. "And for me there was need of a new challenge, a new purpose...[but]...behind me was the greatest command of my service life." (By giving up his P-47, Zemke shortened his war. He scored two kills with the 479th, bringing his final aerial tally to 17¾, but on October 30, on escort duty over Germany, the North American P-51 Mustang he was flying that day came apart in a thunderstorm. Zemke got out safely, only to be captured.)

Zemke's departure marked the Wolfpack's darkest chapter. On September 17 the group was handed the dirtiest ground-attack work of all: anti-aircraft suppression in support of the ill-fated Allied airborne invasion of Holland (Operation Market Garden). In two days of dueling with flak sites, Schilling's men took out 34 emplacements, but 17 P-47s were destroyed and a dozen damaged. Two pilots became prisoners of war and four were killed. The group's old nemesis, JG 26, got through the dazed P-47 pilots the next day to knock down 17 helpless troop transports.

Fortunately, October 1944 was a quiet time for the Eighth Air Force. The *Luftwaffe* was saving its precious planes and fuel reserves

From left, Robert S. Johnson (27 total victories), Hub Zemke (17¾) and Bud Mahurin (20¼) after returning from their March 6, 1944 mission.

for the *grosse Schlag*—the "Great Blow," or Ardennes offensive, in which the Germans hoped to prevent the invasion of their fatherland. As they planned, foul weather initially curtailed Allied fighter cover. Not until December 23 could Schilling lead his men over the battleground, where he lost track of two consecutive enemy formations in the clouds. He angrily took his ground controllers to task, and they replied, "Don't worry about it! There's bigger game on this heading!"

There was. A large enemy formation was located below and 40-plus more were flying ahead, including new Focke Wulf Fw-190D "long-nosed" high-altitude fighters. Sending the 61st and 63rd down to attack the Germans below, Schilling brought the 62nd around behind the group that was ahead. "I managed to hit the right rear Me-109 with about a 20-degree deflection shot at a range of about 700 yards," Schilling recalled. As the Messerschmitt dropped off, Schilling moved up on the next in line, setting it afire. "I then picked another and fired at about 1,000 yards and missed as he broke right and started to dive for the deck. At about 17,000 feet I had closed to about 500 yards and fired, resulting in a heavy concentration of strikes, and the pilot bailed out."

Now separated from his flight, Schilling spotted 35 to 40 Focke Wulfs circling 1,000 feet below him. "I repeated the same tactics as before and attacked one from about 500 yards' range." As the Fw-190 went spinning downward, Schilling latched onto a fifth, which put up more of a fight: "He immediately took violent evasive action, and it took me several minutes of maneuvering to get in a position to fire. I fired from about 300 yards above and to the left, forcing me to pull through him and fire as he went out of sight over the cowling....The pilot immediately bailed out."

Hooking up with a stray 63rd Squadron pilot, Schilling looked for a sixth kill, but when his wingman was attacked he broke off to help him out. Both escaped. When all the gun-camera film was sorted out later, the Wolfpack had chalked up its best day ever— 34 enemy aircraft destroyed. Their tally now stood at more than 800—25 percent of the Eighth Air Force total. (Schilling, who was awarded the Distinguished Service Cross, soon moved up to join 65th Wing Headquarters, finishing the war as a full colonel with 22½ aerial and 11½ ground kills.)

After that, the 56th's only real challengers in the air were the new Messerschmitt Me-262 jet fighters. The Wolfpack had downed jets before with lucky passing shots or by catching them over their runways. They had stuck with the Jug when all other groups went to P-51s, and were the sole recipients of the P-47M—upengined to produce 465 mph (more speed than a Mustang)—with which they could handle combat on the jets' terms. On April 5, 1945, a Wolfpack pilot actually *ran down* a 262 in a shallow dive. Attempting to outturn the P-47, the German pilot was cut off and shot down.

On April 13, the second anniversary of its first combat mission, the Wolfpack celebrated by savaging Eggebeck Airdrome. Coming across the field at 400 to 450 mph, they fired more than 78,000 rounds of .50 caliber ammo, destroying 91 enemy aircraft where they sat and becoming the first Eighth Air Force group to surpass the magic number—1,000 destroyed.

Later that score was reduced, but the 56th Fighter Group finished the war with 992½ confirmed kills, including 664½ in the air, more than any other Eighth Air Force fighter group. Furthermore, the 56th scored 58 probables and 543 damaged in the air and on the ground. At war's end a P-47M was exhibited under the Eiffel Tower, its nose emblazoned with the legend: *Zemke's Wolfpack, 56th Fighter Group, 1,000 Enemy Aircraft Destroyed!*

"A fighter pilot must possess an inner urge for combat," Zemke said. "The will at all times to be offensive will develop into his own tactics. I stay with an enemy until either he's destroyed, I'm out of ammunition, he evades into the clouds, or I'm too low on gasoline to continue the combat."

VI

BATTLING THE ZEROS OVER NEW GUINEA

'Our side believed that the Zero had a gravity-fed carburetor and the engine would not run upside down, whereas the P-40 would. I would soon find out....'

First Person by Richard J. Vodra

I awakened staring up through the mosquito netting at the darkened tent, wet with sweat and my legs on fire from the knees down. Chiggers, they called them. Microscopic red fleas that lived in the jungle grass and burrowed into any living thing. I probably had gotten a new batch during the night. It was the morning of May 14, 1943, and this was New Guinea. Pilots were scheduled to fly every other day if they could. It was my day to fly, and there seemed nothing unusual about it. Yet that sickish little knot that lived in the pit of the stomach of everyone in combat seemed bigger to me this morning. Ominously bigger.

Our fighter squadron (8th Squadron, 49th Fighter Group) had been the first to land on the north, or Japanese side, of the New Guinea mountains, which had, until now, served as an impenetrable barrier between the opposing forces. The audacious move toward the enemy was called "Kenny's Gamble" because it was the brainstorm of our boss, General George C. Kenny. Our job was to stay at that location at all costs, because from there we would be most effective in protecting our ground forces and in making strikes at enemy installations.

We were now less than two miles from the center of our major battle zone, from the same roadblocks, enemy barges, gun emplacements, and airfield at Buna we had been strafing and dive-bombing a few weeks before. Snipers were still a threat, and the squadron had been forbidden to risk sightseeing. Of course, Lieutenant Lowell Lutton, my tent mate, and I had at once sneaked off to investigate the prohibited—the stinking, primeval swamp, the burned-out tanks, the abandoned machine-gun bunkers, the log-covered catacombs—and to learn for ourselves why our diving air attacks, for which we paid so dearly, had invariably ended in bitter frustration.

It was now apparent that our bombs and machine-gun fire had been useless against their improvised log fortresses, which was why it had been necessary to take them out one by one. Somebody should have known. The cost had been beyond belief. Our own suffering from dysentery and malnutrition intensified the horror we felt for our ground troops who had been forced to take out those fortresses. They had had to crawl on their bellies with the seats of their pants cut away to cope with their own dysentery.

A well-armed American burial detail had spotted our prowling

In a painting by Jack Fellows, a Mitsubishi A6M3 Zero falls victim to Squirl Bate, *a Curtiss P-40E of the 8th Squadron, 49th Fighter Group, flown by author Richard J. Vodra.*

and warned us away. Since the beginning of warfare, it has been commonplace that the winners bury their dead, while the losers rot where they fall. Strewn throughout the swamp was grisly evidence that the Japanese had indeed lost this battle.

Perhaps that early morning seemed particularly ominous because of the long night before, broken by air raids and troubling thoughts. Lowell was still shaken and bruised from having belly-landed his airplane the day before. The hydraulic system had failed on his Curtiss P-40E, or "lead sled" as we referred to them because of their relative slowness, weight and lack of maneuverability. He had landed with the gear up into what he had hoped was soft kuani grass to save the plane. Instead, the ground beneath was corrugated with rocks and rotted stumps. He was lucky to walk away from the wreck.

I, too, had had disturbing thoughts. A week or so earlier, I had been climbing with the throttle wide open, to intercept an incoming flight of enemy bombers, when my engine seized because of a worn-out oil line. With my propeller motionless, I managed to maneuver from 15,000 feet back to the field and perform a dead-stick landing just as bombs struck and the strip in front of me became a line of erupting volcanoes.

But it wasn't these experiences we had talked about the previous evening while waiting for the nightly bombs to fall. Wearing undershorts, unlaced GI boots and steel helmets while squatting in 6 inches of slime in the bottom of a slit trench with our knees tucked against our chest, we had swatted mosquitoes and talked of other, more menacing concerns. Lowell had just been awarded the Soldier's Medal. We had all received at least one Distinguished Flying Cross and a number of Air Medals, but the Soldier's Medal was special. He had been awarded it for dashing into a burning bomber and rescuing half its crew before the bomber exploded. He just happened to be on the outside when it did.

Lowell was generally introspective and unflappable, which made this sort of talk unusual. Now, seemingly for the first time, he was worried, and it showed in his voice. We both were worried, but we had never seriously discussed it before. Our planes, what was left of them, were falling apart. They were the same lead sleds with which we had started the war. With no spare parts, we were lucky to keep three out of four in the air for a two-hour patrol if nothing happened during the patrol. And now, suddenly, the Japanese radio was going crazy.

We had never paid any attention to Tokyo Rose's daily radio propaganda broadcasts. The Japanese claims were always absurd, Rose's prating sophomoric. But lately their boasts of our total demise took on an air of disquieting possibility.

One fact was clear to both Lowell and me. Given the disreputable condition of our fighters, just two enemy provocations, spaced an hour apart, would force our planes into the strain of maximum output and leave our squadron decimated—without a shot ever being fired. This had been our best-kept secret since the Battle of the Bismarck Sea two months earlier. Outnumbered and out-gunned, we had won that battle by sheer luck and ingenuity, with much credit due to the unbelievable success of a never-before-tried technique called skip bombing. That innovation allowed our fighter planes without bombsights to get close to Japanese ships and skip bombs across the water at them.

Lately, our intelligence had been reporting even heavier air buildups by the Japanese, and their raids had become more intense. From the Japanese radio histrionics, it seemed that they might well have discovered our "secret" and were intent on finishing off our small force. It was good that Lowell, still bruised from his crash landing, had the day off, for the Japanese had a nasty surprise in store for the duty pilots.

Within a half-hour of getting up that morning, the other duty pilots and I were on our way to the landing strip, 1½ miles from the camp. The hooded headlights on our jeep probed for rotten logs and slime-filled shell holes as we threaded our way through the jungle rot. There were only three functioning jeeps left to haul all 16 pilots. We clung all over the groaning little vehicles like migrant workers heading off to the fields.

No one spoke. No one joked. Three out of four of us had been declared physically unfit to fly, a laudable but useless effort by our flight surgeon. There was no one to take our places. It was a macabre joke that the condition of the pilots so well matched that of their planes.

It was still pitch-black when we broke out of the jungle into a small clearing at one end of the flight strip. Across the clearing, a single lightbulb cast a dirty yellow haze through the open flap of a large square tent—the "alert shack" where we would await any calls to action during our stint. We cut toward the haze. At the far end of the strip, a half-mile away, the low drone of engines could be heard as crew chiefs taxied our fighters out of their jungle hideouts and up the strip, which was no wider than the planes' wingtips. Like blind moles, the planes snaked back and forth up the narrow strip, guided by flickers from flashlights. In the distance the blue flames from the exhausts looked like pilot lights in a gas oven.

The tent was empty except for a few empty boxes and 16 cots dispersed across the dirt floor. A central wooden pole supported the peak of the tent and the unavoidable, omnipotent, brown-leather-cased field telephone that would deliver our "scramble" call. We pushed into the tent as if it were a practiced drill, slung our shoulder holsters over the corner of the nearest cot and, with our brown leather jackets rolled as pillows, were dead out in seconds.

The next morning, the spirit in the tent was high, with laughs and jibes coming as easy as in a fraternity lounge. Then 9 o'clock came and went, and a subtle quietness settled in. Jokes were not so funny, and our eyes roamed inevitably in the direction of the brown leather telephone. One of the pilots who had been reading got up and wandered outside...then the phone went off!

Our heads were down and our knees churning by the time the pilot at the phone screamed out, "Scramble all flights!" Although most of us had at one time lettered in athletics, fever and malnutrition by now had sapped our stamina. I was aching and gasping for breath when I reached my plane, 50 yards away.

I jammed my foot onto the left wing root and swung up into the cockpit with the aplomb of a cowboy in a B Western. There were taboos even here. No one ever entered a cockpit from the right side or allowed his picture to be taken before a mission. Everyone knew about those taboos—most were hangovers from World War I—but there were private ones, also. The second button on my shirt was open, the sixpence a little girl had given me for luck was in my right-hand shirt pocket—anything that had brought you back from the last mission could become a permanent appendage.

A Japanese troop transport falls victim to skip-bombers of the U.S. Fifth Air Force during the Battle of the Bismarck Sea (March 2–5, 1943), in which American and Australian aircraft ravaged Japan's last major daylight convoy, sinking eight transports and four destroyers.

Sergeant George Law, panting almost as hard as I, scrambled up on the wing behind me. I could hear grunts coming from all of the ground crew as one scrambled up on the opposite side of the cockpit while others jerked away the wheel chocks. In one practiced movement, I pulled on my helmet, Law closed the parachute buckles across my chest, and other fingers snapped on my throat mike as I poked my head out the left corner of the windshield and shouted, "Clear!" A voice answered, "Clear!" I could hear other engines starting along the runway.

I would be the last to take off, not the most enviable of positions. I shouted "Contact," then hit the starter button. The propeller turned over slowly, gained speed, the engine kicked in, coughed, started, then quit as the propeller vibrated to a cranky stop. I glanced to my right. One plane was already starting its takeoff run. That would be Ernie "Stone Face" Harris. Others were pulling out behind him. On a scramble, the narrow, one-lane strip forced dangerous nose-to-tail, single-file takeoffs, with each plane fighting the prop wash of the preceding ones. I pushed my starter button again, and again the engine coughed, backfired, roared up, then died. I watched Leo Mayo, on whose wing I was supposed to fly in Red Flight, the last to go, head down the runway.

Ground crews were scattering in all directions for the nearest foxholes. The enemy could be screaming down on us with his guns blazing at that very instant. It had happened before. It's a fighter pilot's dream to be lucky enough to catch an enemy plane on the ground with its pilot and crew. No one was hanging around. Except my crew. My radio was screaming static in my ear. Something sure as hell was happening, but I wasn't picking it up. I pushed the starter button and waved my ground crew away. They stuck. The engine finally caught, flared into a roar and held.

I shoved the throttle forward and jammed the toe of my boot onto the right brake. The tail wheel swiveled, and the plane spun on the right wheel until the nose started to align with the runway. I shoved the throttle the rest of the way forward, released the brake and shot down the strip, straightening out as I went. My tail lifted, and for the first time I could see over the long expanse of cowling in front of me.

It was almost too late. Halfway down the runway there was a plane stopped diagonally across my path, its propeller still. I chopped the throttle and stood on the brakes, working them frantically back and forth to stay in line, and finally came to a stop, not 50 feet from the ailing plane. At best, I'd spared myself having to resort to a ground loop—at worst, there was no time to think about it. Now I waited for the plane to get out of my way. I scanned the sky in front and behind me while trying to watch my engine temperature. Idling, the engine began to overheat. I cracked the air vents. If a strafing party was on its way in, I would not have time to escape its fire anyway.

At last the plane in front of me was wrestled out of the way. I couldn't see who the pilot was, but it wasn't Leo's P-40. Someone had tried to get off after him, but his engine had failed. Now, with full flaps down to shorten my takeoff—a no-no in the old 40—and

full throttle, I screamed on toward the trees at the end of what was left of the runway. When I had barely attained flying speed, I reached down and raised the landing gear, keeping the nose level. The airspeed increased, with the prop skimming the ground by inches, and at the last minute I popped back on the stick.

There was no sensation of flying, just mushing, staggering, stalling with those damnable full flaps down. A treetop flashed by my right wingtip. I pushed the stick forward, bumping up the flaps a bit at a time until at last I felt the sloppiness leave the controls—I began to fly. There was, of course, that feeling of standing still that always comes immediately after leaving the ground.

I glanced over the black control panel in front of me with its empty holes where instruments had been removed to lighten the plane and improve performance. Except for systems necessary to monitor engine functions, only the most rudimentary of dials were left: airspeed, altimeter, turn and bank indicators and, for navigation, a simple compass. Exactly the same as the ones used in World War I. To save even more weight, our total ammunition supply was reduced to last but 10 seconds—one-third less than design.

I pointed the nose upward with full manifold pressure and adjusted the mixture and propeller pitch for maximum rate of climb, but did not get it. Something was wrong. I sensed a definite low, knocking sound in the engine.

I swiveled my head in all directions as I banked over the shoreline, trying to locate my flight. To my left, the sky was polished, the sea glazed, and they fused at the horizon in a thin gray haze. Past my right shoulder, the white mist, not yet burned away by the sun, lay like great lakes and rivers over an unbroken jungle.

My earphones still crackled with static. I pressed my mike button, "Red Flight, Red Flight, this is Red-four. Do you read?" I waited. No answer. I tried again. Nothing. Finally I heard fighter control saying something about "Angels 15," meaning an altitude of 15,000 feet. I could hear them, but they couldn't hear me. My transmitter was out.

Instinctively, I edged eastward. I pushed my thumb out in front of me to eclipse the sun and scanned the surrounding halo. I could see nothing there. The knock in the engine grew louder. Or did it? A knot that felt like a molten baseball formed in the pit of my stomach. I wanted to return to base. But didn't. Not yet. It wasn't all bravado that kept us going.

It took 16 men on the ground to put one plane in the air. Riggers, cooks, clerks, typists, the motor pool, armament, quartermasters, machinists, radio men, intelligence, ground crew. And all of them shared your successes—and died with your failures. You were their trigger, their only means of striking back at an enemy who indiscriminately bombed and strafed them and, given the chance, would overrun them, taking no prisoners.

To return to base with mechanical problems that proved minor or imaginary was to break a trust—and more, having to live with your own questioning conscience. But it took more than even the wizardry of a Sergeant Law to keep these crates in the air. There just was not enough baling wire to go around. The engine was running rough. And to be caught by the enemy under 5,000 feet in a lead sled was suicide. I tried to ignore the engine knock and climbed toward the sun. It took me out to sea.

At last I heard something on the radio that made sense. Fighter control gave a new vector, "Margie-11 Angels 15." I looked down at the postcard-sized map in my lap. A simple ink line representing the coast was divided into square coordinates, with code names changed daily along the side and numbers across the top. The coordinate Margie-11 was most peculiar. It was southwest, near the mountains. The last place to expect an attack. "We're at Margie-11. Can't see anything." I recognized Harris' voice. More static. Harris' voice was taut. "I'm at Angels 20. Nothing! Nothing!"

By now I had reached 10,000 feet and snapped on my oxygen mask. I was still climbing toward the sun, zigzagging as I climbed. I readjusted my safety belt, loosening it so I could raise up higher off my seat to twist my head about. I saw empty sky. The baseball in my stomach pressed up harder. I was still forcing everything wide open, and the engine howled its objection. The knock was faster, louder, more distinct. I was certain now that a rod would throw in a matter of seconds.

At about 12,000 feet, I saw them. Tiny flashes. It was the first thing you always saw. The teardrop glass Mitsubishi A6M canopy on the Zero was made up of a number of panels, and as the fighter flipped and turned, the panels caught the sun's rays and reflected

A Mitsubishi A6M3 Model 32—a clipped-wing Zero variant— flashes past an American camera gun during a dogfight off the New Guinea coast.

them back in all directions. Now I saw them stretching across the sky, twinkling like stars in daylight.

That unexplainable sense of relief settled over me, as it always did. No matter how great the enemy might be or the advantage he might have, it was a relief when he was at last seen.

I squinted my eyes at the area below the flashes and within a few seconds saw a thin black line appear. That would be the bomber formation. They were miles east of the Margie-11 map coordinate. Radar was picking up an echo instead of the real thing.

I pressed the mike button. "Bandits! Bandits! Large formation. About 50. South of Oro Bay, flying north. Come in." No answer. "Do you read, anyone?" My transmitter was dead.

We'd be closing fast, and the Zeros were well over 20,000 feet. It was too late to gain the sun; all I could do was claw for altitude.

I switched gas feeds and released my auxiliary belly tank. The tank was nearly full, so the difference in the lightness of the plane was noticeable.

I flipped on the gunsight. A bead of light encircled by two bright concentric rings appeared, reflected on the windshield in front of me. By knowing the size of the target and seeing how much of the rings the target filled, you could judge the target's distance from your guns. A range finder—but more important, the clever projection system—allowed the pilot to move his head while aiming his plane, unlike the old metal sights that were fixed to the engine cowling.

I turned on my gun switch and tapped the trigger. The loud, low blast of my six .50-caliber machine guns responded reassuringly. Details of the bombers were now discernible. They were heavies, twin-engine Mitsubishi G4Ms, code-named "Bettys" by the Allies. I could see the little gray fighters weaving and turning over them.

We were closing fast. I was almost to the bombers' altitude and was sure every one of them had spotted me, the lone P-40 directly ahead of them. The radio cut in, "Bandits, 12 o'clock level." Somebody else had found them at last. "I don't see anything." Another voice. "There…" The last voice was cut off by screaming static.

All fighters used the same radio frequency, and when any two pilots pressed their mike buttons at the same time, the result was a terrifying howl. For that reason the radio was sometimes referred to as the enemy's secret weapon—in the desperation of a dogfight, mike buttons were constantly being held down only to produce a continuous nerve-racking shriek in all earphones.

The enemy was there now. A neat row of glass-nosed, perfectly round bodies tucked together, wingtips seemingly interlocked. No one flew as beautiful a formation as did the Japanese bombers. I was at their level, maybe slightly above.

My heart was pounding, but the baseball was gone. I was too busy for fear. The entire line in front of me seemed to come alive in unison, forming a continuous row of flashing Christmas tree lights.

I knew those flashes well. I even had mistaken them for some kind of signals the first time I had seen them. They were 20mm cannons firing from nose turrets. Now more flashes from the top turrets. Smaller flashes but more. I ducked instinctively. There had

to be 50 guns trained on me at that instant, if I thought about it. So I didn't. They were still out of range but certainly would keep firing the closer I came.

I picked out the next bomber to the right of the leader, placed my bead of light exactly on the center upper part of his glass nose, and held steady. I focused on that spot, forcing my concentration. When I closed at a combined speed of 700 mph, my guns would be in range no more than a fraction of a second, a rifle shot. I held steady, oblivious to everything but that single glass cone with its flashing 20mm cannon.

Now! I squeezed the trigger, heard the roar, felt the recoil, and saw my cluster of tracers hang directly in front of the glass cone. My blast would hit dead center and pass lengthwise through his fuselage. There was no time to watch.

Since we usually dove our P-40s under enemy formations, I had decided this time to take it over the top. They were not fooled. I flashed by just above their top turrets, but the white smoke trails from their tracers were so thick it was like flying through gauze.

I tipped up on one wing in a sharp bank to the right before the last bomber had slipped under me. I came out on the inside tail of the end bomber on the left of their V formation. This time we were flying in the same direction; time would be no problem. I aimed at the tail gunner, squeezed the trigger and slid my plane around so my bullets tore along the side of his fuselage and into his right engine. But time *was* a problem. Something gray flashed past the corner of my eye. Intuitively I turned toward it, to my left. I started to look back. A black shadow swept over my cockpit and seemed to hang there. A Zero's tail was directly in front of me, not 50 feet away. Almost in my sights.

What had happened was not that unusual. In their eagerness to pounce on me, the Zeros had nearly collided with each other, and the one in front of me had unwittingly dodged into that position. All I wanted to do, and should have done at that point, was to get out of there alive. But the temptation to not miss a kill, which has spelled doom for so many fliers, was too much for me.

I kicked my rudder and fired, not aiming with my sights but just using the tracers. Pieces flew from the Zero in all directions. It flipped up, over and down in one quick maneuver. I tried to follow the plunging fighter with my eyes, but then was startled to find that my guns seemingly were continuing to fire. My tracers continued to spit out ahead of me.

Then, in one sickening rush, I realized that they were not my tracers. Somebody was right on my tail. It was over. Something seemed to explode next to my head, and there was a drumming roar around me like hail crashing down on a tin roof. Worse, my radio went silent, and the sudden lack of noise in my ears added to the terror of the thing. In a flash, the cockpit filled with smoke.

Our side believed that the Zero had a gravity-fed carburetor and the engine would not run upside down, whereas the P-40 would. I would soon find out. But there was a bigger problem. For 100 millennia the visceral structure of the human body has been designed to withstand many times the force of gravity when in a head-up position. Likewise, the orientation of an aircraft in regard to stress is equally critical. To challenge those precepts at the speed I was traveling was to flaunt nature itself.

Foolhardy or not, I had no choice. I shoved the stick straight forward, the nose dropped, I lifted from my seat, pieces of dried mud and debris from dozens of jungle-clogged boots floated up past my face and pressed against the ceiling of my canopy.

My stomach rose like it does when taking the first plunge on a roller coaster. Then my world came completely apart. I had forgotten to retighten my safety belt. My feet left the pedals, my head crushed into the canopy, twisting and stretching my neck sideways. I doubled my knees against my chest to keep from sliding out from under the now biting belt. Every fighter pilot knows the sensation of blacking out in a high-speed turn or quick pull-up, but with experience, learns the exact moment to ease up on the controls. That instant when your neck has turned to rubber, your head wobbles and crushes down between your shoulder blades and a dark tunnel closes in around your eyes—at that precise instant between consciousness and unconsciousness, you ease up. But this was different. Painfully. My stomach kept rising, my jaws clamped shut, the flesh on my cheeks pushed upward, and my neck began to tighten and squeeze as surely as if I was being hanged by a noose. My head wanted to explode. Instead of a dark tunnel, the top of my windshield began changing colors from gray

Dick Vodra beside the checkerboard rudder of his P-40N, which replaced the P-40E in June 1943.

to violet to, at last, a sunburst of scarlet. I felt that I was being catapulted helplessly into space.

By sheer force of will, I reached the throttle, cut it back and, suspended in space, inched back on the stick until I settled down in the seat. My eyes were on fire, partially from smoke and partially, I was to learn later, from burst blood vessels. The plane was in an almost vertical dive, spinning hopelessly. Through the black haze I made out that the needle on my airspeed indicator had swung so far past its critical red line that the wings, by now, should have splintered off.

I slammed open my canopy and pulled down my goggles. If I bailed out now, I'd be used for target practice by every Zero within 10 miles. I fought the stick over against the roll of the plane with all my strength but couldn't hold it until I had spun the trim tab wheel to its limit.

The plane grudgingly steadied into a steep dive; the airspeed slowed back to the red line on the indicator. The wind screaming past my open cockpit sucked away some of the smoke. For the first time I glanced around me. Behind me the sky was filled with planes and thin, black wisps of smoke. No one had followed me down. And I soon saw why: Beautifully familiar silhouettes of P-40s were now streaming in toward the bombers.

I rotated my plane 180 degrees toward the shore. I saw the Zero I had shot, still plummeting. It would crash well inland.

If I could make the shoreline before bailing out, my chances would be much improved, for this corner of the Pacific was the central home of the great white shark. Noise and the underwater concussion from exploding bombs that churned fish into a slick of blood almost guaranteed a shark frenzy.

I leveled my dive as much as possible, but I was already getting low. The heat coming through the fire wall was closing around my legs. I ripped off my oxygen mask and was immediately struck by the acrid odor of burning insulation. Electrical. The dive had evidently blown out the flames, but the smoldering continued.

My luck had held, but with a probable broken fuel line I was sitting inside of a ticking bomb. As I reached to release the buckle of my seat belt, something caught my eye, low to the water out at sea. Sunlight dancing off glass canopies materialized into a swirling flock of tiny, gray, snub-nosed fighters.

And then there was something else. One shape was different and dark, ahead, leading them. In a sinking rush, I realized the tiny dark shape was a lone P-40. He was hopelessly trapped, cut off and headed exactly the wrong way, out to sea. The Zeros were swarming like hungry, screaming hyenas after a wounded antelope.

And now I was heading back out to sea, throttle wide-open. I had made a right turn. The dive had left me at red-line speed, and the fleeing P-40 was not more than 100 feet high—too low for him to get away, but a downhill lunge for me.

There was a chance I could catch up if everything could just hold together. But it wouldn't. The engine howled its defiance, and the whole plane began to vibrate. I felt the molten baseball come back in the pit of my gut and press upward. Always pressing upward so you couldn't breathe. Other pilots admitted that they had that same sensation, an occupational hazard. Suddenly, the engine gave a groan and the plane shook violently. The blood drained from my face as I chopped back on the throttle. I could almost feel the rivets popping out.

I looked down at the empty, flat ocean below, except that now I could make out spuming whitecaps. The lower I got, the more forbidding the water appeared. At half-throttle, the shaking surrendered back to vibration. The nearest Zero was only filling half the smaller ring on my gun sight, still a half-mile away. I was now too low to bail out if I wanted to. I scanned the sky behind and above me. The bomber formation looked unusually ragged. One of them, on fire, had dropped several thousand feet out of formation and, as I watched, exploded into a ball of flame.

A mixture of smoke from tracers, gunfire and burning planes spread a hazy black film across the sky, while fighters, like tiny gnats, darted through and about it. There was nothing close behind me, but I couldn't believe the Zeros directly ahead had not seen me coming. It could be a trap. My momentum was carrying me ever closer, but if they turned on me while I was running at half-throttle, I'd be no better off than the P-40 ahead.

Now, while other Zeros bracketed him from both sides and above, I watched a single Zero drop down directly behind the tail of the lone P-40. There was no smoke from the Zero's guns yet. He was experienced, taking his time, cocky. I was still out of range but had no alternative. I raised the bead of light at the center of my gun sight just above the Zero and held the trigger closed.

The steady recoil from my guns sent me forward against the seat belt. As always, the lazy tracers seemed to just hang still in front of me like miniature ping-pong balls suspended in space.

When the tracers finally reached their mark, taking forever, I forced my eyes to focus on them for aiming instead of watching the sight. The tracers seemed to be going to the right place, but there was no response from any of their pack. I raised my nose a little, then lowered it. I was choking up! Spraying! I was "churning butter," as it's called, crazily rotating the stick around like a buck amateur. I deliberately closed one eye to force concentration.

By now I was right on him, crawling up his tail. And then in one white, blinding flash, the Zero exploded in front of me. As I pulled up to my right, I saw the other P-40 tilt into a bank to his left. With their total focus on making an easy kill, the Zeros had allowed me to limp in from behind unseen.

It was the second time that day that their confident superiority had cost them. The first was when they almost ran into each other in their rush to kill me. Now, the shock of seeing an explosion and flames in their midst, and realizing it was one of their own instead of the lone P-40, scattered the others. I came up behind another Zero quite by accident and again squeezed my trigger. He completed a perfect airshow snap roll, one of their favorite evasive maneuvers, then continued on. My guns gave one quick blurt and quit. I was out of ammunition.

I crawled toward home. It felt like walking on eggs. I was right on the water, too low to bail out, with my throttle cut back to where there was barely flying speed. The vibration was worse, and I was holding the stick completely to one side just to keep the wings level.

Eventually, that ravishingly beautiful, narrow little jungle strip appeared in front of me. I hurled my plane into the worst landing I had ever made. The P-40 had accomplished the single thing for which it was noted. It had brought me home.

The rescued P-40 had landed ahead of me and was pulled off to one side. As I taxied closer, I recognized it from its markings as belonging to Lieutenant Bob White of our squadron. I brought my plane to a stop next to it, cut the ignition, unbuckled my parachute and pulled myself up in the cockpit. As I stood there, I felt a little shiver pass through my body, and I realized that I was soaking wet. My eyes and head were screaming with pain, and I leaned my forehead against the top of the windshield.

Through a red haze, I made out the figure of White trotting over toward me. His face was flushed, his hair still stood on end from having pulled off his flight helmet, but he was grinning from ear to ear. He wiped two fingers across his forehead and snapped off imaginary sweat.

"Man," he shouted, "you should have seen what happened to me!"

Postscript

For his gallantry in action that day, Lieutenant Richard Vodra was decorated with the Silver Star, a medal ranked next to the Distinguished Service Cross.

Japanese reports reveal that one-third of the bombers that participated in that raid were lost, with all of the remainder badly shot up. Two days later, the Japanese 253rd *Kokutai* (naval air group) was withdrawn from the combat zone and sent to Saipan due to its heavy losses.

Within a few weeks of the May 14 aerial fight, the old P-40 lead sleds were replaced by new and faster P-40Ns. Republic P-47 Thunderbolts were introduced in the area for the first time, and additional Lockheed P-38 Lightnings arrived. The Thunderbolts and Lightnings were as superior in performance to the Zero as the Zero had been to the "sleds."

With the Japanese defeat in the air on May 14, 1943, possibly coupled with the recent death of its planner and spark plug, Admiral Isoroko Yamamoto (see chapter XIV), the spirit of the massive naval air counterstrike Operation I flagged and seemed to fade out. Yamamoto's death was a severe blow to the Japanese people and the military—and removed the driving force behind Operation I, which, however, would go on as planned. The failures in the Battle of the Bismarck Sea on March 2–5, 1943, and Operation I were the last attempts by the Japanese to regain the initiative in the Pacific.

THE MACHINES

VII

ZERO: FLIMSY KILLER

A Japanese obsession with weight and maneuverability proved costly for Mitsubishi's masterpiece.

By Bruce Crawford

Few weapons of World War II have gained more fame or enduring notoriety than the Mitsubishi Zero. Within the space of just a few years, the Japanese Zero fighter fell from nearly invincible status to being an easy kill for most American pilots with the proper experience. The story of how this change of fortune came about is among the most fascinating of WWII.

The Zero saga began on May 19, 1937, when the Imperial Japanese Navy tendered requirements for a new shipboard fighter with a speed of at least 310 mph, an armament of two cannons and two machine guns, and exceptional range, climb and maneuverability. Since many land-based fighters of that era had not approached such performance, the navy's standards seemed absurd. Only Mitsubishi accepted the challenge.

Under the direction of chief engineer Jiro Horikoshi, the prototype flew on April 1, 1939. Following the installation of a more powerful, 14-cylinder Nakajima NK1C Sakae 12 radial engine, it was found that the new fighter amply exceeded the requirements that had been considered impossible only a few months before.

In order to obtain maximum range and agility, Horikoshi used a complex single-unit wing assembly designed for low wing loading coupled with a newly developed lightweight metal. Contrary to a widely held belief that persists to this day, no wood was used in the Zero's construction.

The finished product was in many ways a technological masterpiece. It boasted unsurpassed climb and maneuverability in addition to a 1,930-mile maximum range that was nearly three times that of concurrent Western designs. It was the first shipboard fighter that clearly outperformed its land-based rivals, and the built-in factors that would limit its performance would not become evident for several years.

In order to test its new weapon under operational conditions, the Japanese navy committed several pre-production Zeros to China in the summer of 1940—much as the Germans had done with the Bf-109 in the Spanish Civil War nearly five years before. The new fighter promptly wiped out all the defending Chinese fighters during its first combat use in August. This initial encounter set the tone for the next few months, since the new machines—officially designated A6M1s—swiftly eliminated all opposition. In more than a year of operational use, over 100 Chinese fighters were shot down without the loss of a single Zero.

Thus started the Zero legend. General Claire Chennault—later to gain fame as the leader of the "Flying Tigers"—attempted to warn the U.S. Army Air Corps of the Zero threat, but the warnings were filed and ignored. As a result, the Mitsubishis that swarmed over Pearl Harbor on December 7, 1941, came as a complete surprise to American forces, despite the fact that the aircraft had been in combat

In a painting by Tony Weddel, Mitsubishi Zero ace Saburo Sakai evades a pack of Grumman F6F Hellcats off Iwo Jima on June 24, 1944. Demonstrating what the Zero could still do with the right pilot at the controls, Sakai's A6M5 returned without a single bullet hole.

A Zero shot down at Pearl Harbor. It would be another half year before Americans would get their hands on a flyable specimen and learn about the fighter's true capabilities.

haustively trained in aerobatics, while the Zero's light weight and low wing loading made it ideal for dogfights. The end results were downed American, British Commonwealth and Dutch aircraft—and a Japanese sweep across the Pacific.

So rapid and complete were these victories that the Zero soon gained a reputation for invincibility. The new weapon perhaps reached its zenith during the Java–East Indies campaign of February 1942, when Allied air units were simply wiped out. Gregory Richmond-Board recalled that his No. 453 Royal Australian Air Force Squadron lost 11 of its 13 Brewster Buffalos to Zeros in its first combat, while No. 21 Squadron was "wiped out to a man....We realized what we had in the Buffalo—a barrel which the Zero could outfly, outgun, outmaneuver and outdo almost everything else that was in the book for a fighter plane. No one yet knew what the Zeros were, but they were not slow, ancient, fabric-covered biplanes."

The problem faced by the Allies was that obsolete aircraft such as the Buffalo, P-35 and P-36 had little chance against the Zero. Like the aircraft used earlier in China, they could not fly high enough nor gain enough speed to take advantage of the Zero's poor performance at high speeds. But the Allies learned that better aircraft were equally ineffective if the proper tactics were not used—over Darwin, Australia, Zeros shot down 11 of 12 defending Curtiss P-40 Warhawks. Even the Spitfire, considered by some to be the best fighter of the war, lost 17 of 27 to the marauding Zeros when their Australian pilots tried to dogfight with the Japanese.

"It was simply a matter of tactics," observed Chennault. "The RAAF [Royal Australian Air Force] pilots were trained in tactics that were excellent against German and Italian equipment but suicide against the acrobatic Japanese."

Chennault's Flying Tigers, operating from Burma and China, repeatedly demonstrated the Zero's vulnerability to fast diving and rolling attacks. In a single combat, Flying Tiger P-40s ripped into a Japanese formation and destroyed 17 fighters and bombers without loss. While many Tiger actions were against Japanese army aircraft rather than navy Zeros, the point is irrelevant—because combat after combat revealed the Zeros could be defeated if their weaknesses were exploited.

Over New Guinea, the Imperial Japanese Navy's crack Lae Wing

for nearly a year and a half and had been seen by dozens of foreign observers. Americans did not seem ready to accept the fact that Japan could produce an airplane of such impressive performance.

Over China, the Zero faced Russian-built Polikarpov I-15 and I-16 fighters, in addition to a wide assortment of other airplanes from around the world. All had one thing in common: They were inferior to the Mitsubishi product in every respect. In the opening stages of the war in the Pacific, the Zero faced more modern opposition, ranging from the already obsolete Republic Seversky P-35 to the outstanding Supermarine Spitfire. The performance of these Allied machines still varied widely, but all were inferior to Japan's A6M in low-speed, close-quarters combat. And with few exceptions, Allied pilots allowed themselves to be drawn into twisting, turning dogfights with the Japanese. That played directly to the Zero's strengths, since Japanese Imperial Navy pilots were ex-

On December 7, 1941, A6M2s from the aircraft carrier Akagi *strafe Pearl Harbor, in* Waking of a Giant, *by Lance Kitchens.*

encountered the Bell P-39 Airacobra flown by the U.S. Army. To be sure, the P-39 was a modern fighter, but it had been designed for a close-support, tactical role rather than for air superiority missions. The mid-engine plane weighed twice as much as a Zero, yet had a low-altitude-rated engine of only slightly more power; it should be no surprise that this heavy machine did not fare well against the agile Zero. Yet Saburo Sakai, the Japanese navy's leading surviving ace, described how an 8th Fighter Group P-39 destroyed a bomber after diving at great speed. "No one could move in time to disrupt the attack…it rolled and dived beyond our range," Sakai recalled.

In theory, few aircraft should have been less qualified to take on the Zero than the Grumman F4F Wildcat. The squat, bulldoglike

F4F was several years older in design than the Zero but, like most American fighters, it was rugged and heavily armed. Most important, Marine and Navy pilots did not allow the Zeros to dictate the terms of combat.

James Flatley, commander of the carrier *Yorktown's* Wildcats during the Midway engagement, stressed that the proper way to take the Zero was to dive at full throttle and maintain speed, no matter what the enemy did. "Sooner or later they had to take you on, on your terms," Flatley said. "If you should be jumped from

The Spartan cockpit of a Mitsubishi Zero includes a touch of World War I. Note the 7.7mm machine guns protruding through the instrument panel.

behind, they had difficulty following, particularly when you rolled at high speed."

Using similar tactics, Wildcats virtually wiped out Sakai's Lae Wing in the fall of 1942 over Guadalcanal, where many of the Japanese navy's ace pilots were shot down and killed by American pilots such as Joe Foss, Marion Carl and John L. Smith.

The question quickly comes to mind: How could a simple change in tactics enable the Wildcat to defeat the supposedly invincible Zero only a few short months after it decimated everything the Allies could field against it? At least part of the answer is that the Zero's "invincibility" was an illusion. The Mitsubishi's formidable reputation was forged in China in the early months of the war, when the quality of its opposition often was poor. This manifested itself in poorly trained or inexperienced pilots, with obsolete aircraft and poor tactics based on an Allied lack of intelligence on the Zero. Sometimes only one of these factors was present, sometimes two and sometimes (especially during the air actions over China) all three.

Prewar Japanese naval flight training was possibly the most rigorous in the world, as Sakai noted in his book *Samurai*. In contrast, some of the pilots thrown against the Zeros had barely learned the rudiments of flying, much less the skills needed to best the Japanese. During an aerial melee with Zeros on September 13, 1940, three Chinese pilots startled the Japanese by bailing out before joining combat. Two others—flying Russian-built, fixed-gear I-15 biplane fighters—collided with each other and smashed into a mountain. While this was an extreme case, few of the Allied pilots could boast the training and experience possessed by the Japanese. In addition, they faced the crushing handicap of disorganization and mass confusion brought about by the Japanese onslaught.

Even before the outset of the Guadalcanal campaign, the Americans obtained a priceless gift when an intact Zero was found in the Aleutian Islands in June 1942. U.S. Navy technicians soon learned that while the Zero enjoyed unparalleled maneuverability at speeds below 150 mph, aileron control became sluggish at 180 mph and nearly immovable at 230 mph. A few astute American strategists like Chennault and Flatley had already guessed this glaring liability.

It had always been apparent, however, that the Zero could not withstand the firepower of American fighters. Hits that were shrugged off by a P-40 resulted in a downed Zero and, most important, a dead pilot. This shortcoming became more serious as the war progressed and highly skilled veteran Zero pilots were killed.

The obsession with light weight and maneuverability cost the Zero in other ways. The single-unit wing assembly was difficult to mass-produce. The A6M could not absorb the groundfire damage or carry the ordnance needed for close-support duties. The low wing loading was responsible not only for the Zero's poor rolling ability but also for top speeds limited to the 330- to 350-mph range. With the introduction of more modern fighters such as the 400-plus-mph Vought F4U-1 Corsair and Lockheed P-38 Lightning, American pilots could break off and initiate combat at will.

While 1936-vintage aircraft like the Spitfire and Me-109 could be upgraded to performance levels that were on a par with more modern aircraft throughout the war, the Zero practically stagnated despite desperate attempts to improve its performance. This was partially due to the inability of the Japanese to wring more power from the Sakae radial engine, but was also due to the fact that options were restricted by the emphasis on maneuverability and light weight at all costs. Mitsubishi had belatedly seen the need for armor protection and self-sealing fuel tanks for the A6M5, but the addition of these badly needed items negated some of the small performance gains netted from the Nakajima NK1F Sakae 21, which had undergone only a 200-hp gain through the entire range of Zero development.

Near the close of the war, Mitsubishi extensively redesigned the Zero to install the larger 1,560-hp Mitsubishi MK8P Kinsei 62 engine. The resulting machine, the A6M8, was a great improvement over earlier Zeros, but its top speed was still only 367 mph.

Grumman, meanwhile, had hiked the performance of its Hellcat from 376 to 420 mph in the F6F-6 model with the addition of little more than a modified engine and a four-blade propeller. But the U.S. Navy did not bother to adopt the experimental F6F-6 model because it was not needed. The Navy had found during 1944 tests that the ultimate production A6M5 version of the Zero had been hard pressed to take on the latest model of the elderly Wildcat, much less the Hellcat, Corsair, F8F Bearcat and a host of Army Air Force fighters.

In accounts following the war, designer Horikoshi declined to shoulder all the blame for the Zero's shortcomings, insisting that some of these were forced on his design staff through various outmoded concepts held by the Japanese Imperial Navy, including the emphasis on maneuverability and maximum performance at the expense of all armor protection. His charges ring true, since the Japanese military seemed to have little grasp of the type of fighter needed for modern warfare. While the early Zero obtained tremen-

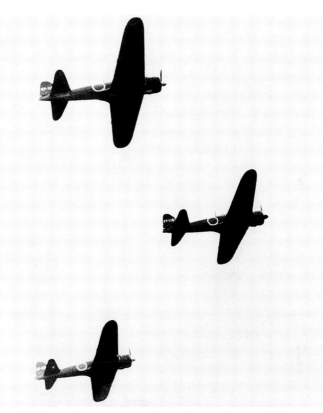

A trio of A6M2s in late-war camouflage. Even as late as 1944, A6M2s were serving not only as trainers but also as second-line fighters and kamikazes.

dous range and performance from its relatively small Sakae radial engine, it lacked the inherent versatility and capacity for development and improvement present in American designs.

The Japanese attitude toward air combat was perhaps best expressed by writer Thomas G. Miller, who observed that "Japanese air tactics never evolved beyond World War I–style dogfighting...they could not cope very well with adversaries who declined to fight them on their own terms."

Unfortunately for Japan, the Zero was the material result of that strategy.

VIII

EAGLE FLIES A MUSTANG

Don Gentile and his P-51 seared the skies over Europe in his quest to be the best of the best.

By John Stanaway

January 14, 1944, was a bright, clear day for the American 4th Fighter Group as it searched for German fighters in the skies over France. Blue section of the 4th's 336th Fighter Squadron was being led by Captain Don Gentile, known in the group as "Gentle," but renowned as a skilled and aggressive aerial fighter. By this point in the war, the *Jagdwaffe* (the German *Luftwaffe's* fighter arm) was already feeling the net tighten as its losses in skilled fighter pilots mounted, and American units like the 4th, with their Republic P-47D Thunderbolts, were ranging over Europe in ever more offensive thrusts.

The 336th Squadron crossed the coast at approximately 2:30 in the afternoon and arrived at the target area at Magny, near Paris, about 15 minutes later. Orbiting over the area at 25,000 feet, Gentile sighted and called out 15 enemy fighters to the east, about 3,000 feet below and far off to the left. He immediately led his flight down to the attack.

As the Americans dove to the attack, the enemy dots grew into recognizable shapes, and Gentile could see that they were Focke Wulf Fw-190 fighters. They had seen the U.S. attackers and fanned out into two groups to meet the threat.

The P-47D Thunderbolt flown by Gentile was able to dive faster than any other aircraft of the day, and Gentile quickly closed on the tails of two straggling Fw-190s. His wingman, Lieutenant Bob Richards, tucked in close while the other two P-47s of the flight—flown by Lieutenants Louis Norley and Vermont Garrison—went after another pair of German fighters that were diving away to the right.

Gentile approached the trailing Focke Wulf, which was diving away at a 50-degree angle. The big Thunderbolt opened fire from about 300 yards back, and the German took hits around the cockpit, finally rolling over and going straight down from 8,000 feet after black smoke began streaming back from his engine.

Panic probably began to assail the lead German pilot when Gentile next slid into firing position at about 250 yards behind him, and the uprushing ground forced him to level out his dive. Gentile

One of the Eighth Air Force's deadliest duos provides top cover for an Allied bomber stream, in Gentile and Godfrey, *by Harley Copic. While strafing a German airfield, Captain John T. Godfrey was downed by flak and taken prisoner on August 24, 1944.*

Back from a mission on March 30, 1944, Dominic S. Gentile prepares to brief his essential teammate—his crew chief, Staff Sgt. John Ferra.

began firing and closed to about 150 yards. His .50-caliber bullets found their mark.

The dark treetops of the Compiégne Woods were blurring just below when the concentrated fire from the eight machine guns in the wings of the Thunderbolt finally ripped the heart out of the Focke Wulf. The German aircraft dissolved into a flaming orange spray the moment it plunged into the ground.

German reprisal came in the form of two other Fw-190s, arriving a bit late to help the first pair but in time to surprise Gentile. When he turned around in his seat, he could see the first Focke Wulf close behind—so close that he heard the chug of the four heavy 20mm cannons that sent high-explosive shells crashing into the Thunderbolt with sledgehammer blows.

Only his fighter pilot instincts, developed over the past two years in both the Royal Air Force and the U.S. Army Air Forces, saved Gen-

tile when he turned left inside the enemy's line of fire. The German had to pull up and fly over the P-47 to avoid a collision.

Gentile kept the Thunderbolt in the left turn until the second Focke Wulf passed overhead without firing. The first German fighter was quickly turning around to come back onto the Thunderbolt's tail as Gentile maneuvered to get on the other German's tail when the pilot apparently lost his nerve and began to tear away from the combat at high speed. Gentile fired a couple of harmless bursts and realized with a shock that his ammunition was gone.

A quick look around confirmed his worst fear—the first German was approaching for another gunnery pass. Bob Richards had lost contact with the hard-flying Gentile in the last stages of the dive over the woods and was frantically trying to find him when Gentile's calls for assistance reached him—"Help! Help! I'm being clobbered!"

Gentile, racing flat-out to escape, was down almost to the very ground with no room to dive or to turn away. Fortunately for the American, the German pilot offered Gentile an opening by using too much lead on his aim—his tracers were arcing 30 to 40 feet in front of the Thunderbolt's nose.

With amazing coolness, Gentile waited until the last second before breaking into a turn that would take him out of the German's line of fire. "Don, hold on to yourself," he muttered aloud. "Keep yourself steady and you'll get out of this all right. Don't panic, Don." He often talked to himself in times of stress.

At the precise moment that the German tracers reached the edge of his cockpit, Gentile threw the airplane as hard as he could in the direction of his attacker. The Thunderbolt shuddered on the verge of a stall as the beleaguered American pilot heaved back on the stick and kicked left rudder as hard as he dared.

Gentile reported later that he could "feel that spin in my teeth," before he eased out of his suicidal turn. Within no time at all he was calling up all sorts of damnation in the vexing realization that the tracers were still coming at him—not as close now, thanks to his wild maneuvering, but inching their way toward him. The German may not have known how to lead his aim properly, but he was good enough to stay on the Thunderbolt's tail.

Three or four times the American repeated the nerve-shattering process of waiting while the tracers worked their way almost into his face before he turned suddenly, risking death in a high-speed stall, and escaped under the line of fire.

He alternately talked to himself and called for help on the radio. Some of his squadron mates heard him and asked for his position, but he could only report that he was over the Compiégne Woods, and all he could see was a railroad track below.

This mortal game of tag lasted for 10 to 15 minutes before Gentile noticed that the tracers had stopped coming in his direction. He looked back at the Focke Wulf and could practically see the pilot boiling in rage because his guns, too, were out of ammunition. As the German pilot flew away in frustration, Gentile gently coaxed his P-47, with all its engine temperatures gauges in the red, into a shallow climb. He felt he would "like to find a cloud and get out and dance on it."

The two victories he scored on this mission gave Gentile a total of 5⅓ kills since he had started flying combat a year and a half before. As he later reported to correspondent Ira Wolfert for their joint book, *One Man Air Force*: "That fight was, perhaps, the most critical I have ever fought. I have had bigger triumphs, easier ones, but this one taxed every last bit of me. It showed me what I had learned and it taught me what I was. After it, I felt there was no German alive anywhere who could keep me from killing when I had an even break in the fight; or if the breaks went against me and he got them all, I felt I could keep him from killing me."

Dominic Salvatore Gentile had wanted to fly ever since he was a young boy in the west-central Ohio town of Piqua. His parents dreaded the prospect of his following up the dangerous notion, but he persisted and pleaded with his father to help him buy a World War I–vintage biplane that was advertised for sale in Baltimore.

The elder Gentile was doubtful, but gave in to the supplications of his then 17-year-old son. He agreed that if the owner could fly the thing to a nearby airfield, they could consider buying it. Not only did the owner get it to the Ohio airfield, but Don actually soloed on the same day. They paid $1,400 for the plane, and from that time on Don Gentile seemed to spend more time in the air than on the ground. It was autumn 1939; the war in Europe had just started.

Unknown to his parents, Don was using his practice time to prepare for pilot training in the Royal Canadian Air Force (RCAF). When

John Godfrey and Don Gentile stand beside Gentile's Mustang, in Shangri-La, *by George D. Guzzi, Jr. The two pilots became a nearly inseparable team during Gentile's tour with the 4th Fighter Group.*

he finally broke the news to his father and asked him to sign the enlistment papers—necessary because of Don's age—the elder Gentile kindly put forward a sensible proposition. Don's father was a restaurant owner who had come to America from Italy with little education. He realized how difficult life could be without at least a high school education, and he wanted his son to have a diploma. Don agreed enthusiastically and surprised his father by getting top grades in his senior year and graduating with honors.

Then, keeping his promise, the elder Gentile went with his son as Don drove the family's old Oldsmobile to the recruiting station in Canada. At the RCAF station, Don passed his medical examination easily, but his father had renewed anxieties about signing his son over to an unknown fate. Don and the RCAF prevailed. After he signed up, Don leaned over the desk and kissed his father.

Next, Gentile went to England and worked his way through Britain's Royal Air Force (RAF) pilot training from July 1941 until he graduated as a pilot officer in December. He served in various RAF squadrons until June 1942, when he was assigned a billet in Supermarine Spitfire No. 133 Eagle Squadron with other Americans who wanted to enter the war before their country did. By the time he joined the RAF, he had already logged more than 300 hours of flight time.

Gentile had not gone into combat very quickly, though. Because the young American was so impressive as a pilot, the RAF made an instructor out him, much to his disgust. One day when flying over an English dog track while a race was in progress, he was struck by an idea. He repeatedly buzzed the track, and spectators as well as racing dogs took off in every direction while Gentile laughed like a maniac above them. That did it. The British were very particular about the standard of conduct expected from RAF flight instructors, and Gentile was posted to an operational squadron before he could think much about it.

If his confidence was ever to be shaken, it was probably on the mission of July 31, 1942, when his leader was shot down and Gentile found himself all alone with a Focke Wulf Fw-190 on his tail. There was nothing to do but try to maneuver out of danger, so Gentile threw his Spitfire into tighter and tighter turns until he momentarily blacked out. Somehow, he shook off his German pursuer and made it back in one piece.

On August 19, Gentile made three sorties over the German-occupied and highly fortified Dieppe beachhead during an Allied commando raid. The *Luftwaffe* accounted for more RAF aircraft than it lost during this operation, but Gentile claimed an Fw-190 and a Junkers Ju-88 bomber just as it was making a run on Allied troops on the beach.

The next month, all three Eagle Squadrons were inducted into the U.S. Army Air Forces, and Gentile's No. 133 Squadron became the 336th Squadron of the 4th Fighter Group, soon to gain recognition as one of the most famous fighter units on the Allied side. On September 29, 1942, Don Gentile became a second lieutenant in the U.S. Army Air Forces.

During March and April of 1943, the 4th Fighter Group converted from Spitfires to P-47Cs, much to the displeasure of Eagle Squadron veterans, who valued the Spitfire's excellent maneuverability and climb rate. But the P-47 had a marginal range advantage over the Spitfire, and better yet, it also had heavier firepower with a much flatter trajectory and an ability to dive from altitude that was legendary for most of the war.

Gentile didn't score again until he shared another Ju-88 with Louis Norley and Vermont Garrison over Holland on December 16, 1943. On January 5, 1944, he got another Fw-190 at about 7,000 feet over the southern border of Holland.

Lieutenant John T. Godfrey was to play a large part in of Don Gentile's career. He had been with Gentile in No. 133 Squadron and had transferred over to the 4th Fighter Group at the same time. In about the middle of 1943, Godfrey was first assigned to Gentile's wing on a B-17 support mission. On the way back, Gentile went into a tight spiral, and Godfrey dutifully followed all the way down through the clouds until they pulled out at a scant 1,500 feet. When they landed, Godfrey was going to ask why they had made such an unorthodox descent when Gentile came over to him and praised him for staying on his wing. It seems that Gentile's gyrocompass had gone out, and he very nearly had ended up crashing.

The two men became an inseparable team. Gentile trusted Godfrey as a capable and faithful teammate, and Godfrey trusted Gentile as an experienced leader and destroyer of the enemy. By the end of their tour the two men had become renowned because of press coverage of their exploits. President Franklin D. Roosevelt referred to them as "Captains Courageous," and Winston Churchill dubbed them the "Damon and Pythias of the Twentieth Century."

On February 25, 1944, Gentile bagged another Fw-190 a few miles southeast of Luxembourg for his sixth whole victory and last confirmed in the P-47. The legendary combat leader Colonel Don Blakeslee had taken command of the 4th Fighter Group in January and almost immediately began working for conversion to the North American P-51 Mustang fighter.

It is now accepted that the P-51 was an outstanding fighter of the war, but at the end of 1943 and early in 1944 the airplane had not yet established its reputation. For one thing, it was generally feared that the vulnerable liquid-cooling system of the P-51 made it a "one-way ticket" on sorties into Germany. Other items that caused concern among pilots were its poor cockpit canopy defroster and its armament. The latter was unusually light for contemporary American fighters, comprising only four wing-mounted .50-caliber guns that showed a propensity for jamming. Even though the Mustang would eventually be considered an especially easy fighter to fly, it required much attention to proper trimming techniques to land without incident.

Gentile took to the Mustang with relish, although his first missions were fraught with dangerous problems. He was leading Red Section on an abortive March 3, 1944, mission to Berlin when about 50 Messerschmitt Me-110s, Dornier Do-217s, Junkers Ju-88s and Focke Wulf Fw-190s seemed to appear from everywhere.

It was hardly an auspicious debut in the Mustang, because Gentile had to scrape away the frost from the inside of his canopy and wait for the defroster to work before he saw a twin-engine Me-110 right beside him, firing away like mad. He broke away, only to have three Fw-190s attack him head-on. He escaped these pests also and attacked a Do-217, scoring strikes on it while his gunsight light went out and two more Focke Wulfs flashed by.

Lieutenant Willard Millikin, who had been covering Gentile until that time, called in that he himself was battling 10 Fw-190s. Gentile rolled his Mustang over to lend a hand and found himself in the midst of a host of Fw-190s. He rolled and climbed like a corkscrew and finally hit one German hard enough to convince the pilot to abandon his airplane. By this time, some of his Mustang's guns had

Captain Gentile poses at the propeller of his P-51B Shangri-La *in the spring of 1944.*

jammed, so Gentile simply outmaneuvered his attackers until he had a definite target.

His opportunity came when he was able to get a proper lead on an Fw-190 from behind; he fired short bursts until the enemy plane started to burn and went into a slow spiral into the clouds far below. Gentile kept jumping back into the battle to assist his squadron mates under attack until he joined up with two other Mustangs and made it back home. It had been a harrowing morning.

Five days later, Gentile was back on the Berlin route with his trusted wingman, Lieutenant Godfrey. They were just nearing the German capital at about 1:50 in the afternoon when a large group of Messerschmitt Me-109s made a head-on attack on the lead formation of B-17s.

Gentile led Godfrey into a fast bounce on the German fighters and went into a whirling circle of combat with two of the 109s. Godfrey shot down his first target with an accurate burst, but Gentile had trouble turning with his prey until he decided to use his landing flaps. With flaps slightly lowered, he drew to within 75 yards and fired until white smoke trailed back from the Messerschmitt, and it fell into an uncontrollable spiral.

The two Americans then attacked another Me-109. Gentile slipped in behind the target and fired from 100 yards until the German pilot bailed out. Another two Messerschmitts were observed flying together, and the Mustang pilots simply drew up behind them. Godfrey's target exploded while Gentile's opponent went into a spin, trailing smoke; the pilot bailed out far below.

Another Messerschmitt with an inordinately brave pilot made an attack on Godfrey, and the two Americans smoothly maneuvered onto his tail. Godfrey fired and could see his ammunition striking the enemy plane until his bullets ran out. Gentile took over and kept hitting the 109 until its belly tank caught fire and the pilot bailed out.

Discovering a lone B-17 Flying Fortress on its way back from the Berlin area, the two Mustangs escorted it home. Gratitude for Gentile and Godfrey poured over the radio from the appreciative Fortress crew.

Gentile's score now stood at 11.84 confirmed air victories, but his star was just beginning to rise. On March 18, he was flying in Colonel Blakeslee's flight and, in a wild fight with six Fw-190s, chased one of them down to 6,000 feet near Augsburg and hammered it until the pilot bailed out. Less than two weeks later, on March 29, Gentile and Godfrey were on an escort mission to the Brunswick area when a swarm of German fighters hit the bombers. By the time the battle was over, Gentile had two more Fw-190s and an Me-109 to his credit. Godfrey shot down two more Fw-190s and shared a stray Heinkel bomber with two other pilots.

Gentile was the leading ace in P-51s by the end of March and was competing with Thunderbolt pilot Bob Johnson of the 56th Fighter Group and Duane Beeson of his own 4th Fighter Group's 334th Squadron. Johnson had 22 confirmed air victories by the beginning of April, and Beeson had 16.

The primary motivation for Gentile to score was the prospect of postwar life. He was a complete optimist who saved all his money and planned for the future. His lack of college training bothered him in relation to his life beyond the war. He dreaded the idea of becoming an "airborne bus driver." His hope was to do something dramatic enough to give him a leg up in the time to come.

His next chance came on April 1, when he again flew in Blakeslee's flight on a B-24 cover mission in the Stuttgart area. Four Me-109s had shot down one of the Liberators before Gentile arrived, but he chased one down from 23,000 feet to the cloud tops around 6,000 feet. The two planes were in a steep spiral, and Gentile got good strikes on the German before he had to pull out of the dive. The German was not so lucky, and Godfrey came down in time to see him explode in a field below.

At the time, Gentile was credited with a total of 21 air and three ground victories for a total of 24. After the war his score was revised, but for the moment he was high-scorer in the European theater.

On April 5, the 4th Fighter Group made a successful strafing raid on Stendel Airdome and claimed 25 Junkers, Messerschmitt and Focke Wulf aircraft in a wild, confused action. Gentile is variously credited with four or five Junkers destroyed. He became the first pilot in the theater to be recognized by Eighth Air Force headquarters for having more than 26 air and ground victories, topping Captain Eddie Rickenbacker's World War I record of 26 victories. Beeson was shot down and captured on the same mission, which ended his challenge with 25 air and ground kills (later revised to 24.08).

Gentile rounded out his own score on April 8, when he claimed two more Fw-190s around the Brunswick area. This was his final combat action in the air. He aroused the full fury of Colonel Blakeslee on April 13, when he used his famed P-51B, *Shangri-La*, to buzz the 4th's base at Debden for the benefit of the media and ended up in a crash. He was not hurt, but Blakeslee ordered him off the base and out of England.

Gentile went on a bond-selling tour with Godfrey and other top American aces and enjoyed some instant fame. However, Bob Johnson and Major Dick Bong of Lockheed P-38 fame in the Pacific both claimed their 27th air kills later in April and became more generally associated with breaking Rickenbacker's WWI record. Gentile had

Don Gentile finished the war with 21.84 confirmed air victories.

made a great effort to achieve the fame that would tide him over into civilian life and had come within a razor's edge of both his goal and getting killed. What he did accomplish was to become the first great Mustang ace of the war, with 15.5 of his eventual 21.84 confirmed air victories scored in that airplane. He remained the P-51 ace with the most air kills until Captain George Preddy, the top-scoring Mustang ace of the war, got six Me-109s in a single battle on August 6, 1944, for a total of 20 Mustang victories.

John Godfrey returned to the front in August 1944, and promptly added an Me-109 to his score on the 5th and Me-110 on the 6th. On August 24, however, he was brought down by anti-aircraft fire during a strafing attack near Norhausen. He escaped from his POW camp on April 3, 1945.

Gentile remained at Wright-Patterson Air Force Base, testing Lockheed P-80 jet fighters and other types, until he was discharged in April 1946. Apparently, he soon decided his chances were better in the Air Force, so he reclaimed his commission in December 1947. Gentile married another Ohioan, Isabella Masdea, became the father of three children and settled into the relatively happy routine of military family life.

Tragically, it was a routine flight that ended the outstanding life and Air Force career of Captain Dominic Salvatore Gentile. Sergeant Lawrence Kirsch was not quite satisfied with the T-33 trainer that he was preparing for Gentile's proficiency flight from Andrews Air Force Base on January 28, 1951. He asked the captain to delay the flight for a few hours while he checked the airplane thoroughly. When Gentile returned, Kirsch was still not at ease about the airplane but offered to go along on the flight to advise if an abort became necessary. The two men boarded the jet and made a normal takeoff. About 25 minutes later, witnesses between Ritchie and Forestville, Md., saw the jet come out of the sky at a steep angle, clip the tops of several trees and crash in a fiery explosion in a field near some woods. Gentile and his passenger were killed instantly.

For a time, Gentile Air Station in Ohio served as a memorial to the career of the extraordinary combat pilot. Don Gentile was one of the most outstanding of World War II fighter pilots and will be remembered as such.

IX

AVENGER!

Tubby but deadly, the U.S. Navy's multirole Grumman TBF lived up to its name, bringing retribution to the Japanese in the Pacific.

By Jerry Scutts

A low, gray overcast, punctuated by rain squalls, hung like a tattered shroud over the Pacific Ocean on April 7, 1945. Through the murk, pilots and crewmen of Navy Grumman TBF Avengers and Curtiss SB2C Helldivers strained their eyes to spot the telltale wake of ships. Down there, somewhere below, was a floating kamikaze force spearheaded by *Yamato*, the world's largest battleship.

Suddenly, there she was, defiantly moving toward units of the U.S. fleet off Okinawa. The Imperial Japanese Navy intended for *Yamato*, surrounded by her destroyer shield, to force her way to Okinawa, scuttle herself in the shallows offshore, and pound the American landing force with her big guns. The mission of the U.S. Navy fliers was to prevent that from happening.

As they sighted their quarry, each TBF and SB2C crew selected a target and lined up to make its run. The portly TBFs chose a shallow dive, leveling out to release their "tin fish"; the SB2Cs came in steeper, their bomb bays agape, to drop their bombs.

By the time *Yorktown's* fliers made their torpedo drops, *Yamato* was already crippled by the Helldiver attacks but still capable of fight. She would not last much longer, though. One after another, the TBFs released their deadly cargos, and within minutes *Yamato* was wreathed in flame and smoke as the torpedoes and more bombs struck home. The mighty ship, pride of the Imperial Japanese Navy, finally succumbed to the battering. She sank at 2:35 p.m.

Helping deliver the *coup de grâce* to the world's biggest battleship was a high point in the career of the TBF Avenger, one of the aeronautical success stories of World War II. Conceived before the attack on Pearl Harbor, Grumman's replacement for the Douglas TBD Devastator was destined to serve through most of the Pacific War. It became the most important attack bomber in the Navy's inventory and was ordered in greater numbers than any previous type.

In March 1939, the U.S. Navy requested a new torpedo bomber. The specifications included a crew of three—pilot, radioman and gunner—a 300-mph top speed with a stalling speed of 70 mph, and a range of

On June 20, 1944, TBF Avengers from the Belleau Wood pass the damaged Japanese carrier Zuikaku *and launch their torpedoes at light carrier* Hiyo *(not shown), in a painting by Robert Watts.*

1,000 miles carrying a torpedo or three 500-pound bombs. In addition, the new aircraft had to have adequate crew armor and be able to withstand the stresses of low flying during attacks on ships.

Also paramount was machine-gun armament, both for strafing during the target run-in and to provide the aircraft with some protection from intercepting enemy fighters. Wing folding, to assist hangaring aboard carriers, and an internal ordnance bay were also specified—all previous Navy attack aircraft had carried their offensive loads externally, with the inevitable drag penalty.

Out of 13 proposals submitted by different companies, the Navy ordered prototypes from Vought and Brewster, as well as one from Grumman—the G-40, similar to that company's F4F Wildcat fighter but appreciably larger. That similarity was no accident on Grumman's part. If the G-40 was selected by the Navy, the new bomber could be built in less time, using construction techniques familiar to the work force.

On April 8, 1940, the Navy's Bureau of Aeronautics, which acted as that service's official contractor for airplanes, ordered two prototypes of Grumman's single-engine, three-place aircraft. It was to be powered by a 1,700-hp, two-stage Wright R-2600-8 engine, one of two power plants proposed.

The design team for the Grumman G-40 was led by engineer William T. Schwendler, one of the three joint founders of the company. The Navy, convinced that Grumman had the right aircraft to replace the TBD, ordered 285 production aircraft some seven months before either of the prototypes flew.

Designated XTBF-1 and XTBF-2, the first Avengers differed in details, the XTBF-1 machine lacking a dorsal fin and having a smaller empennage area. In that guise, the XTBF-1 made its first flight on August 1, 1941, with test pilot Bob Hall immediately beginning an intensive test program. The testing lasted until November 28, when the plane was destroyed in a crash after the crew's forced bailout following a fire in the bomb bay. By then the second aircraft was well on its way to completion, with a large dorsal fin added to improve stability.

Flight tests with the XTBF-2 began on December 20. They showed that the greater tail area had cured any tendency for the new attack bomber to become unstable and that few further design changes were necessary before production began. After the attack on Pearl Harbor, the nation was swept by a wave of anger, and the name "Avenger" seemed highly appropriate for a new Navy attack bomber.

Modern fighters and bombers for all the U.S. services were vital if the final victory was to be won. Grumman, already committed to building the F4F Wildcat, realized that production space at its Bethpage plant on Long Island was about to run out. The General Motors Corporation was therefore brought in to take over TBF production at its Eastern Aircraft Division as soon as practicable. Eastern Aircraft–built Avengers would have a slight change in designation and be known as TBMs rather than TBFs.

While GM tooled up, Grumman began building Avengers. The first TBF-1 was rolled out on January 2, 1942, and two months later Navy crews from torpedo squadron VT-8 were visiting Bethpage to see their new aircraft. Initial handover of TBF-1s to VT-8 was made at the end of March.

The squadron detachment was given barely enough time to evaluate the Avenger at Naval Air Station, Norfolk, Va., before the men received new orders. Their destination now was the Pacific and the carrier *Hornet*, already at sea and conveying the rest of VT-8 to war.

Forewarned of Japanese plans to occupy Midway Island, the Navy called for volunteers to fly six TBFs to be based there to provide some additional defense for the small garrison. On June 1, 1942, the six TBF-1s with their volunteer crews departed Ford Island, Hawaii, and set course for Midway, 1,500 miles away. Once on Midway, the Avenger crews had but three days to wait for action—on June 4, the Japanese fleet was reported to be only 100 miles away.

Taking off to attack the enemy carriers, the small U.S. force passed enemy aircraft heading in to bomb and strafe Midway. Lieutenant Langdon K. Fieberling, leading the force, noted three Mitsubishi A6M2 Zero fighters setting up for a firing pass on them.

Like all Japanese aircraft, the A6M had been given an Allied code name for rapid identification, with male names signifying fighters—in this case "Zeke," which sounded similar to the airplane's popular nickname, among Japanese and Americans alike, of Zero. Luckily, the enemy pilots did not press home their attack, and the TBFs soon sighted their own primary target, the Japanese carriers.

Trying to evade the strong combat air patrol put up by the carriers and ignoring flak from the ships, the TBFs ran in for their torpedo drop. It was no fault of the crews or their new aircraft that VT-8 failed to damage any of the Japanese carriers with their torpedoes. Five aircraft were quickly shot down.

The sixth TBF, piloted by Ensign Albert Earnest and crewed by turret gunner J.D. Manning and radio operator/tunnel gunner Radioman 3rd Class Harry H. Ferrier, limped away. Earnest made it back to Midway with his turret gunner dead and his hydraulics shot out. He landed on one good main wheel and without flaps.

With the loss of five TBFs from Midway added to those TBDs that were slaughtered in the Midway sea battle, VT-8 suffered griev-

Jack Fellows depicts Grumman TBF Avengers of Squadron VT-1 from the carrier Yorktown *in June 1944.*

ously that day—44 men and 20 aircraft were lost. It was left to other units flying the older Douglas SBD Dauntless dive bombers to do the avenging at Midway, striking a blow from which the Japanese navy was never to fully recover. By sinking four carriers, U.S. Navy aircraft all but wiped out the cream of the Japanese navy's fliers, men who had spent years in training. They could be replaced only by individuals whose training, under war conditions, would not be as thorough.

Despite the TBF's disappointing combat debut, Navy leaders recognized that it had promise—good performance, load-carrying capability and range. Throughout the rest of 1942, production increased, enabling the Navy to rapidly retire its remaining obsolete torpedo bombers and to commission new TBF squadrons. Once the TBF-1 was in service, its adaptability enabled the Navy, and later the Marine Corps, to fill numerous specialized roles without introducing completely different aircraft.

Grumman's Bethpage plant continued to build the TBF-1 until the end of 1943, by which time General Motors' Eastern Aircraft Division at Trenton, N.J., was in full production. Grumman built 2,293 TBF-1s, completing the last aircraft in December 1943. Eastern's first TBM-1 was delivered by the Trenton plant on November 12, 1942, General Motors having signed a contract to build 1,200 aircraft.

Before finalizing plans for an all-encompassing thrust back across the Pacific, the U.S. Navy wanted the carrier force equipped with the best bombers, torpedo planes and fighters that could be obtained. Thus the obsolete TBD Devastator passed from the scene, and even the rugged and reliable SBD Dauntless began passing the torch to the TBF, which combined the torpedo attack role with equally effective bombing capability.

Improved models of the SB2C Helldiver, restricted to bomb delivery with a useful strafing capability from cannon or machine-gun armament, joined the fleet late in 1943. Together, the Avenger and the Helldiver proved to be a highly effective team.

The tough fighting at the Battle of Midway was still a very recent memory when the TBF embarked on its first major operation to support the U.S. landings on Guadalcanal in the Solomon Islands beginning on August 7, 1942. For that operation, Task Force 61's air element included squadrons VT-3, VT-7 and VT-8, equipped with TBFs and assigned respectively to the carriers *Enterprise*, *Wasp* and *Saratoga*.

During those dark, backs-to-the-wall days, the versatile Avenger proved it could fight as well from a land base as from the deck of a carrier, as part of the *Enterprise* Air Group would find out in November 1942. Forced to return to action while one of her elevators was still under repair, *Enterprise* disembarked part of her TBF force to bolster the Guadalcanal defenses. Among the targets these land-based TBF crews successfully attacked was the battleship *Hiei*, which had been previously crippled in a night surface action on November 13-14.

Earlier, in the Battle of the Eastern Solomons, *Saratoga's* air group of TBFs and SBDs sank the light carrier *Ryujo* on August 24, 1942. Principal honors went to the 28 dive-bombing SBDs of VS-3 and VB-3, although one VT-8 Avenger's torpedo struck home to contribute to the demise of the sixth Japanese carrier to be sunk in World War II.

The fight to secure the Solomons also recorded the combat debut of the TBF in the hands of Marine aviators when VMSB-131 took up station on Henderson Field, Guadalcanal, in November 1942. This Marine squadron designation was something of a throwback to prewar days, standing as it did for Marine Scout-Bombing Squadron. The term "Scout" was finally dropped in 1946.

Initiating combat operations by using its TBFs in an unfamiliar torpedo bombing role, VMSB-131 also scored hits on *Hiei* on November 13. The Marine tin fish helped send the wrecked *Hiei* to the bottom—becoming the first Japanese battleship to be lost in action.

Thereafter, Marine TBFs concentrated on the traditional leatherneck role of close air support of infantry and land operations, using bombs and rockets rather than torpedoes. Although they were to be land based for much of the war, Marine TBF crews were also no strangers to carrier decks. But it was December 1944 before the first all-Marine escort carrier *Block Island* was commissioned. *Block Island* put Marine aviators back in the mainstream of the war, flying strike missions in TBMs in support of the Okinawa campaign.

With the Avenger firmly established as an integral part of the Navy-Marine attack elements on land and aboard both fleet carriers and the "baby flattops" (escort carriers, or CVEs), Grumman and Eastern developed the Avenger to undertake more specialized tasks. Having established the TBF-1B in production to follow the TBF-1 and TBF-1A, the latter for Lend-Lease delivery to Britain's fleet air arm, Grumman subsequently built its final variant, the TBF-1C.

Among the changes introduced in the 1C was an increase in fixed armament over the TBF-1. Finding the original cowling-mounted .50-caliber machine gun useful during strafing runs, combat pilots wanted greater firepower. In the TBF-1C, the fixed gun in the forward upper fuselage was removed, and a single .50-caliber machine gun was installed in each wing just outboard of the folding back breakpoint. Other changes included mountings for a 275-gallon auxiliary fuel tank in the bomb bay and wing racks for two 58-gallon external tanks. These increased the overall fuel capacity to 725 gallons, giving the TBF-1C a range of 1,105 miles.

In common with most TBF/TBM models, minor in-service modifications were made without need to change the aircraft's basic designation in Bureau of Aeronautics records, although more specialized duty did require such identification. The Grumman TBF-1C had its equivalent Eastern (General Motors) TBM-1C, and the TBF/TBM-1D aircraft were C models fitted with anti-submarine radar in a starboard wing pod, plus underwing rocket launching points.

Finding the ideal radar for Navy aircraft, so seaborne targets could be detected early enough for an attack to be planned and launched, occupied many man-hours and millions of dollars. Among the ideas tried for the TBF was a massive radome housing the radar scanner positioned above the cockpit center section. The idea was scrapped.

Surface search radar, or ASB (air to surface, Type B), employed a pair of antennas mounted below the aircraft's wings, fixed in azimuth to provide a 60-degree beam. ASB could detect surface targets 40 nautical miles away and submarines five miles away. Microwave radar generally replaced ASB, and the Western Electric Model APS-3 radar was fitted to many TBFs/TBMs. With a 14-inch parabolic antenna built into a pod located on the starboard wing leading edge, it could pick up ships at 50 miles and submarines at 15 miles, with the added advantage of distinguishing the size of airborne targets.

Reconnaissance was also vital to effective carrier strikes, and in common with other shipboard aircraft, Avengers were modified to carry cameras. Both the TBF and TBM-1P versions had their bomb bay space partially occupied by cameras. Night photography was occasionally assisted on individual aircraft by a powerful searchlight (primarily to spot submarines) mounted on a port wing rack.

An escort carrier–based TBF-1 Avenger fitted with ASH radar (the port antenna mast of which can be seen under the left wing) conducts an anti-submarine patrol over the Atlantic Ocean.

The TBF/TBM proved numerous new systems, including a turbojet that was experimentally fitted in the aft lower fuselage of the first XTBF-3, and a wide variety of attack loads such as mines, sonobuoys and 3.5-inch and 5-inch rockets. The best of these features of earlier model Avengers were combined in the TBM-3, the last major wartime production model.

Built exclusively by Eastern Aircraft, 4,657 TBM-3s were manufactured. Externally similar to earlier Avengers, this TBM series introduced further equipment changes, including an autopilot. The late-model TBM-3s, mainly the 3D and 3E versions, were powered by the Pratt and Whitney R-2600-20 engine, which provided 1,900 hp for takeoff.

Weighing approximately 1 ton less than earlier versions, the TBM-3D was a radar-equipped version intended for anti-submarine warfare work with a wing searchlight. The TBM-3E had APS-4

A TBM-1C of VT-1 warms up for takeoff from the carrier Yorktown *during the Marianas campaign in June 1944. Note the unique Grumman method of folding wings on the TBM in the background.*

radar in an underwing pod and reduced armament. The original "stinger" ventral gun position, a design feature of most Avengers, was deleted and the transparent sighting panels were faired over. An external tailhook was usually fitted to the TBM-3 in place of the retractable unit of earlier models, which added 11 inches to the aircraft's overall length.

The weight-saving exercise improved the Avenger's performance, enabling the TBM-3 to attain 276 mph at 16,500 feet, with rate of climb increasing to 2,060 feet per minute. While these figures represented a relatively small gain over the performance of the TBF-1, crews appreciated every mph, especially if enemy fighters put in an appearance.

Although it was stretching things a little to call the Avenger a fighter, Navy and Marine TBF/TBM crews were credited with a highly respectable score of 98 Japanese aircraft destroyed by the end of the war. Avenger crews thought nothing of mixing it up with the Japanese, often throwing their big airplanes all over the sky to bring their fixed and flexible (turret and lower fuselage) guns to bear. The results were often spectacular, making a fallacy of the Japanese theory that light, unarmored warplanes could beat heavier and well-protected aircraft in combat.

All remaining TBM models completed during the war were based on the TBM-3 and included the winterized TBM-3J, with extra protection for equipment operating under Arctic conditions. The TBM-1L was fitted with a retractable searchlight; the TBM-3N was specially equipped for night attack, with reduced or deleted flexible armament; and the TBM-3W was equipped as an early warning aircraft. Like a number of other TBF models, the development of an early warning version was begun during hostilities but was destined not to see operational service before the Japanese surrender.

In February 1943, with Guadalcanal out of danger of recapture by the Japanese, the Marines were able to base additional TBF squadrons on Henderson Field. Those included VMTB-132 (equipped with both TBFs and SBDs) and VMTB-143. VMSB-131, which became VMTB-131 in January 1943, left the Solomons during the year and subsequently saw action flying from Guam. In general terms, all TBF squadrons were redesignated as torpedo bomber units, even though the torpedo was used far less than bombs. A force of Marine TBF units remained available to harry the remaining enemy forces in the South Pacific while the buildup of TBF squadrons for duty aboard fleet and escort carriers continued in preparation for a series of raids on Japanese island strongpoints.

Small air groups composed of attack bombers and fighters, operating from escort carriers, proved to be invaluable because they could maintain a limited offensive, particularly against enemy submarines and surface transports, away from the main battle areas. They freed the larger fast-carrier force from such time-consuming second-line duty so that the carrier force could concentrate on the main task of defeating the Imperial fleet. A mix of Avengers and Wildcats became standard aboard most Pacific theater CVEs, the ratio of fighters to TBFs varying according to operational needs.

As operations in the Solomons area continued throughout 1943, the TBF squadrons added aerial mining to their increasingly wide combat role. Extremely hazardous work, mining was deemed essential to help prevent a resurgence of the "Tokyo Express," the general name given to Japanese seaborne supply runs to their island garrisons.

Small enemy units were left on islands of no major strategic importance so far as U.S. war plans were concerned. Navy Avengers often attacked targets in and around Rabaul, the principal Japanese naval base on New Britain, which was to more or less hold out right to the end of the war. These enemy garrisons were contained by an Allied sea and air blockade, making invasion unnecessary. By the fall of 1943, the United States had taken the atolls of Tarawa, Makin and Betio in the Gilbert Islands.

In November, carriers launched the first Avenger night missions designed to reduce nocturnal enemy forays against the fleet. In those early "hunter-killer" operations, the TBF teamed with radar-equipped F6F Hellcat fighters. They met with some success, further eroding any advantage the Imperial Navy might still believe it had at night.

After the capture of the Marshall Islands, the United States had a substantial foothold from which to launch more ambitious operations. When a short, sharp campaign against the atoll of Truk was undertaken on February 17 and 18, 1944, *Enterprise* launched the first TBF night bombing attack. On the 17th, Navy torpedo squadron VT-10 sent 12 TBF-1Cs to carry out a highly successful penetration of the harbor in which they scored 13 hits on enemy ships. On the following day, aircraft from four carriers found few worthwhile seaborne targets and instead plastered harbor facilities, airfields and storage/ammunition dumps.

Before February 1944 was over, it was Eniwetok's turn. That island in the Marshalls had been secured by February 21, and before month's end, Navy strikes had been made on the principal islands in the Marianas group. A period of close-support sorties followed before a force of 15 U.S. carriers was unleashed against the Marianas in June.

During the pre-invasion assault on Saipan on June 13, VT-16's skipper, Robert H. Isely, was lost. Making a shallow-angle approach to fire rockets at targets on Aslito airfield, Isely's Avenger was hit by flak. The TBF, which had flown from *Lexington*, crashed in flames. Later, when the United States had transformed Aslito into

Displaying a mixed bag of markings, TBF-1s from VT-12, VC-38, VC-40 and Marine squadrons VMTB-143 and VMTB-233 make a sortie from Espiritu Santo in the New Hebrides Islands on October 5, 1943.

a major Boeing B-29 base, it was renamed Isely Field to honor the gallant Avenger pilot.

The Navy took a serious view of TBF losses in the Marianas, citing rocket attack missions on enemy positions as a primary cause. The necessary low and slow approach to ground targets was decidedly dangerous, and, for a time, the use of rockets was restricted to specific targets that minimized the risk to TBF crews. Rockets continued to be a major item of ordnance in the Navy's armory, however, as a full salvo was equivalent to a destroyer's broadside in terms of destructive power.

These early Navy rockets were the 3.5-inch kind carried on British-type underwing mounting rails, which were found to reduce the aircraft's speed by as much as 17 knots. Rails were subsequently found to be unnecessary and gave way to so-called zero-length launchers. Each rocket was clipped to a pair of stub launchers and fired electrically, the ignition sequence being enough to

With their rear gun turrets removed, many Avengers fought a different enemy after World War II, "bombing" forest fires with water and chemicals. This surviving TBM-3 has been restored to flyable condition by the Confederate Air Force, but it lacks the wartime gun turret.

propel it forward without any other guidance.

Apart from suffering combat attrition over the islands themselves, the Japanese were taking a hammering in the famed "Marianas Turkey Shoot," the resounding victory for the U.S. carrier air groups over successive waves of attacking Japanese planes. This series of air battles all but broke the back of remaining Japanese carrier-based air power. However, U.S. admirals wanted the jackpot. If they could sink the enemy carriers that had launched the ill-fated air groups slaughtered by the Navy Hellcats, future U.S.

operations would be considerably safer. At 3:40 p.m. on June 20, 1944, the retiring Japanese carrier force was sighted by a TBF from *Enterprise*.

Although the targets lay at extreme range from the U.S. carriers, Admiral Marc Mitscher gave the order to go, and at 4:11 the first of 54 TBFs, 77 dive bombers and 85 fighters roared off into the evening sky.

At 6:40, Mitscher's fliers sighted the Japanese, who had already lost two carriers to American submarines—Vice Admiral Jisaburo Ozawa's flagship, *Taiho*, fatally torpedoed by *Albacore*, and *Shokaku*, sunk by *Cavalla*. Pressing their attacks through flak and the 75 remaining aircraft that Ozawa's carriers got into the air, the American dive bombers damaged several warships and disabled two oilers, *Genyo* and *Seiyo Maru*, which were subsequently abandoned and scuttled.

The only other Japanese loss occurred when four TBM Avengers from VT-24 off the light carrier *Belleau Wood*, led by Lt. j.g. George B. Brown, attacked the light carrier *Hiyo*. Although struck by anti-aircraft fire, Brown, who had sworn earlier that he would torpedo an enemy carrier at any cost, probably did succeed in scoring a hit, while the torpedo of one of his comrades, Lt. j.g. Warren Omark, definitely found its mark. His plane badly shot-up, the wounded Brown ordered his radioman and gunner to bail out, but then tried to bring his Avenger back to *Belleau Wood*. He never made it, disappearing into a cloud as Omark tried to guide him home. Parachuting safely and floating in their life jackets, Brown's crewmen were later rescued by a ship from Task Force 58 and reported that they had the satisfaction of seeing *Hiyo* go down.

Heading back to their ships, the aircrews weighed their chances of bringing off a night landing on the blacked-out decks of the carriers, even if their fuel tanks did not run dry long before the flattops were sighted. Recognizing the pilots' difficulties, Mitscher won heartfelt thanks from the carriers' plane crews by ordering the fleet to turn on every available light, enabling many tired men to avoid ditching. Even so, 23 Avengers and 39 SB2Cs were lost that night, mainly from ditchings.

As more and more island bases were secured, including Noemfoor, Peleliu and Ulithi, Marine squadrons, a number of which were TBF-equipped, filled any gap left when the carriers had departed. They guarded the surrounding sea lanes and attacked enemy shipping, particularly transports and submarines. Guam and Tinian became home for VMTB-131 and VMTB-242, respectively, during the summer of 1944.

The fleet, meantime, was gearing up for operations against Formosa and the Philippines. The October 1944 invasion of Leyte saw TBFs heavily engaged against shore installations while the enemy gambled on a major sea engagement to thwart the American plans. Such a "decisive" sea battle had long figured in Japanese plans, although the time when the Imperial Navy could hope to win a straight fight with the U.S. Navy had since passed.

At Leyte, however, the Japanese scored heavily, crippling the U.S. carrier *Princeton* so badly she had to be abandoned. Leyte also witnessed the first mass use of kamikaze planes, which mauled the

A TBF of AG-37 sits with wings folded aboard the escort carrier Sangamon *while a Japanese suicide plane hits the flight deck of sister ship* Suwannee *on October 26, 1944.*

strong American escort carrier force. Offsetting any Japanese success was the sinking of the battleship *Musashi* by Avengers and Helldivers, plus the continuing depletion of enemy air power, for which there were few well-trained pilot replacements.

When the Philippine landings had established a beachhead, Navy and Marine TBFs once more spearheaded the push inland. At sea, *Independence* carried the first night air group into combat. Composed of fighters and the TBM-1Ds of VTM-41, this group continued the earlier success of coordinated Avenger/fighter strikes, pointing the way to true round-the-clock carrier operations. In December 1944, *Enterprise* became the first night carrier, and with *Independence*, their air groups conducted radar-directed operations until the war's end.

By early 1945, the carrier force was pounding on the enemy's front door, having decimated Japanese shipping so badly that its merchant fleet had virtually ceased to exist. Damage inflicted largely by TBM and Curtis SB2C attacks had also brought the Imperial Navy almost to its knees. Increasingly, the desperate enemy resorted to suicide tactics to stave off the inevitable defeat. In far from favorable weather, with rain squalls and low visibility, the carrier air groups were heavily engaged that January in the seizure of Iwo Jima. The island was taken primarily to provide an emergency bomber airfield roughly halfway between the Marianas and Japan.

On February 19, TBFs made their debut over the Japanese home islands. So far as conventional warfare was concerned, the April 1 invasion of Okinawa, 450 miles from Japan, should have been relatively safe for naval sea and air forces—which were strong enough to deal with numerous targets simultaneously, including the mighty *Yamato* and her escort.

Although the terrible kamikazes tried their best to secure some kind of victory off Okinawa, the U.S. carrier air groups maintained the pressure on Japan. TBFs made a series of successful airstrikes on the home islands between July 10 and August 15, by which time the two Boeing B-29 Superfortress atomic bomb strikes had wiped out the cities of Hiroshima and Nagasaki. Japan agreed to surrender on August 15.

Termination of TBM production more or less coincided with the final surrender of Japan in September 1945. By then a grand total of 9,839 aircraft had been manufactured by Eastern. Having participated in every major operation, plus numerous minor ones, throughout most of the Pacific War, the Grumman Avenger had earned an honorable place in the history of aviation. Luckily, enough examples still exist today to give younger people some impression of what it was like to go to war in the tough, reliable old aircraft that, because it was tubby and relatively slow, was nicknamed "Turkey."

One of history's small ironies is the fact that, in 1954, the Grumman Avenger became the first military aircraft to be operated by the newly formed Japanese Maritime Self-Defense Force. Ten TBM-3W2s were delivered that year, with 10 TBM-3S2 models following in 1955. Those machines were flown on patrol duties until their retirement in 1960, the year in which other nations also replaced their Grumman patrol bombers. The Avengers served the Japanese well. No aircraft from the small force were lost during the six years or so that the planes were used to provide valuable training for many patrol crews.

X

BUZZ BOMB BLASTS BRITAIN

Hitler unleashed the V-1, precursor of the cruise missile, against London in 1944.
The British responded with high-speed interceptors, including the first Allied jet.

By David Alan Johnson

"Hey! They got one! They got one!" At BBC Broadcasting House in London's West End, an American Army officer suddenly began shouting and pointing out the window. Technical Sergeant Dick Dudley and everyone else in the room got up to see what the noise was all about. Sergeant Dudley arrived at the window just in time to see an aircraft rushing by, its tail brightly aflame. It looked as though the local anti-aircraft gunners had hit a German bomber and set it on fire. But it was not a bomber. It was a new German weapon, quite literally a "flying bomb."

The air raid sirens had already sounded—"deep-throated, three-toned jobs that sounded as though they really meant it," was one American's description of them. When the flying bombs reached Greater London's southern boundary, the guns of the London Defence Region opened up. Anyone who missed the sirens was jolted awake by the roaring bark of the guns, which rattled windows and frightened children. Anyone who opened his blackout curtains could watch the searchlights trying to pinpoint the intruders—odd little airplanes with flaming tails—through a steady drizzle.

What observers caught sight of was a very odd aircraft, a pilotless, jet-propelled aerial torpedo that would bear many names. Officially, it was simply FZG-76—*Flakzielgerät* (anti-aircraft target device)-76. The anti-aircraft designation was a ruse to throw Allied spies off the track. In Britain, it was known as the "doodlebug," "buzz bomb" and "farting fury," along with a number of other comic names.

The Fieseler company that designed it designated it the Fi-103. The Nazi Propaganda Ministry called the pilotless aircraft *Vergeltungswaffe* (retaliation weapon) 1, or V-1. But the name almost universally favored by Britons and Americans alike was "buzz bomb."

A V-1 flying bomb resembled a small aircraft with a stovepipe mounted over its tail and no cockpit. Its overall length was just over 25 feet, with a wingspan of 17 ½ feet. Standard 80-octane gasoline kept its jet engine running, which was housed in the stovepipe assembly; this was the same fuel used by trucks. The flying bomb was easy and cheap ($500) to build and carried a 1,870-pound warhead. But while the flying bomb may have been cheap and simple, it was not very accurate—it could not hit small targets, or even moderate-sized villages. It was accurate enough to hit a target the size of Greater London, however, and that was all that was expected—a way to hit back at the Allies without risking the depleted reserves of the *Luftwaffe's* bomber fleet.

During the early months of 1943, extensive tests were carried out involving the FZG-76. Only nine months had passed between the beginning of work on the project in March 1942 and the first successful launch, which took place on Christmas Eve, although

With lives at stake, a Supermarine Spitfire Mark IX races alongside a V-1 guided bomb in hopes of forcing it over with its wingtip, and thereby disrupting its controls, in Deadly Chase, *by Ronald Wong.*

the flying bomb still had its share of teething problems. One question involved the proper type of launching site for the flying bombs. Some favored large concrete emplacements; others proposed small, portable sites. As head of the *Luftwaffe, Reichsmarschall* Hermann Göring compromised, ordering four concrete bunkers and 96 smaller sites begun immediately.

Next, men had to be trained to handle and fire the flying bomb. A new *Luftwaffe* unit was formed in August 1943, called *Flakregiment* 155 (W). The anti-aircraft designation was, once again, aimed at deceiving Allied intelligence.

The new unit was placed under the command of *Luftwaffe* Colonel Max Wachtel, who had been in charge of all the experimental flying bomb launches. Wachtel was instructed to get his men ready for firing the bomb under actual combat conditions, and he took his orders to heart; his *Flakregiment* began exercises within days of the unit's creation. From the western side of Peenemünde, on Usedom Island in the Baltic Sea, the launching crews began readying the small, jet-propelled planes and firing them downrange over the Baltic.

Troops of Flakregiment *155 (W)—a unit that, despite its name, had nothing to do with anti-aircraft operations—push V-1s into position for assembly and launching in 1944.*

Under Wachtel, *Flakregiment* 155 (W) continued its training through the winter of 1943 and into 1944. By June 1944, Wachtel and his unit were in France, ready to begin operations. But few others connected with the flying bomb project were as efficient as Wachtel.

One of the main problems was with the production of the flying bombs themselves. Because of the many defects that plagued the bomb, it did not go into production until March 1944. Engineers at the Volkswagen plant at Fallersleben, near Hamburg, did their best to work out the problems, but the pilotless planes kept crashing immediately after launching. Full production did not begin until April 1944, when 1,000 flying bombs rolled off the Volkswagen assembly line.

Wachtel had been ordered to begin launching the pilotless bombs against England by June, but his unit had no equipment, no launching rails and no supplies. It had been decided that light-weight launching ramps, called modified sites, would be used in place of larger ramps that had proved too vulnerable to Allied bombing attacks.

The supplies and equipment that Wachtel needed to begin operations did not arrive until June 12, 1944, only a few hours before he was to begin launching V-1s against southern England. Only 10 ramps were ready for launching; 55 were supposed to have been prepared, but not enough spare parts and equipment had been sent for all of them.

By 3:30 a.m. on June 13, the 10 firing ramps were ready. The *Luftwaffe* high command decided to go ahead despite the fact that so few ramps were operational.

Months of practice made the pre-launch procedure a set routine for the crews. First, the flying bomb's fuel tank was checked, to make certain that it had been topped off. Following this, the wooden wings were attached—these had been folded over the fuselage to make storing and moving the aircraft easier. After assembly, the plane was aligned precisely with its firing ramp—which was pointed directly at London—and its gyrocompass was set at zero to ensure it flew the straight course on which it had been aimed.

The flying bomb, now ready for launching, was moved onto its firing ramp. After it was loaded onto its catapult, a lug on the underside of the fuselage was attached to the catapult's firing piston. When the piston was released, it accelerated the V-1 off the launch rails in the same way that a jet plane is catapulted off the flight deck of an aircraft carrier.

With the stubby-winged flying bomb poised for takeoff, the launching crew took cover inside the "control bunker," a heavily armored trailer that housed the catapult's firing controls, or jumped into a nearby slit trench. The firing officer gave an order, a technician pulled a lever, and the flying bomb's pulse-jet engine came to life with a throbbing, ear-numbing roar.

This simple jet engine was the flying bomb's most unique feature. Housed outside the fuselage, above the tail, the jet is usually described as looking like either a stovepipe or a giant blow torch.

At the front end of the engine housing was a set of intake flaps

A "ski site" launcher for V-1 missiles, installed in France and pointed directly at London. Only 10 of the 55 intended launchers were ready to begin operations on June 13, 1944.

that resembled a Venetian blind. These flaps opened at the beginning of the engine's cycle, allowing air to be drawn into the combustion chamber, where it was mixed with 80-octane fuel. In the second stage of the combustion cycle, the flaps closed and the fuel-oxygen mixture was ignited. With a tremendous flash, a burst of hot exhaust shot out from the rear of the engine to provide forward thrust. Immediately following the exhaust stage, the intake flaps opened again, allowing air into the combustion chamber and repeating the cycle.

This simple jet engine could complete up to 500 combustion cycles every minute, giving the flying bomb a maximum speed of about 400 mph. The engine's pulsing combustion process also gave the flying bomb its distinctive *duv-duv-duv* sound in flight, a sound that Londoners would soon come to recognize.

After listening for a moment to ensure that the engine was firing

Vengeance for D-Day: A row of shops at London's Clapham Junction, three minutes after being hit by a V-1 on June 17, 1944.

properly, the firing officer gave the order to launch. A second lever was pulled, releasing the catapult's piston. The flying bomb lurched forward, shot along the length of steel rail, and jumped uncer-

tainly into the night sky. During the next half-hour, between about 3:30 and 4 a.m., nine more of the bombs bolted from their catapults. The launching crews watched as the small aircraft left their ramps, brilliant flashes of fire trailing from their exhausts.

Four of the shots failed, the flying bombs crashing just after take-off, with explosions loud enough to hurt the eardrums of the catapult crews.

Two of the successfully launched flying bombs crashed into the English Channel. The other four reached England; two landed in Kent, one in Surry, and one crashed in London, the intended target of all of them. The London bomb came down in Bethnal Green, East London, about three miles away from its Tower Bridge target point. The explosion killed three people and knocked out a railway bridge.

Although only four flying bombs reached England during this first launch, hundreds more would be launched during the next several weeks.

An inexpensive, and not very accurate, mechanism sent the flying bomb diving into its target upon arrival. Each bomb had a small, propellerlike anemometer device on its nose that was connected to the bomb's autopilot. As the flying bomb flew through the air, its forward motion turned the propeller like a pinwheel in the wind.

After a preset number of revolutions, the propeller tripped the diving controls, pointing the bomb earthward at a steep angle. The mechanism was set by the catapult crew before launching; the setting of how many revolutions were needed to trip the diving controls was based upon calculations involving the flying bomb's speed and the distance to target.

Any number of factors could undo this inherently imprecise system. Headwinds or tailwinds could alter the machine's ground-speed, ruining carefully worked-out calculations that were usually a lot more accurate than the mechanism itself. The autopilot might go haywire and send the bomb plunging into the Channel. Or it might not work at all, causing the bomb to overfly London and keep going until it ran out of fuel.

When the windmill device tilted the bomb toward the earth, all the fuel ran to one end of the tank—the end away from the fuel pump. The pump began drawing air, and the engine, cut off from its fuel supply, stopped running.

People in London and southern England very quickly learned to use this "cutting out" of the engine to their advantage. Between the time the pulsing *duv-duv-duv* ended and the bomb hit the ground, an average of between five and 15 seconds would pass—enough time for people to dive under a table or some sort of cover. This characteristic undoubtedly saved many lives.

A Spitfire chases a V-1 (circled) above the English countryside. Shooting at a V-1 risked damage or destruction to the pursuer if its warhead exploded, so "tipping" became a more popular means of "doodlebug" disposal.

In spite of the machine's defects, Wachtel's *Flakregiment* 155 (W) kept launching the bombs at a steady rate. On Saturday, June 18, 1944, his unit launched its 500th flying bomb. One of them landed on Hungerford Bridge, the railway bridge across the Thames River to Charing Cross Station in London.

Buzz bomb buster supreme: Squadron Leader Joseph Berry added 59½ V-1s to a Junkers Ju-88 he had downed in 1943.

The explosion blew a gaping hole in the middle of the bridge, forcing one of London's major rail terminals to shut down. Later in the day, an American intelligence officer saw the damage done to the bridge—it had been blown almost in half by the explosion. He also noticed that several large buildings on the Thames embankment had all the windows facing the river blown out.

Each flying bomb had an efficient system of sensitive fuses and pressure switches that detonated the warhead on first contact, before the machine could bury its nose (and warhead) in the earth. When the 1,900 pounds of high explosives went off on the surface of a roadway, the blast cut down everything within reach. Solid walls crumbled—often, even individual bricks in a wall would be reduced to pebble-sized bits. Windows a quarter of a mile away cracked from the force of the explosion.

A central London fire station got a firsthand look at the effects from the blast of a flying bomb. The firemen had opened the station's big front doors, trying to enjoy a sunny but not very warm June day, when a buzz bomb landed less than a block away. The blast waves first slammed the heavy wooden doors shut; then, a second later, the vacuum created by the explosion wrenched them open again. When the bomb's warhead detonated, shock waves flew out in concentric circles, like gigantic ripples. As the blast waves pulsed outward, they created a vacuum behind them. One London fireman called it a "double whammy" effect—the vacuum was capable of creating as much damage as the blast itself.

In an effort to stop the flying bomb attacks, anti-aircraft defenses and more than 1,000 barrage balloons were sent to Kent, southeast of London. Bombs launched from the Pas de Calais would have to fly over this "gun belt" on their way to London. Also, eight fighter squadrons, equipped with Hawker Typhoons, Supermarine Spitfire IXs and XIVs, and Hawker Tempest Vs, flew standing patrols.

Fighters assigned to combat the flying bombs underwent modifications to squeeze every last bit of power from their engines to help them chase the speedy flying bombs. All armor and excess weight were removed. The leading edges of wings and stabilizers were polished to a high gloss. The engines themselves received particular care, with meticulous tuning and overhauling at frequent intervals. After all the cutting and streamlining, the flying bomb interceptors consisted of little more than machine guns and cannons, a fuel tank, and a finely tuned engine. Because the buzz bombs traveled at more than 400 miles per hour, the piston-engine fighters needed all the speed they could muster.

Pilots of the modified Spitfires and Tempests could now close with the flying bombs more easily. Some could even fly right alongside the bombs, close enough to read the German writing on the fuselages. A few enterprising pilots discovered that they could slide a wing under the wingtip of the "flying blowlamp" and lift it, tipping the flying bomb out of control. That quickly became a standard method of destroying the bombs.

"Tipping the doodlebugs" nearly always worked. The flying bombs had a very delicate gyro mechanism; any sudden, violent movement—such as wing-lifting—would cause it to malfunction. With the gyroscope out of order, the machine would spiral earthward and crash. From the air, the concentric shock wave of the crashed bomb was said to look like "a single ripple on a lake."

But this maneuver was not without its risks. The flying bomb was made of rolled sheet steel, while the RAF fighters had a skin of light aluminum alloy. Many a Spitfire and Tempest hobbled back to base with one of its highly polished wings bent and twisted out of shape from the "wing wrestling."

Bringing down a buzz bomb with gunfire also presented problems for Allied pilots. The most frequent method of attack was the deflection shot, approaching from the side and opening fire when the bomb crossed the pilot's line of sight.

"It's like firing at a large flame with wings sprouting out of it," the pilot of a Tempest V said. "Your cannon scores hits, and suddenly there is a big red flash."

The top "doodlebug ace" was Squadron Leader Joseph Berry, who flew Tempest Vs with the Fighter Interception Unit, and then No. 501 Squadron. Berry's final score was 59½ V-1s, including a one-night record of seven on July 23. During a low-level chase four days later, he closed to 100 feet before downing the doodlebug, and his plane was damaged in the ensuing explosion. To his chagrin, he had to share the credit with a de Havilland Mosquito that had fired at the V-1 from 1,000 yards and, in the opinion of his unit, had "missed hopelessly."

Another noted V-1 specialist was Flying Officer R.F. Burgwal, a Dutch pilot who flew Rolls-Royce Grifon-engined Spitfire XIVs with No. 322 Squadron, a Dutch unit based in southeast England. Burgwal was credited with 21 V-1s, while a squadron mate and fellow Hollander, Flight Lt. J.L. Plesman, accounted for 12.

Number 616 Squadron could combat the pilotless planes on an equal footing. In July 1944, the unit received seven Gloster Meteors, the RAF's first jet fighter. The Meteor had a maximum speed in excess of 400 miles per hour, and could easily overtake the missiles. But the Meteor suffered from constant gun trouble—its 20mm cannons had a habit of jamming.

In spite of the balky cannons, however, the Meteors accounted for 13 flying bombs. When the guns failed, pilots could always rely upon the tipping techniques.

Meteor pilot T.D. Dean had a problem with his Meteor's cannons on August 4; he attacked a flying bomb, but his guns jammed. Undeterred, Dean maneuvered his aircraft alongside the bomb, slid a wingtip under the missile's, and executed a sharp bank, using the tipping maneuver. The V-1's gyro mechanism was thrown out of balance, and the flying bomb crashed. This was the first combat victory for an Allied jet fighter.

When a flying bomb was disabled by gunfire, it behaved in the same way as any conventional airplane—it went out of control, sometimes trailing smoke, and smashed into the earth. But the V-1s presented some problems that fighter pilots had not encountered before. One of the main problems was with the sheet steel skin—it deflected .303-caliber machine-gun bullets like armor plate.

Cannon fire was most effective against the V-1; a shell from a 20mm cannon would blow a hole right through the steel outer covering. But a 20mm cannon had a much shorter range than a .303-caliber machine gun, forcing the attacking pilot to move in at close range before pressing the firing button. And if a cannon shell should hit the flying bomb's 2,000-pound warhead, the result could be disastrous for the attacker. When a buzz bomb exploded in midair, great chunks of metal sprayed in all directions. The result could be the same as having a huge anti-aircraft shell explode nearby.

Jagged shrapnel holes and blasted-away control surfaces were the reward of a careless or overeager pilot who attacked a flying bomb. At least five aircraft were destroyed by midair flying bomb explosions. One such aircraft, a Spitfire, was flown by a Free French pilot, Jean-Marie Maridor, who attacked a flying bomb at point-blank range near the south coast. The bomb's ton of Trialen exploded, blasting the Spitfire apart and killing Maridor instantly.

The flying bomb offensive against London and southern England continued throughout the summer of 1944. In late summer, the launch sites on the Normandy coast were captured by the

A Gloster Meteor III of No. 616 Squadron at Manston. Never destined to engage Messerschmitt Me-262 jet fighters, the Meteors of 616 did account for 13 unmanned V-1s.

Allied armies as they moved inland from the D-Day beaches. By the first week of September, the flying bomb attacks had all but ended. More than 2,000 of them had hit London, with many others coming down on the surrounding suburbs.

But in mid-September, the bombs began to be fired at England by a new method—launched in midair from two-engine Heinkel He-111 bombers. The V-1 was slung under the Heinkel's port wing, inboard of the engine.

The Heinkels approached England at low altitudes to avoid radar detection. The pilot climbed to about 20,000 feet when the bomber neared the flying bomb's launching point, and he instructed the crew to start the bomb's engine and gyroscope. When everything was ready and the bomber had reached its required altitude, the V-1 was released. The pilotless plane dropped for several hundred feet before it leveled out and headed toward its target. Some never pulled out, and crashed into the North Sea. But most leveled off and continued along their preset course toward the eastern coastline of England.

Only one or two of those air-launched bombs hit London every day; some shots were aimed at the port of Southampton. Apart from putting an added strain on Britain's defenses, as well as on already taut British nerves, this new attack had little effect. The last flying bomb was launched at London on March 29, 1945, only six weeks before Germany surrendered.

By later standards, the FZG-76 seems primitive. It was designed by engineers at the Gerhard Fiesler Werke under pressure by the *Luftwaffe* and was produced in such haste that it suffered from major flaws. The pilotless aircraft looks especially primitive when compared with its present-day descendent, the Tomahawk cruise missile. In addition to an efficient fuel and propulsion system, the Tomahawk also has a computerized guidance system. Its computerized autopilot can actually read a built-in map and follow the map right to its target. The FZG-76 was simply pointed in the direction of its target—with luck, it struck within several miles of it.

Although the FZG-76 flying bomb was not the miracle weapon that the Nazi Propaganda Ministry had promised, its accomplishments far outweighed any of its negative aspects. During the flying bomb assault from mid-June to early September 1944, 2,419 of the pilotless aircraft hit London. Rail and transportation networks were seriously disrupted, and war production fell off dramatically. Damages inflicted, including lost factory production, totaled $150 million. About 6,000 Londoners were killed in V-1 attacks, with another 40,000 wounded or injured. German casualties were 185.

The flying bomb was an expedient of war. It was not sophisticated, but it did the same job as the Tomahawk cruise missile—it penetrated enemy defenses without endangering a human pilot. And, despite its shortcomings, it had an impact on the Allied war effort.

XI

THE BOMB THAT ENDED WORLD WAR II

It was the second atomic bomb, dropped on Nagasaki, that induced the Japanese to surrender.

By C.V. Glines

The atomic bombing of Hiroshima on August 6, 1945, has been the subject of numerous books and articles since that time, many by scientists and others who participated in the development of the world's first atomic bombs. The personal story of Brigadier General Paul W. Tibbets, who flew the Boeing B-29 *Enola Gay*, and the individual accounts of its crew members have also been published since that eventful mission more than a half century ago.

Strangely, however, the story of the second mission, which bombed Nagasaki, has not been fully told, mostly because of the concurrent rush of events leading to Japan's complete surrender. Then, too, it may be because that second A-bomb strike nearly ended disastrously. It further proved the verity of Murphy's Law that anything that can go wrong will go wrong.

Tibbets, then a colonel in charge of the 509th Composite Group, had honed his unit of 15 B-29 Superfortresses into one of the finest Air Force bombardment outfits ever assembled. Operating from Tinian Island in the Marianas, then considered the largest air base in the world, he and his crew had made a picture-perfect 2,900-mile flight and had dropped the uranium bomb called "Little Boy" squarely on target. That single bomb, weighing 8,900 pounds, wiped out nearly five square miles of Hiroshima—60 percent of the city. More than 78,000 of the city's total population of 348,000 were killed; an estimated 51,000 were injured or missing.

It had been an exhausting 12-hour mission. After returning to Tinian, Tibbets was greeted on the tarmac by General Carl Spaatz, commander of the Strategic Air Force, who pinned the Distinguished Service Cross on his rumpled, sweat-stained flying suit. Meanwhile, U.S. President Harry S. Truman was aboard USS *Augusta*, returning from a conference with Winston Churchill and Josef Stalin at Potsdam, Germany. Upon hearing the news, Truman exclaimed, "This is the greatest thing in history!" He promptly announced to the world the existence of an atomic bomb that had been developed under the code name "Manhattan Project."

The War Department then issued a number of press releases giving the history of the project, information about production facilities, and the biographies of key people. In an unusual example of military and press cooperation, the releases had actually been drafted by William L. Laurence, a science reporter for *The New York Times* who had known about the A-bomb for several months prior to the Hiroshima mission. Apprised of the need for complete secrecy, he had visited the production facilities and had followed the group to Tinian.

On August 9, 1945, a Boeing B-29 of the 509th Composite Group drops a single deadly bomb on its secondary target, in Bockscar Over Nagasaki, *by Randy Green.*

Weighing 10,800 pounds and measuring 10 feet 8 inches in length and 5 feet in diameter, the plutonium bomb called Fat Man was larger and more complex than Little Boy, the U-235-based bomb that had been dropped on Hiroshima.

Within hours, newspapers around the world were carrying stories about the bomb and the principles involved in splitting the atom. They chronicled the bomb's development, the devastation it caused, the role of Maj. Gen. Leslie R. Groves in directing the Manhattan Project, and the contributions of some 30,000 engineers and scientists in solving the mystery of the atom's energy potential.

Secretary of War Henry L. Stimson was one of the few top leaders who had been totally informed of the bomb's top-secret development every step of the way, and he had approved the target selections. He announced that improvements would be forthcoming soon "which will increase by several fold the effectiveness" of the Hiroshima bomb.

The populace of the target cities had been warned. Leaflets had been dropped on 11 Japanese cities on July 27, telling the citizens that America was "in possession of the most destructive explosive ever devised by man." There had been other warnings given to the Japanese during the preceding weeks, while the Twentieth Air Force's Superforts firebombed the country's principal industrial cities.

But the immense havoc a single bomb could produce was unimaginable, and the warnings were not taken very seriously. Just the day before, July 26, a declaration had been issued at Potsdam that notified the world of the intentions of three of the Allied nations concerning Japan: "The prodigious land, sea and air forces of the United States, the British Empire and of China, many times reinforced by their armies and air fleets of the west, are poised to strike the final blows upon Japan. This military power is sustained and inspired by the determination of all the Allied Nations to prosecute the war against Japan until she ceases to resist.

"…We call upon the Government of Japan to proclaim now the unconditional surrender of all the Japanese armed forces, and to provide proper and adequate assurance of their good faith in such action. The alternative for Japan is prompt and utter destruction."

The Potsdam Declaration was debated vigorously at the highest levels of the Japanese government. A delegation was sent to Moscow to request that the Soviet Union, then still at peace with Japan, act as a mediator. It was hoped that if the Soviets would agree to that role, it might be possible to negotiate terms that would be the most favorable to Japan.

There was great dissension among the Japanese military leaders, for few wanted to submit to a demand for unconditional surrender. Senior diplomats and influential citizens, however, privately urged Marquis Koichi Kido and members of the Japanese cabinet to take advantage of the offer in order to bring a prompt end to the war. On the other hand, War Minister Korechika Anami and the chiefs of the army and navy staffs adamantly refused to accept the terms of the Potsdam agreement. The result was that the Japanese government appeared to ignore the Allied declaration. There was no suspicion that the declaration itself constituted a warning that the most devastating weapon ever devised would be forthcoming. The people of Hiroshima tragically learned otherwise.

Because of the complete disruption of communications in Hiroshima after the atomic attack, the initial reports of damage were meager and fragmentary. While the world waited for their reaction, shocked Japanese officials were trying to grasp the extent of the damage. Meanwhile, President Truman issued the following statement: "It was to spare the Japanese people from utter de-

Setting out on "Special Mission No. 16," Bockscar *carries out her* Lonely Flight to Destiny, *in a painting by Craig Kodera.*

struction that the ultimatum of July 26 was issued at Potsdam. Their leaders promptly rejected that ultimatum. If they do not now accept our terms, they may expect a rain of ruin from the air the likes of which has never been seen on this earth."

It was known that there had been other diplomatic moves, made previously by Japanese emissaries through neutral nations, that intimated Japan might surrender under certain terms that were unacceptable to America and its allies. But when nothing definitive was heard from the Japanese, plans proceeded to drop the second atomic bomb.

The second mission was designated "Special Mission No. 16." A B-29 would carry "Fat Man," heavier than Little Boy and more complex. The primary target was Kokura. The secondary target was Nagasaki.

The 509th's Operations Order No. 39 of August 8, 1945, assigned Major Charles W. Sweeney, commanding officer of the 393rd Squadron, as the pilot in command of aircraft No. 297, nicknamed *Bockscar.* Major James I. Hopkins, Jr., group operations officer, was assigned to fly a second B-29 named *Full House*, which would carry photographic equipment and scientific personnel. On board would be Group Captain Leonard Cheshire, Winston Churchill's official representative.

Captain Fred Bock, instead of flying his own plane, would pilot *The Great Artiste*, named for Captain Kermit K. Beahan's ability as a bombardier and his alleged expertise with the opposite sex. That plane would be carrying the same special electronic measuring instruments used when Major Sweeney flew it on the Hiroshima flight. It would also be carrying William L. Laurence, the *New York Times* reporter who had been chosen at the inception of the Manhattan Project. His reporting would win him a Pulitzer Prize. A fourth aircraft was to proceed to Iwo Jima and stand by in case of an early abort by either of the backup aircraft.

Two weather observation planes were to proceed to the target areas one hour ahead of the strike aircraft. Since the order was to bomb visually for the greatest accuracy, it was essential that the area be visible to the bombardier.

Sweeney's crew normally had 10 men. Three others were added: Lt. Cmdr. Frederick L. Ashworth, U.S. Navy, the weaponeer in charge of the bomb; his assistant, Lieutenant Phillip M. Barnes; and the radar-countermeasures specialist, Lieutenant Jacob Beser. Captain Charles D. Albury was the co-pilot; Lieutenant Frederick J. Olivi, a third pilot; Captain James F. Van Pelt, Jr., navigator; Captain Kermit Beahan, bombardier; Staff Sgt. Abe M. Spitzer, radioman; Staff Sgt. Edward K. Buckley, radar operator; Staff Sgt. Albert T. DeHart, central fire control gunner; Master Sgt. John D. Kuharek, flight engineer; and Staff Sgt. Raymond G. Gallagher, mechanic/gunner. Beser was the only man who flew on both atomic bomb missions as a member of the crew of the strike aircraft. Many of the others in the formation, including Sweeney, had flown the other aircraft on the Hiroshima flight.

The crews of the 509th had trained together for almost a year under top-secret conditions. They had first gathered at Wendover Field, an isolated base in western Utah, and then had flown individual long-range, over-water navigation missions from Batista Field, Cuba. The personnel of the 509th moved to Tinian by air and sea in late May and early June 1945, where their top-secret status was the subject of much curiosity and constant ribbing. The crews designated for the atomic missions practiced by dropping giant 10,000-pound "pumpkins" on 12 Japanese targets. Each pumpkin contained 5,500 pounds of explosives.

The B-29s of the 509th had been modified to deliver the atomic bomb and were thus unable to carry conventional bombs. Instead, they carried the pumpkins, painted orange and shaped like Fat Man. The pumpkins also had been used during their Stateside training. Proximity fuses that produced an air burst, a feature of the atomic bombs, were installed. About 45 of the pumpkin bombs had been brought from the States. According to Tibbets, his crews were so accurate with them that Maj. Gen. Curtis E. LeMay, then commanding the Twentieth Air Force, ordered 100 more.

The carefully planned elements of one of the world's most sin-gular air units came together on schedule, backed by the highest national priority for supplies. The two atomic bombs were the result of the work of thousands of people. They had accepted the responsibility to try to split the atom, and to explore its potential as a bomb that could be controlled and released on demand.

The development of the atomic bomb can be said to have begun in the 1920s and early 1930s. It was then that several physicists, most of them in Europe, originated theories about ways to unlock the energy they believed existed within the atom. One of those physicists was Leo Szilard, a Hungarian who had fled from Nazi Germany to England in 1933. Szilard theorized that "in certain circumstances, it might be possible to set up a nuclear chain reaction, liberate energy on an industrial scale and construct atomic bombs." He urged British officials to conduct research to prove or disprove his theory.

Meanwhile, two German physicists, Otto Hahn and Lise Meitner, experimented with radioactive uranium in an effort to produce a chain reaction. Meitner fled from Nazi Germany to Sweden in 1938 and, together with Otto Frisch, passed the results of their experiments to physicist Niels Bohr, who left soon after for the United States. Bohr contacted Albert Einstein, also a refugee scientist, and winner of the 1921 Nobel Prize for physics, to explain the military potential of atomic energy.

Einstein, by then well-known in America, wrote a letter in August 1939 to President Franklin D. Roosevelt. "Some recent work," his letter said, "...leads me to expect that the element uranium may be turned into a new and important source of energy in the immediate future and it is conceivable...that extremely powerful bombs of a new type may thus be constructed."

Roosevelt appointed a group of scientists to an advisory committee on uranium, but at the time there was no real stimulus to proceed with any definitive action. Meanwhile, scientists in Germany and Japan were also considering the potential of atomic energy for war use. It took the attack on Pearl Harbor to stir the United States into action.

In 1942, Dr. Vannevar Bush, head of the U.S. Office of Scientific Research and Development, confirmed to the president that an atomic weapon could be developed. The Manhattan Project was authorized. General Leslie R. Groves, a tough, no-nonsense Army Corps of Engineers officer, was put in charge.

Enrico Fermi, an Italian physicist working with a team of fellow scientists at the University of Chicago, built the first nuclear reactor on a squash court under the stands of the university's football stadium. On December 2, 1942, the world's first self-sustaining, controlled nuclear reaction was achieved.

There were at least two methods that could be used to produce an explosion, both expensive but possible. Extensive facilities were built at Oak Ridge, Tenn., and Hanford, Wash., to produce uranium and plutonium, the fissionable material needed for the bombs. A central laboratory to design both bombs was established at the so-called Site Y near Los Alamos, N.M., with Dr. J. Robert Oppenheimer in charge.

Little Boy, 10 feet long and 28 inches in diameter, was similar to a gun in which a "bullet" made of uranium-235 was fired into a target also of uranium-235. When the two collided, a supercritical mass was attained, and a chain reaction and explosion would occur. No preliminary firing tests were made.

Fat Man measured 10 feet 8 inches long and 5 feet in diameter. It contained a sphere of plutonium. Conventional explosives surrounding the plutonium were fired so that the plutonium was compressed into a supercritical mass, producing a chain reaction and an explosion. Fat Man was tested in the New Mexico desert, near Alamogordo, on July 16, 1945. A blinding explosion, the world's first nuclear blast, was equivalent to 18,600 tons of TNT. By the time the more complicated Fat Man had been tested, most of Little Boy's elements were already en route to Tinian.

After Tibbets returned from Hiroshima, Sweeney's crews watched as Fat Man was loaded on August 8. Sweeney's greatest fear, he said later, was of "goofing up." He said, "I'd rather face the Japanese than Tibbets in shame if I made a stupid mistake."

Sweeney did not make any "stupid mistakes," but the second atomic mission seemed jinxed from the start. When queried recently, General Tibbets called the second mission a "fiasco" through no fault of Sweeney's.

The two target cities had been carefully selected. They had purposely not been bombed heavily by LeMay's B-29s so that, as the

On a hillside leading to the prison in Nagasaki on September 8, 1945, Dr. Nagai, medical instructor and X-ray specialist at the city's hospital, surveys the results of the bomb blast—unaware that the residual radiation is killing him.

after-action report noted, "The assessment of the atomic bomb damage would not be confused by having to eliminate previous incendiary or high explosive damage."

Kokura, on the northeast corner of Kyushu, was chosen as the primary target for Fat Man because it was the enemy's principal production source for automatic weapons. It was also the site of the Mitsubishi Steel and Arms Works and was one of the largest shipbuilding and naval centers in Japan.

Nagasaki, the secondary target, was the third largest city on Kyushu. It was also one of Japan's leading shipbuilding and repair centers. It was not considered a completely "virgin" target, however, because it had been bombed many weeks before by Twentieth Air Force bombers. Niigata was originally considered as a third target, but it was too far away from the other two cities.

The crews were given their final briefing during the early morning hours of August 9. They would cruise-climb to the bombing altitude of 31,000 feet. Meanwhile, the two weather planes would report the conditions over both targets. Radio silence between the bombers was to be absolute. If any of the planes had to ditch, rescue ships and submarines were in position; also, aircraft were on alert, to be dispatched to locate a downed plane or its crew.

With his airplane stripped of all armament except two .50-caliber tail guns, Sweeney lifted *Bockscar* off at 3:49 a.m., Tinian time. The flight route to Kokura was originally planned to proceed via Iwo Jima, but bad weather forced a change to Yaku-Shima in the Ryukus. En route, Commander Ashworth armed Fat Man.

When *Bockscar* arrived at the rendezvous point, only *The Great Artiste* was there. Due to poor visibility, Hopkins, in *Full House*, had lost contact with the other planes.

It had been agreed that Sweeney would not linger more than 15 minutes over the rendezvous point, but he circled for 45 minutes looking for Hopkins. Meanwhile, Hopkins was circling at another point many miles to the south. Breaking radio silence, Hopkins called out, "Chuck, where in the hell are you?"

Sweeney did not answer. Frustrated, he told the crew, "We can't wait any longer," and turned toward Kokura with the single B-29 escort. He wanted the mission to be a complete success, but it would be difficult to call it that if the explosion was not properly documented by the photography that the equipment on Hopkins' plane would produce. Meanwhile, in the bomb bay, something had gone wrong. The black box containing the electrical switches that armed the bomb had a red light. As long as the light blinked in a regular rhythm, it meant that the bomb was properly armed. If it blinked irregularly, something was malfunctioning.

Lieutenant Barnes, the electronics test officer, was the first to notice that the red light suddenly began to flash wildly. He and Ashworth frantically removed the black box's cover to search for the trouble. Quickly tracing all the wiring, Barnes found the problem: The wiring on two small rotary switches had been reversed somehow. He quickly hooked them properly. It could have been worse. If it had been the timing fuses, they would have had less than one minute to find the trouble before Fat Man might have gone off.

Although Sweeney had heard fragmentary reports that the weather over Kokura would be favorable for visual bombing, it wasn't. Instead of the three-tenths cloud cover originally reported, the city was now obscured by heavy cloud cover. In addition, smoke from a firebomb raid the previous night on nearby Yawata made conditions worse. Staff Sergeant DeHart, in the tail-gun position, reported flak "wide, but altitude is perfect." Fighters were detected on radar; Staff Sgt. Gallagher thought he saw fighters through the haze.

Lieutenant Olivi recalled what happened next: "We spent about 50 minutes and made three passes from different directions, but Beahan [the bombardier] reported he couldn't bomb visually. It was at this time that the crew chief [Master Sgt. Kuharek] reported that the 600 gallons of fuel in the bomb bay auxiliary tanks could not be transferred. We needed that extra 600 gallons badly."

They had no choice now. After conferring with Ashworth, Sweeney turned toward Nagasaki, hoping that the weather there was better. When they arrived, the city was obscured by nine-tenths cloud cover with very few holes. Ashworth and Sweeney considered bombing by radar against orders. Despite the risk of having an armed bomb aboard, they had been ordered to bring it back if they could not bomb visually. Niigata, the unofficial tertiary target, was too far away, especially considering their reduced fuel supply. No one wanted to have to ditch in the East China Sea or try to land on Okinawa, the nearest friendly base, with the armed Fat Man aboard.

"We started an approach [to Nagasaki]," Olivi said, "but Beahan couldn't see the target area [in the city east of the harbor]. Van Pelt, the navigator, was checking by radar to make sure we had the right city, and it looked like we would be dropping the bomb automatically by radar. At the last few seconds of the bomb run, Beahan yelled into his mike, 'I've got a hole! I can see it! I can see the target!' Apparently, he had spotted an opening in the clouds only 20 seconds before releasing the bomb."

In his debriefing later, Beahan told Tibbets, "I saw my aiming point; there was no problem about it. I got the cross hairs on it; I'd killed my rate; I'd killed my drift. The bomb had to go."

When Beahan shouted, "Bombs away!" over the intercom,

Sweeney wheeled the B-29 around in a sharp, 60-degree left bank and turned 150 degrees away from the area as they had all practiced many times before. Approximately 50 seconds after release, a bright flash lit up the cockpit, where everyone had donned dark goggles. "It was more dazzling than sunlight," according to Olivi, "even with my Polaroid glasses on. I could see fires starting and dust and smoke spreading in all directions. An ugly-looking mushroom began to emerge from the center. It spread and began rising directly toward our B-29.

"Right after the blast, we had lunged downward and away from the radioactive cloud. We felt three separate shock waves, the first being the most severe. As the mushroom cloud kept on climbing toward us, bright flames, a sickly pink, were shooting out of its interior. I had a sickish feeling in the pit of my stomach that we were going to be enveloped by the cloud. We had been warned many times about the possibility of radiation poisoning if we flew into it.

"Actually, I think the mushroom cloud missed us by about 125 yards before we pulled away from it. The briefings and all the practice we had on evasive tactics now had special meaning."

Reporter Laurence, flying nearby in *The Great Artiste*, was transfixed in awe at the scene. "We watched a giant pillar of purple fire, 10,000 feet high, shoot upward like a meteor coming from the earth instead of from outer space," he wrote later in his award-winning book *Dawn Over Zero*. "It was no longer smoke, or dust, or even a cloud of fire. It was a living thing, a new species of being, born right before our incredulous eyes.

"Even as we watched, a giant mushroom came shooting out of the top to 45,000 feet, a mushroom top that was even more alive than the pillar, seething and boiling in a white fury of creamy foam, a thousand geysers rolled into one. It kept struggling in an elemental fury, like a creature in the act of breaking the bonds that held it down.

"When we last saw it, it had changed its shape into a flowerlike form, its giant petals curving downward, creamy white outside, rose-colored inside. The boiling pillar had become a giant mountain of jumbled rainbows. Much living substance had gone into those rainbows."

Major Hopkins saw the column of smoke from 100 miles away

Photographed at Boswell Air Force Base, N.M., on March 29, 1945, Bockscar *shows off some revised nose art, with her target added.*

and flew toward the area after the explosion. However, the area was completely covered by clouds and smoke, hence no ground damage could be observed.

Sweeney made one wide circle of the mushroom cloud, then headed toward Tinian. Now they had a new danger confronting them. The fuel supply was dangerously low. They changed course for Okinawa with everyone on the flight deck watching the fuel gauges on Kuharek's flight engineer console. Sweeney had pulled the props back to a range-extending low rpm and leaned out the fuel mixture controls as far back as he dared while he descended; he figured they would land about 50 miles short of the island. Even when they spotted Yontan Field, it still seemed likely they would have to ditch short of the runway.

While Sweeney flew, Albury called the tower for landing instructions. He received no reply. He broadcast a Mayday while Sweeney told Van Pelt and Olivi to fire every emergency flare on board. No one seemed to pay any attention. In desperation, Sweeney took the mike and shouted, "I'm coming straight in!"

"Someone must have gotten the message," Olivi recalled, "because when we lined up on the approach, we could see emergency equipment racing out to the runway. We had only enough gas for one pass, so if we didn't make it, we were going to end up in the ocean.

"Sweeney came in high and fast—too fast. Normal landing speed for the B-29 was about 130 mph. We used up half the strip before we touched down at about 150 mph, a dangerous speed, with nearly empty gas tanks.

"As we touched down, the plane began to swerve to the left and we nearly plowed into a line of B-24s parked along the active runway. Sweeney finally brought the plane under control, and as we taxied off the runway the No. 2 engine quit. Ambulance, staff cars, jeeps, and fire engines quickly surrounded us and a bunch of very jittery people debarked, very glad to be safe on the ground."

What Olivi did not mention was that the airplane used up all of the runway trying to come to a halt. Sweeney stood on the brakes and made a swerving 90-degree turn at the end of the runway to avoid going over the cliff into the ocean. Beser recalled that two engines had died, while "the centrifugal force resulting from the turn was almost enough to put us through the side of the airplane."

Kuharek, before refilling the tanks, estimated that there were exactly seven gallons left in them. The Nagasaki mission had taken 10½ hours from the takeoff at Tinian to the landing at Okinawa. After they landed, the crewmen were told that the Russians had just entered the war against Japan.

For Sweeney and his crew, a nagging question haunted all of them: Had they hit the target? Ashworth didn't think they had. In his anxiety about obeying the order to bomb visually, Beahan had released the weapon about 1½ miles northeast of the city, up the valley of the Urakami River. The bomb had exploded over the center of the industrial area, not the densely populated residential area.

While their Superfort was being gassed, Sweeney and Ashworth commandeered a jeep and went to the base communications center to send a report to Tinian. They were refused permission to send such a message without the commanding general's personal permission. Lieutenant General Jimmy Doolittle had been newly sent to Okinawa to oversee the arrival of Eighth Air Force units from Europe to prepare them for future combat.

Doolittle, not privy to any of the A-bomb plans or operations, listened intently as Sweeney and Ashworth explained what had happened. Both men were nervous about telling a three-star general that they did not believe the bomb had hit the target directly. As they talked, Doolittle pulled out a map of Japan where they pointed out the industrial area over which they thought the bomb had exploded. Doolittle said, reassuringly, "I'm sure General Spaatz will be much happier that the bomb went off in the river valley rather than over the city with the resulting much lower number of casualties." He promptly authorized the communications section to send Sweeney's coded after-action report.

Sweeney and his crew, thoroughly exhausted, took off for Tinian after a three-hour layover and arrived there about midnight. Sweeney received the Distinguished Service Cross as pilot-in-command. All of the other crew members received the Distinguished Flying Cross as "members of a B-29 aircraft carrying the second atomic bomb employed in the history of warfare….Despite a rapidly dwindling gasoline reserve, they reached the target and released the bomb on the important industrial city of Nagasaki with devastating effect. The power of this missile was so great as to threaten the disintegration of the aircraft if it had been detonated while still in the bomb bay by a burst of flak, or a hit by enemy fighters, or if it was dropped while the B-29 was close to the ground, as might have occurred during engine failure."

In his 1962 book, *Now It Can Be Told: The Story of the Manhattan Project*, General Groves answered the question about the results of the Nagasaki mission: "Because of the bad weather conditions at the target, we could not get good photo reconnaissance pictures until almost a week later. They showed 44 percent of the city destroyed. The difference between the results obtained there and at Hiroshima was due to the unfavorable terrain at Nagasaki, where the ridges and valleys limited the area of greatest destruction to 2.3 miles by 1.9 miles. The United States Strategic Bombing Survey later estimated the casualties at 35,000 killed and 60,000 injured."

The force of the Fat Man explosion was estimated at 22,000 tons of TNT. The steep hills had confined the larger explosion. Although the industrial area had been flattened, the bomb caused less loss of life than Little Boy.

The events that followed the Nagasaki mission transpired quickly. Russia declared war on Japan on August 9. On that day, Emperor Hirohito spoke to the Japanese Supreme Council. "I cannot bear to see my innocent people suffer any longer," he said. "Ending the war is the only way to restore world peace and to relieve the nation from the terrible distress with which it is burdened."

The Japanese announced their acceptance of unconditional surrender on August 14. World War II officially ended at 10:30 a.m. Tokyo time, September 2, 1945, when Japanese emissaries signed the surrender document aboard the battleship USS *Missouri* in Tokyo Bay.

Although a few pumpkin bombing missions were flown by the 509th between the second A-bomb drop and the surrender announcement on August 14, for all practical purposes, the Nagasaki mission had ended the war.

THE MISSIONS

XII

FIRST STRIKE AGAINST JAPAN

In April 1942, Jimmy Doolittle's raiders made history when
their B-25s dropped the first bombs on Tokyo.

By C.V. Glines

The surprise Japanese raid on Pearl Harbor on December 7, 1941, was only the beginning of bad news from the Pacific. In the ensuing weeks, Wake Island, Singapore, Hong Kong and most of the Philippines were overrun by the Japanese army.

Within an incredibly short time, the Japanese had invaded and conquered huge land areas on a front that extended from Burma to Polynesia. By April 1, 1942, Bataan had fallen, and 3,500 Americans and Filipinos were making a brave last stand on the tiny island of Corregidor. There seemed to be no end to the Japanese aggression. Never before had America's future looked so grim.

Soon after the death toll at Pearl Harbor had been totaled, President Franklin D. Roosevelt asked America's top military leaders, Army Generals George C. Marshall and Henry H. "Hap" Arnold and Admiral Ernest J. King, to figure out a way to strike back at Japan's homeland as quickly as possible. Although there was nothing they wanted to do more, it seemed an impossible request to carry out.

In response to the president's persistent urging, Captain Francis S. Low, a submariner on Admiral King's staff, approached King and asked cautiously if it might be possible for Army medium bombers to take off from a Navy carrier. If so, could they be launched against Japan?

The question was passed to Captain Donald B. "Wu" Duncan, King's air operations officer. After studying the capabilities of several Army Air Forces (AAF) medium bombers, Duncan concluded that the North American B-25 might be capable of taking off from a carrier deck. He recommended takeoff tests be conducted before any definite plans were made.

When this basic idea was passed to General Arnold, he called in Lt. Col. James H. "Jimmy" Doolittle, a noted racing and stunt pilot who had returned to active duty in 1940 and was now assigned to Arnold's Washington staff. He asked Doolittle to recommend an AAF bomber that could take off in 500 feet from a space not more than 75 feet wide with a 2,000-pound bombload and fly 2,000 miles. Arnold did not

On a flight deck full of North American B-25B Mitchell medium bombers, recently promoted Lt. Col. James H. Doolittle and the captain of the aircraft carrier Hornet *confer before launching a daring raid on Japan, in John D. Shaw's* The Hornet's Nest.

say why he wanted the information.

Doolittle checked the manufacturers' data on the AAF's medium bombers—the Douglas B-18 and B-23, North American's B-25 and the Martin B-26. He concluded that the B-25, if modified with extra fuel tanks, could fulfill the requirements. The B-18 could not carry enough fuel and bombs, the wingspan of the B-23 was too great, and the B-26 needed too much takeoff distance.

Arnold then told Doolittle why he had asked for the information, cautioning him that because such an unprecedented mission was possible, it must be kept top-secret by all concerned. Doolittle promptly volunteered to lead the effort, and Arnold promised him his complete personal backing for whatever support he felt necessary.

The plan called for a Navy task force to take 15 B-25s to a point about 450 miles off Japan. There, they would be launched from a carrier to attack military targets at low altitude in five major Japanese cities, including Tokyo, the capital. The planes would then fly to bases in China, where the planes and the crews would be absorbed into the Tenth Air Force, then being organized to fight in the China-Burma-India (CBI) theater.

On February 2, 1942, two B-25s were hoisted aboard USS *Hornet*, the Navy's newest carrier, at Norfolk, Va. A few miles off the Virginia coast, the lightly loaded bombers were fired up and took off without difficulty. *Hornet* was then ordered to proceed to the West Coast for its first war assignment.

Jimmy Doolittle, a very energetic man, decided that the B-25 crews would consist of five men: pilot, co-pilot, navigator, bombardier and engineer-gunner. Twenty-four B-25s and their crews would be assigned to the mission from the three squadrons of the 17th Bomb Group and its associated 89th Reconnaissance Squadron, located at Pendleton, Ore. To preserve secrecy, Doolittle personally began making all the arrangements for the training and special equipment without revealing why he wanted things done.

The four squadrons were ordered to Columbia, S.C. En route, the designated planes were modified with extra fuel tanks and associated plumbing at Minneapolis, Minn. New incendiary bombs and shackles were ordered, along with electrically operated motion-picture cameras that would be activated when the bombs were released. Intelligence information, maps and target folders for the five major Japanese cities were prepared.

When the four squadrons arrived at Columbia, the word was passed that volunteers were needed for "a dangerous mission." Almost every man in the four squadrons volunteered; the squadron commanders chose 24 crews, plus extra armament specialists and mechanics to ready the aircraft. The selected men and the planes were sent to Eglin Field, Fla., beginning in the last week of February.

Doolittle arrived at Eglin on March 3 and assembled the entire group of 140 men. "My name's Doolittle," he said. "I've been put in charge of the project you men have volunteered for. It's a tough one, and it will be the most dangerous thing any of you have ever done. Anyone can drop out and nothing will ever be said about it."

Doolittle paused and the room was quiet. Several hands went up, and a lieutenant asked if Doolittle could give them any more information. "Sorry, I can't right now. " he said. "I'm sure you will start getting some ideas about it when we get down to work. Now that brings up the most important point I want to make, and you're going to hear this over and over again. This entire mission must be kept top-secret. I not only don't want you to tell your wives or buddies about it, I don't even want you to discuss it among yourselves."

From the first day of training, it was understood that all the volunteer crews would participate in the training; however, only 15 planes would eventually go on the mission. This was done to ensure that there would be plenty of spare crews on hand to replace anyone who became ill or decided to drop out.

As the takeoff training of the pilots progressed, it proved to be a harrowing experience for most of them. Army Air Force pilots were not taught during their training to take off over extremely short distances at bare minimum airspeed. Taking off in a medium bomber with the tail skid occasionally striking the ground was unnatural and scary to them. But under U.S. Navy Lieutenant Henry L. Miller's patient instruction, they all soon learned the required skills.

In addition to takeoff practice, it was hoped that each crew would receive 50 hours of flying time to be divided into day and night navigation, gunnery, bombing and formation flying. But maintenance problems kept the planes on the ground most of the time.

Crew No. 1 (Aircraft No. 40-2344) after its crash landing in China. The Americans are: (from left) Staff Sgt. Fred A. Baemer (bombardier), Staff Sgt. Paul J. Leonard (engineer-gunner), Lieutenant Richard E. Cole (co-pilot), Lt. Col. James H. Doolittle (pilot and group leader), and Lieutenant Henry A. Potter (navigator).

Every B-25 model at that time was equipped with one upper and one lower turret, each with twin .50-caliber machine guns. But the upper and lower turret mechanisms continually malfunctioned; the lower turret was especially difficult to operate. Doolittle ordered the lower turrets removed and additional gas tanks installed in their place.

There was a single .30-caliber movable machine gun in the B-52's nose, which was placed in a gunport by the bombardier when needed. There were no guns in the tail, so Captain C. Ross Greening, the armament officer, suggested that two broomsticks be painted black and installed there to deceive enemy fighters. Since the bombing was to be at 1,500 feet or less, Greening also designed a simple bombsight he called "Mark Twain" to replace the top-secret Norden bombsight. It was made from two pieces of aluminum that cost about 20 cents.

One of the volunteer gunners had other duties. When 1st Lt. T. Robert "Doc" White, a physician attached to the 89th Reconnaissance Squadron, heard of the call for volunteers, he asked to be included. He was told there was no room for a passenger; the only

Doolittle leads his specially trained flight off Hornet's *deck on a course for Tokyo and other Japanese targets, in* I Could Never Be So Lucky Again, *by William S. Phillips.*

way he could go would be as a gunner. White said that was all right with him. He took gunnery training, qualified with the second highest score with the twin .50s on the ground targets, and was assigned to a crew. His presence on the mission would prove to be fortuitous.

Doolittle wanted to fly the mission as a pilot. "But I wanted to go only on the basis that I could do as well as or better than the other pilots who took the training," he said. "I took Hank Miller's course and was graded along with the others. I made it, but if I hadn't I intended to go along as a co-pilot and let one of the younger, more proficient pilots occupy the left seat."

On one of his training flights, Doolittle flew with Lieutenant Richard E. Cole, co-pilot; Lieutenant Henry A. Potter, navigator; Sergeant Fred A. Braemer, bombardier; and Sergeant Paul J. Leonard, engineer-gunner. The original pilot had become ill and did not return to flying duty. These men became Doolittle's crew.

Meanwhile, Captain Wu Duncan had arrived in Honolulu and conferred with Admiral Chester W. Nimitz, commander in chief of the Pacific Fleet, and conveyed the plan for a Navy task force to transport the Army bombers to the launch point. Nimitz liked the idea and gave the task of carrying it out to Admiral William "Bull" Halsey, who was anxious to tangle with the enemy any way he could.

Duncan worked with the CINCPAC (commander in chief, Pacific) planning staff on the details for a 16-ship task force. It was decided that seven ships would accompany *Hornet* from the Alameda Naval Air Station near San Francisco and rendezvous with an eight-ship force that included Halsey's flagship, the carrier *Enterprise*. The linkup would take place near the 180th meridian.

By the middle of March, *Hornet,* now destined to be the ship that would deliver the B-25s to the takeoff point, had passed through the Panama Canal and proceeded to Alameda. At the end of the third week in March, Captain Duncan wired Washington from Honolulu: "Tell Jimmy to get on his horse."

This coded message was all Doolittle needed to get his men and planes moving to the West Coast. Since two of the B-25s had been damaged in training, the 22 remaining were flown to McClellan Field, in Sacramento, Calif., for final inspections before proceeding to Alameda. All of these crews would go aboard the carrier.

Captain Duncan flew to San Diego to confer with Captain Marc A. Mitscher, skipper of *Hornet.* Mitscher had not been told about the mission until then and was delighted to have a part in it. Since he had watched the first two B-25s take off successfully several weeks earlier, he was confident it could be done. Duncan then went to San Francisco to await the arrival of Doolittle from Florida, Halsey from Hawaii and *Hornet* from San Diego.

The three men, joined by Captain Miles Browning, Halsey's chief of staff, met informally in downtown San Francisco to discuss the details and determine if anything had been left undone. The plan was for *Hornet,* in company with the cruisers *Nashville* and *Vincennes,* the oiler *Cimarron,* and the destroyers *Gwin, Meredith, Monssen* and *Grayson*—-to be known as Task Force 16.2—to leave San Francisco April 2. Halsey, aboard *Enterprise,* was in charge of Task Force 16.1 and would leave Hawaii on April 7, accompanied by the cruisers *Northampton* and *Salt Lake City,* the oiler *Sabine,* and destroyers *Balch, Benham, Ellet* and *Fanning.*

The rendezvous of the two forces would become Task Force 16 and would take place on Sunday, April 12, at approximately 38 degrees 0 minutes north latitude and 180 degrees 0 minutes west longitude. The force would then proceed westward and refuel about 800 miles off the coast of Japan. Then the oilers would detach themselves while the rest of the task force dashed to the launch point.

Halsey later reported in his memoirs, "Our talk boiled down to this: we would carry Jimmy within 400 miles of Tokyo, if we could

Sixteen B-25Bs crowd Hornet's *flight deck as the aircraft carrier steams to the launch point. Unbeknown to the Americans, a five-carrier Japanese task force was close enough to have intercepted them if the original takeoff point had been reached.*

sneak in that close; but if we were discovered sooner, we would have to launch him anyway, provided he was in reach of either Tokyo or Midway."

What Halsey did not discuss was the tremendous risk the Navy was taking. If marauding Japanese submarines discovered the task force steaming westward, it would be an excellent opportunity to cripple what was left of the Navy's strength in the Pacific. Doolittle knew full well that if Halsey's ships were under heavy attack, the B-25s stored topside would be pushed over the side to make the flight deck available so *Hornet's* fighters could be brought up on deck to help protect the task force.

When the B-25s landed at Alameda on April 1, Doolittle and Captain Ski York greeted each crew. "Anything wrong with your plane?" they asked. If a pilot admitted some malfunction, he was directed to a nearby parking ramp instead of the wharf.

Originally, only 15 planes were to be loaded, but Doolittle asked for one more to be hoisted aboard. When the carrier was at sea, it would take off and return to the mainland to show the other B-25 crews that takeoffs were not only possible but could be made easily. Although the bomber crews had been told that B-25s had made carrier takeoffs previously, none had ever seen it done, nor had they done it themselves. Lieutenant Miller, the Navy pilot who had instructed them in carrier takeoffs, would be aboard that B-25.

The next morning, Task Force 16.2 prepared to depart from San Francisco Bay. Just before *Hornet* was to depart, Doolittle was ordered ashore to receive an urgent phone call from Washington. He recalled: "I thought it was going to be either General Hap Arnold or General George Marshall telling me I couldn't go. My heart sank because I wanted to go on that mission more than anything....

"It was General Marshall. 'Doolittle?' he said. 'I just called to wish you the best of luck. Our thoughts and our prayers will be with you. Goodbye, good luck, and come home safely.' All I could think of to say was, 'Thank you, Sir, thank you.' I returned to the *Hornet* feeling much better."

Shortly before noon, *Hornet* passed under Golden Gate Bridge. That afternoon, Mitscher decided to tell his men where they were going. He signaled to the other ships, "This force is bound for Tokyo." As he recalled later, when he made the announcement on *Hornet,* "Cheers from every section of the ship greeted the announcement, and morale reached a new high, there to remain until after the attack was launched and the ship was well clear of combat areas."

The next day, April 3, Doolittle changed his mind about sending the 16th plane back to the mainland. A Navy blimp, the L-8, arrived overhead with spare parts for the B-25s. Air-patrol coverage was provided as far as possible by a Consolidated PBY Catalina.

Doolittle assembled his crews and introduced Commander Apollo Soucek and Lt. Cmdr. Stephen Jurika. Soucek was the ship's air officer, and he described the basics of carrier operations. Jurika, *Hornet's* intelligence officer, briefed them on the target cities and surrounding areas.

Jurika had been an assistant naval attaché in Japan in 1939 and had obtained much valuable information about Japanese industry and military installations. He spoke to the crews almost every day, telling them about Japanese customs, political ideologies and history. Doolittle allowed the pilots to choose their targets in the assigned cities. Lieutenant Frank Akers, the carrier's navigator, gave the pilots a refresher course on navigation. Doc White, the physician-gunner on Lieutenant Don Smith's crew, gave talks on sanitation and first aid.

Doolittle made it a practice to meet with the crews two or three times a day. He continually warned them not to bomb the Imperial Palace and to avoid hospitals, schools and other nonmilitary targets. He said that most planes would carry three 500-pound demolition bombs and one 500-pound incendiary. He planned to take off in the late afternoon with four incendiaries and drop them on Tokyo in darkness. The resulting fires would light up the sky and serve as a beacon for those following and guide them toward their respective targets in Tokyo, Yokohama, Kobe, Nagoya and Osaka. All aircraft would then proceed to China and be guided by homing beacons to landing fields where they would refuel before proceeding to Chungking, the ultimate destination.

Mitscher and Halsey joined forces as planned. Meanwhile, arrangements in China were not going well. Japanese ground forces were moving in strength toward the airfields where the B-25s were to refuel. Although the Americans and Chinese in Chungking were told that they could expect some aircraft to arrive and to prepare for them by placing fuel and setting up homing beacons, they were not told that the planes would be arriving from the east after bombing Japan. Misunderstandings developed and were compounded when Generalissimo Chiang Kai-shek asked that the arrival of the planes be delayed so he could move his ground forces into position to prevent occupation of the Chuchow area where one of the refueling airfields was located.

As the task force continued westward, the Japanese knew from intercepted radio messages as early as April 10 that an enemy carrier force was steaming toward them. However, it was estimated

that it would have to approach to within 300 miles of their coast in order to launch any carrier planes. If that was where the task force was headed, there would be plenty of time to intercept it.

Unknown to the Americans, a line of radio-equipped picket ships was positioned about 650 miles off Japan, and they could signal the approach of any large force and warn the land-based air defense forces to prepare for an attack.

Meanwhile, a Japanese navy air flotilla was alerted to back up homeland air defenses. Patrol bombers would be dispatched when the enemy force was estimated to be about 600 miles out. However, when the American task force observed radio silence for the last 1,000 miles, the Japanese cautiously decided that it might be headed elsewhere.

In the early morning hours of April 18, *Enterprise's* radar spotted two small ships. The force changed course briefly to avoid them. The weather turned sour; light rain was falling, and green water was plunging down *Hornet's* deck. A dawn patrol was sent up from *Enterprise* to scout the area. One of the pilots sighted an enemy surface ship and dropped a message to the "Big E's" deck, noting the ship's position and adding, "Believed seen by enemy."

Admiral Halsey promptly flashed a message to Captain Mitscher:

Arriving at its target, Lieutenant Ted W. Lawson's B-25B commences its bombing run, in Thirty Seconds Over Tokyo, *by Craig Kodera.*

"Launch planes to Colonel Doolittle and gallant command, good luck and God bless you."

The B-25s were quickly loaded and one by one moved into take-off position. Doolittle was first off at 0820 hours; the 16th B-25 was off an hour later. Just as the pilot of the last plane had started his engines, a deckhand slipped on the wet deck and fell into the B-25's whirling left propeller, which severed his arm.

One by one, the B-25s droned on toward Japan. None flew in close formation with another, and only a few actually saw any other B-25s as they proceeded toward their respective target cities.

Shortly after noon, Tokyo time, Doolittle called for bomb doors open, and Sergeant Fred Braemer sighted down the 20-cent bomb-sight and triggered off four incendiaries into the capital city's factory area. Fourteen other crews found their respective targets; however, one B-25, with its top turret inoperative and under attack by fighters, dropped its bombs in Tokyo Bay. Several others were also attacked, but none suffered any noticeable damage.

All of the planes except one turned southward off the east coast of Japan and then westward toward China. Captain York had a difficult decision to make. Both of his B-25's engines had burned excessive amounts of fuel on the way to Japan, and he knew he and his crew would have to ditch in the shark-infested China Sea if they followed the planned route to China. He elected to proceed against orders to Soviet territory and landed near Vladivostok. He had hoped he could persuade the Soviets to refuel the plane and allow them to continue to China, but the aircraft and crew were promptly interned because the Soviet Union wanted to retain its neutral status with Japan. The crew finally escaped into Iran 14 months later.

As the other aircraft turned toward China, they experienced head winds, and it appeared that few, if any, would reach the coast before running out of fuel. Although the head winds then fortuitously turned into tail winds, the weather worsened in the late afternoon as they were approaching the coastline. Doolittle and 11 other pilots elected to climb into the clouds and proceed inland on instruments. When their fuel reached the zero mark, the crews bailed out. One crew member was killed attempting to depart the airplane. All others made it with only bruises, slight cuts or sprained ankles and slowly made their way to Chuchow and Chungking with the help of Chinese peasants. More than a quarter-million Chinese subsequently paid with their lives when ruthless Japanese soldiers murdered anyone suspected of helping the Americans and even people whose villages the Americans had passed through.

Four pilots elected to crash-land or ditch their aircraft. Two crewmen drowned while trying to swim to shore. Four members of one crew were seriously injured; they were assisted by the rear gunner, Corporal David Thatcher, and friendly Chinese to a hospital run by missionaries and were joined there by Lieutenant White and his crew. It was there that "Doc" White amputated the leg of the pilot, Lieutenant Ted W. Lawson, and gave two pints of his own blood to save Lawson's life. Lawson later wrote about his experiences in *Thirty Seconds over Tokyo*. Thatcher and White later received the Silver Star for their gallantry.

Sixty-four of Doolittle's "Raiders" eventually arrived in Chungking; some were retained in the theater to serve in the Tenth Air Force; others were returned to the States and assigned to new units. Three pilots and one navigator later became prisoners of the Germans.

Eight crewmen were captured by the Japanese, tortured, given a mock court-martial and sentenced to die. Three of them were executed by firing squad; one died of malnutrition. The remaining four—George Barr, Jacob DeShazer, Robert L. Hite and Chase J. Nielson—survived 40 months of captivity, most of it in solitary confinement, and returned to the States after the war.

The question has been asked: Can this raid be considered successful if all aircraft were lost and relatively little damage was done to the targets?

The answer is a strong affirmative. The mission provided the first good news of the war and was a tremendous morale boost for America and her allies. Japanese morale, on the other hand, was shattered because their leaders had promised that their homeland could never be attacked.

The original purpose of the raid, as stated by Doolittle before he departed, was to prove that "Japan was vulnerable and that a surprise air raid would create confusion, impede production and cause air defense forces to be withdrawn from the war zones to defend the home islands against further attacks." All of that occurred.

Besides being the first offensive air action against the Japanese home islands, the Doolittle-led raid accomplished some other historic firsts. It was the first combat mission in which the U.S. Army Air Forces and the U.S. Navy teamed up in a full-scale operation against the enemy. Jimmy Doolittle and his raiders were the first to fly land-based bombers from a carrier deck on a combat mission and first to use new cruise-control techniques in attacking a distant target. The incendiary bombs they carried were forerunners of those used later in the war. The special camera equipment specified by Doolittle to record the bomb hits was later adopted by the AAF. The after-action crew recommendations concerning armament, tactics and survival equipment were used as a basis for other improvements.

Jimmy Doolittle's famous air raid against Japan marked the beginning of the turnaround toward victory for America and her allies in World War II.

XIII

THE CACTUS AIR FORCE: A THORN IN JAPAN'S SIDE

A small group of die-hard aviators fended off Japanese invaders
at Guadalcanal, code-named 'Cactus.'

By Don Hollway

The Japanese Mitsubishi A6M2 Zero fighter swept in low over the sweltering jungle of Guadalcanal, as if to land on the nearly completed crushed-coral runway at Lunga Point. Once the air base was completed the Japanese planned to fly long-range bombers from it to cut off Australia from the east.

But as the Zero buzzed the field, the pilot was startled to see enemy troops on the runway—10,000 U.S. Marines had landed the day before, August 7, 1942, and now held the field. He hastily climbed away, leaving this little clearing in the jungle that would become the objective of the pivotal campaign of the war in the Pacific.

Believing the amphibious assault to be a temporary, diversionary raid (and seeing that they were outnumbered 3-to-1), Japanese ground forces on Guadalcanal initially withdrew into the jungle, expecting air attacks to drive the Americans off. Over the next two days, land-based Japanese navy planes, including Mitsubishi G4M bombers (Allied code name "Betty") and Zero ("Zeke") fighters, downed 20 percent of the U.S. Navy fighters sent against them but lost nearly half their own. The loss of four cruisers and a destroyer in the sea battle of Savo on the night of August 9, combined with the continuing threat of daylight air attack, caused the U.S. Navy to withdraw. The Marines were left on "the Canal" with what they referred to as the only unsinkable aircraft carrier in the Solomons—

the island's airfield. They used captured construction equipment to finish the 2,600-foot runway, adding an extra 1,200 feet for good measure.

Although bereft of taxiways, revetments, drainage and radar, the airfield—christened Henderson Field after Marine Major Lofton Henderson, who died leading a dive-bomber attack in the June 4 Battle of Midway—boasted Japanese hangars, machine shops and radio installations, a pagodalike control tower complete with a warning siren for air raids, and even an ice plant. But not until August 20 did Guadalcanal—code-named "Cactus"—take delivery of 12 Douglas SBD Dauntless dive bombers and their escort of 19 Grumman F4F-4 Wildcat fighters, the advance squadrons of Marine Air Group (MAG) 23. "I was close to tears and I was not alone," said Maj. Gen. Archer Vandergrift, the Marine ground commander, "when the first SBD taxied up and this handsome and dashing aviator jumped to the ground. 'Thank God you have come,' I told him."

Defending Henderson Field on Guadalcanal on October 13, 1942, Captain Joseph J. Foss of Marine Fighter Squadron (VMF) 121 has a Zero Encounter with a Mitsubishi A6M2 of the Tainan Kokutai, in a painting by Robert Taylor.

Within 12 hours the fledgling "Cactus Air Force" helped finish off a Japanese infantry assault. The next day, the American fliers gave an enemy bomber raid from Rabaul, New Britain, a rude welcome. In his first combat engagement, Captain John Lucien Smith, commanding Marine Fighter Squadron (VMF) 223, and four F4Fs met the fighter escort, 13 Zeros of the crack *Tainan Kokutai* (naval air group) led by Lieutenant Shiro Kawai, head-on. All four Wildcats survived, though two were badly damaged and one cracked up attempting a dead-stick landing. No Zeros were destroyed, but Smith thought the skirmish "did a great deal of good" by giving the Marines a better idea of the Zero's capabilities while instilling confidence in the performance and durability of their own Wildcats. Later that week Captain Marion Carl, who had downed a Zero at Midway, got two Bettys and another Zero. Carl and Smith were to become friendly rivals.

The balance of power on Guadalcanal seesawed with the waxing and waning of fighter strength at Henderson. By the end of August the Cactus Air Force included 14 Bell P-400 Airacobra fighter-bombers (export versions of the company's P-39) of the 67th Fighter Squadron, U.S. Army Air Forces (USAAF), and 19 F4Fs of VMF-224, under Major Robert E. Galer. (In less than two weeks Galer would knock down four enemy planes, go down in the water and swim ashore. His gallantry would eventually garner him 13 kills and the Medal of Honor.)

By the afternoon of September 10, however, only three P-400s remained, along with 22 SBDs and 11 F4Fs. (Among the missing was Marion Carl.) Two dozen Navy Wildcats hurriedly flew in to reinforce them; the Airacobras proved barely enough to help repulse an attack on Bloody Ridge, just south of the airfield.

During the course of the Bloody Ridge battle, Henderson received 60 planes, including 18 more F4Fs, 12 SBDs and six Grumman TBF Avenger torpedo bombers, but the Japanese reinforced Rabaul with 60 fighters and 72 medium bombers.

By mid-October, 224 Japanese planes had fallen to the Cactus Air Force, including 111½ to VMF-223 and 19 to Smith, who, as the highest-scoring American airman to date, was awarded the Navy Cross and the Medal of Honor. His erstwhile opponent as top gun,

Major John L. Smith scored 19 aerial victories and earned the Navy Cross and Medal of Honor over Guadalcanal.

Carl, had actually made it back to Henderson after spending five days with the natives, only to find that Smith had pulled ahead of him in victories. ("Dammit, General," he told Brig. Gen. Roy S. Geiger, the Marine air commander, "ground *him* for five days!") Carl finished with 18½ kills and a Navy Cross.

Seven of the pilots who had arrived with Smith and Carl in August went out as aces; six were killed and six wounded. Of the Dauntless squadron, only the commander, Lt. Col. Richard C. Mangrum, was able to walk away when he was evacuated on October 12; all his men had been killed, wounded or hospitalized.

"These guys had stopped [the Japanese] cold," said Captain Joseph J. Foss, who would become Cactus' premier ace, "and now it was our turn." Foss—nicknamed "Smokey Joe" for his cigar habit—was executive officer of Major Leonard K. "Duke" Davis' VMF-121, which moved up to relieve VMF-223 on October 9.

"We were fired upon by Japanese troops as we landed," recalled Lieutenant Jefferson J. DeBlanc of VMF-112, some of whose pilots arrived a month later in transport planes. "We were always under fire on takeoffs and landings."

Pilots were quartered in mud-floored tents in the frequently flooded coconut grove called "Mosquito Grove," between the airstrip and the beach. The latrine was a trench, with a log for a seat; the bathtub was the Lunga River. There were only two meals a day—dehydrated potatoes, Spam, cold hash and captured Japanese rice—and cigarettes. Malaria, dysentery, dengue fever, beriberi and myriad lesser-known tropical diseases stalked the garrison. No man could get out of duty with less than a 102-degree fever, but by October more than 2,000 had been hospitalized.

Working conditions were also daunting. Fuel had to be hand-pumped out of 55-gallon drums (and strained through chamois, since native porters sometimes cooled their feet in it) into 12-quart buckets before being poured into airplanes. There were plenty of bombs but no bomb hoists; the SBDs' 500-pounders had to be hand-loaded. The Wildcats' turbochargers, not to be engaged below 10,000 feet but wired open anyway, wore out the engines in 25 to 50 flying hours.

"Almost daily," wrote the 67th Squadron historian, "and almost always at the same time—noon, 'Tojo Time'—the bombers came." Advance notice arrived from coast-watchers up the archipelago or, once incoming Japanese bombers learned to detour out of their sight, via Henderson's new long-range SCR (signal corps radio) 270 radar. The Wildcats, Dauntlesses and P-400s scrambled to take off two at a time—through a blinding pall of dust or, if it had rained, through wheel-sucking mud—on a treacherous runway pocked with half-filled bomb and shell craters and rutted by the solid rubber tail wheels of carrier aircraft. Almost invariably one or two planes failed to take off.

The "ground pounders," the SBDs and P-400s, scuttled off over the treetops to work over enemy ground positions—or at least to keep out of the way of the impending airstrike. The Wildcat pilots had their work cut out for them just raising their landing gear (which took 29 turns of a hand crank), struggling to form up, trimming their aircraft and testing their guns. (Early Wildcat guns had a tendency to jam during hard maneuvers; furthermore, if the oil

Major Robert E. Galer, commander of VMF-224, scored 13 victories and also received the Medal of Honor.

necessary to prevent rust on the guns in the humid sea-level air was not removed before takeoff, it froze at altitude, jamming the actions.) Most important, the pilots had to reach the Japanese bombers' altitude before the Zekes fell on them.

In his first combat mission, attempting to intercept bombers at 24,000 feet, Lieutenant James Percy of VMF-112 suffered a partial turbocharger failure 10,000 feet short of the enemy formation. "I continued to climb very slowly on low blower, but it was obvious I wasn't going to reach [the enemy's] altitude in time to intercept," Percy recalled. "As the bombers passed about 3,000 feet over me, I noticed their bomb bay doors were open. As I grasped what that meant, their bombs started falling toward me. All I could do was duck my head and pray. Bombs passed all around me, but I was not hit." (Percy's luck held; in June 1943 he survived a 2,000-foot fall with a shot-up parachute into the waters off the Russell Islands.)

Down below, a black flag would go up at the "Pagoda"—air raid imminent—and the triple-A (anti-aircraft artillery) would open up. Around the runway, slit trenches and bomb shelters rapidly filled (a sign over one shelter entrance read, "Beneath these portals pass the fastest men in the world") as the first bombs began to fall at one end of the field and the explosions "walked" across to the other side.

Diving, whether to attack or to escape, was the one maneuver at which the Wildcat bested the Zero. "The Zeros had superior maneuverability," said 2nd Lt. Roger A. "Jughead" Haberman, a division leader in Foss' flight who ultimately scored seven victories. "In two and a half turns against a Wildcat they could have you boresighted. But our planes were heavier than theirs, so if you got into trouble, you could dive earthward away from them."

Usually.

Joe Foss (standing second from left) and pilots of VMF-121 at Henderson Field in February 1943. By that time, Captain Foss was in command of the squadron and had earned the Medal of Honor.

On October 13, in Foss' first combat, he was jumped by a Zeke flown by Petty Officer 1st Class Kozaburo Yasui of the *Tainan Kokutai*. Foss later recalled: "That bird came by like a freight train and gave me a good sprinkling, but I knew I had him. I pulled up and gave him a short burst, and down he went." But while Foss was credited with the kill, Yasui in fact survived (he would bring his own score up to 11 before he was killed over Guam on June 19, 1944)—and his two wingmen, Petty Officer 2nd Class Nobutaka Yanami and Seaman 1st Class Tadashi Yoneda, bounced Foss. Their bullets hit his oil cooler, and his engine seized. "The only thing I could do to get out—I was right over the field—was to just wheel over and dive straight down," Foss recalled. He plunged from 22,000 feet right down to the deck. "I'd read that a Zero couldn't

follow such a dive; its wings would come off trying to pull out. Well, whoever wrote that was a fiction writer because those boys just kept on my tail, pumping lead!" Anti-aircraft gunners cleared the Zekes from his tail, and Foss coasted in to a dead-stick crash landing.

The Americans knew the Japanese had the edge in experience. Most Yanks were straight out of flying school, with less than 300 hours in training aircraft. "Some of the pilots," wrote Percy, "barely had enough time in the F4Fs to get safely airborne." Many Zero aces, veterans of the Sino-Japanese War, counted 800 hours of flying time even before the United States entered the war.

The Japanese bombers were the Americans' real targets. Bettys, with their 20mm tail cannon, were typically attacked from above and to the side, leaving the Wildcat with enough energy to zoom-climb back up for another pass. Missing on one attempt, Foss dove right through a Betty formation. "A thousand feet below," Foss recalled, "I suddenly turned back up and headed toward the belly of the last plane on the left wing of the V echelon. Directly under the bomber, nose pointed straight up, I waited until my plane had lost almost all of its speed and I was on the verge of stalling before pulling the trigger." Not just for its streamlined hull did the Japanese call the Betty the "Flying Cigar"; its fuel tanks hit, this one exploded right on top of Foss—his fifth kill.

But Bettys could drop more than bombs. DeBlanc's first victory was a G4M just 50 feet above the water, making a torpedo run against U.S. ships. "I flew through the [anti-aircraft] barrage from the fleet and locked onto the tail of a Betty and opened fire, killing the rear gunner and watching my tracers strike the engines," DeBlanc said. Target-fixated, the American pilot nearly collided with the flaming bomber, but he recovered to nail two more—three kills in one mission. (At the end of January, in a wild dogfight over Vella Gulf, DeBlanc shot down three Japanese floatplanes and two Zekes before being shot down himself. He bailed out, was rescued by a coastwatcher and eventually was flown back to the Canal. Credited with nine kills, he was awarded the Medal of Honor.)

The Navy fighters' radio frequency, meant for communication over the uninterrupted expanses of the sea, was susceptible to interference from intervening land masses. Henderson's Japanese transceiver could only transmit to the fighters out to about 20 miles but could receive their radios from 100 miles. The control-

In a painting by William S. Phillips, Joe Foss puts his motto, "When You See Zeros, Fight 'Em," into practice. Wildcat pilots used hit-and-run tactics and teamwork to cancel out the Zero's superior maneuverability—and take full advantage of the Japanese fighter's frailties.

lers in the Pagoda often could only sit helplessly and listen as the battle played out, unable to help direct the action.

"The ground crews would count [the survivors] as they landed," said the 67th's historian. "The ambulance would stand, engine running, ready for those who crashed, landed dead stick, or hit the bomb craters in the runway. Then the work of patching and repairing the battered fighters would start again."

Probably the Americans' greatest advantage was simply their proximity to the base. Pilots had a very good chance of making it back to Henderson Field—if they could survive being shot down.

After downing three other Zeros during a dogfight on October 25, 1st Lt. Jack E. Conger of VMF-212 went into the drink after he rammed a fourth Zero—since he had no ammunition left. The Japanese pilot also parachuted and insisted the Marine rescue boat

Lockheed P-38F Lightnings of Captain John W. Mitchell's 339th Fighter Squadron join the Marine Wildcats at Henderson. First seeing action escorting a bombing mission in November 1942, the P-38s provided the Cactus Air Force with a longer-ranging offensive punch.

pick up Conger first. Conger had to convince the Marines not to shoot the chivalrous enemy pilot and was the first to reach down to pull him aboard. Taking umbrage at the dishonorable prospect of capture, the Japanese pilot, 19-year-old Petty Officer 2nd Class Shiro Ishikawa of the 2nd *Kokutai,* thrust his 8mm Nambu pistol out of the water into Conger's face and pulled the trigger. The wet ammo misfired and then misfired again when Ishikawa tried to shoot himself. Having had enough, Conger (who would finish with 10½ kills) brained his recent aerial adversary with a five-gallon gas can and hauled him into the boat.

Nighttime brought a new set of annoyances: Tokyo Rose propaganda on the radio; nuisance bombers ("Louie the Louse" and "Washing Machine Charlie," named for the chugging sound of his unsynchronized propellers), mixing the occasional bomb with whistling bottles dropped just to rattle nerves; and troop convoys

(the "Cactus Express," later redubbed "Tokyo Express"), coming down the Solomons' central channel ("the Slot") to offload troops at Cape Esperance under cover of naval bombardment.

"Throughout most of my first night on Guadalcanal," recalled Foss, "shells streamed above our tents in both directions as Japanese ships in the channel targeted our artillerymen on the island, who returned the fire. The veterans…assured us that the night's shelling was 'light.'" By the end of his first week, Foss believed them. On October 13, Japanese 105mm and 150mm artillery pieces, dubbed "Pistol Pete" and "Millimeter Mike" by the Marines, began lobbing random shells from the surrounding hills, beyond the range of the Marines' 105mm and 5-inch fieldpieces. A heavily escorted Japanese bomber raid arrived over Henderson at noon, cratering the airfield and setting 5,000 gallons of aviation fuel ablaze. That night, in what was to be known ever after as "the Bombardment," the Japanese battleships *Haruna* and *Kongo* dropped more than 900 14-inch shells onto Henderson.

Come dawn, Henderson was a scene of destruction, the steel-matted main runway a twisted ruin and the Pagoda damaged. (Geiger ordered the Pagoda demolished to deny the Japanese a target in the future.) More than three-quarters of the SBDs and all of the TBFs were destroyed. Forty-one Americans were dead.

But the Americans had a surprise up their sleeves—an auxiliary airstrip, Fighter One, carved out of the coconut grove southeast of the main field. From there, the Cactus Air Force launched strikes against incoming air raids and the Tokyo Express. On the night of October 14, however, heavy cruisers *Chokai* and *Kinugasa* paid a follow-up visit, pelting Henderson with 752 8-inch rounds. The morning of October 15 found Japanese transports calmly offloading at Tassafaronga, just 10 miles from Lunga.

But the Japanese were to rediscover a truth that has blessed and bedeviled air forces since the dawn of military aviation—runways, though easily cratered, are easily repaired. Henderson put every available plane in the air to bomb and strafe the ships as well as the troops and supplies already ashore. Flying General Geiger's personal Consolidated PBY-5A Catalina amphibian, *Blue Goose,* Major Jack R. Cram torpedoed one of the transports, *Sasago Maru,* an action for which he would receive the Navy Cross.

The accompanying destroyers riddled the PBY, and three Zeros of the *Tainan Kokutai* chased it back to Lunga. Haberman, attempting to put his smoking F4F down, pulled off from his approach to Fighter One and shot the last Zeke off Cram's tail (killing Petty Officer 2nd Class Chuji Sakurai). During the action, three transport ships were set afire and beached; one was sunk by more B-17s sent up from Espíritu Santo.

Again, before dawn on October 16, the cruisers *Myoko* and *Maya* came down the Slot to hammer Henderson, this time firing 1,500 8-inch shells. By dawn Geiger put his total losses at 23 Dauntlesses, six Wildcats, eight Avengers and four Airacobras. Even including those planes that the ground crews cobbled up from cannibalized parts, the Cactus Air Force had only 34 planes left, including just nine Wildcats.

Just as nine Aichi D4Y1 "Val" dive bombers plunged down to finish off the Cactus Air Force, Lt. Col. Harold W. "Indian Joe" Bauer arrived from New Hebrides with 19 Wildcats and seven Dauntlesses. His fuel tanks almost empty, Bauer nevertheless shot down four Vals.

Both sides needed time to recover from the shock. Because Fighter One was too frequently flooded, another strip, called Fighter Two, was smoothed out across the Lunga River. Geiger, 57, who at one point had personally taken an SBD up to drop a 1,000-pound bomb on Japanese troops, finally was transferred out with combat fatigue.

Meanwhile, Japanese cruisers and destroyers landed more troops on the island, and on November 13 the battleships *Hiei* and *Kirishima* came down the Slot to smash Henderson once and for all. Alerted to their approach, American cruisers and destroyers ambushed them. Dawn found *Hiei,* hit 85 times, almost dead in the water just 10 miles north of Savo Island and less than 40 miles from Henderson. It was payback time.

All day *Hiei* lay prostrate while SBDs and TBFs punched bombs and torpedoes into her. The Wildcat fighter escort, finding no Zeros, went down to strafe as well. That night the Japanese scuttled *Hiei.* An American report noted, "It should be recorded that the first battleship to be sunk by Americans in the Second World War was sunk because of a handful of Marine and Navy aircraft."

On November 14, a cruiser force under Vice Adm. Gunichi

As a pursuing Wildcat's bullets strike home, a Mitsubishi G4M2 attempting to bomb Henderson Field bursts into flame.

Mikawa tried to achieve what the battleships had failed to do, shelling Henderson Field once more while an 11-ship troop convoy under Rear Adm. Raizo Tanaka headed for Guadalcanal. Both Japanese forces soon found themselves under attack by every available Cactus Air Force plane and the entire air group off the American carrier USS *Enterprise*, which had flown in to reinforce Henderson. In the ensuing fight, Indian Joe Bauer, by now an 11-victory ace, went into the water; he was seen swimming but disappeared before he could be rescued. (Bauer was posthumously awarded the Medal of Honor.) Mikawa lost the heavy cruiser *Kinugasa* to *Enterprise's* dive bombers, which also succeeded in damaging the heavy cruiser *Maya.* Seven transports went down; the others, beached, were destroyed the next day. Only 40 percent of the 10,000 Japanese troops made it onto Guadalcanal, with just 5 tons of supplies.

Mortally stricken by aircraft from Henderson on November 14, 1942, Kinugawa Maru, *one of "Tenacious Tanaka's" troopships, lies close to the mouth of the Bonegi River, near Tassafaronga, after being deliberately run ashore as an alternative to sinking in deep water.*

It was a turning point. After mid-November the Japanese, although they continued trying to destroy Henderson, gave up trying to recapture it. Instead, they secretly built their own airfield, at Munda on New Georgia, stretching a wire net over the construction to conceal the runway and leaving the tops of palm trees on it as camouflage.

Foss, with a Distinguished Flying Cross and severe malaria to show for his stint on Guadalcanal, had rotated rearward but returned to Henderson on New Year's Day 1943. Placed in command of VMF-121, he soon shot down three of the new, square-winged A6M3 Type 32 Zekes to raise his score to 26—tied with American World War I ace Eddie Rickenbacker. The bet was that Foss would be first to break Rickenbacker's record.

Foss' chance came on January 25, when Japan sent a last-ditch aerial armada down the Slot—30 Army bombers and fighters, recently moved to Rabaul from Malaya to assist the depleted naval units. Against them Foss had only his eight-plane Wildcat flight—the "Flying Circus"—and four Lockheed P-38F Lightning fighters of the 339th Fighter Squadron.

The bombers stayed out of range until their Nakajima Ki.43 fighter escorts could deal with the Americans. But the Ki.43 pilots feared a trap. "By refusing to run away when the odds were clearly and overwhelmingly against us, we instilled [in the Japanese] the deep suspicion that we had many more planes in the air," said Foss. The P-38s were more than capable of handling the few Ki.43s that ran the gantlet, two of which were shot down by Lieutenants Ray W. Bezner and Besby F. Holmes.

With the Wildcats still blocking the way—and accounting for two more Japanese fighters—the bombers soon gave up and went home. For turning back that air raid without firing a shot—and for giving Henderson's safety higher priority than his personal score—Foss received the Medal of Honor; a few days later he transferred out for good. His 26 kills would make him the highest scoring Marine fighter pilot of the war except for Major Gregory "Pappy" Boyington (who technically scored six of his 28 kills over China as one of the "Flying Tigers"). Foss retired a brigadier general, later serving as governor of his native South Dakota.

The Japanese military saved face by evacuating their remaining ground forces in early February, literally under the Americans' noses. The campaign for Guadalcanal was over; Henderson's role in history, however, was not. It was from Fighter Two that 16 P-38s of the 339th Squadron took off on April 18, 1943, to intercept and shoot down a Betty bomber carrying the mastermind of Pearl Harbor, Admiral Isoroku Yamamoto, as it approached Bougainville. But one of the returning Lightnings landed at a new forward airstrip in the Russell Islands. The war was leaving Henderson behind.

Through January 1943 the Cactus Air Force had lost 148 aircraft shot down and 94 airmen killed or missing. In addition, between August and November 1942, 43 planes were destroyed on Henderson Field and 86 were lost operationally. During that same period, the U.S. Navy carriers supporting the Guadalcanal campaign lost a total of 49 planes in combat, 72 destroyed on their ships and 184 operational losses. Estimates of total Japanese losses ranged as high as 900 aircraft and more than 2,400 aircrew members. The latter statistic reflected the beginning of a talent drain that would ultimately prove fatal to the Japanese land and naval air forces.

"None realized more the importance of the field that they had so obligingly begun, and so precipitantly abandoned, than the Japanese," wrote one historian. "For they never regained their strategic airfield, and for the lack of it they lost Guadalcanal, the Solomons, and ultimately New Guinea, the Bismarck Archipelago and their bases to the north. Probably never in history have a few acres of cleared ground cost so much in ships, men and treasure as...Henderson Field."

XIV

WHOSE KILL WAS IT?

Controversy has long persisted over which P-38 pilot downed Japan's planner of
Pearl Harbor, Admiral Yamamoto. Despite a thorough Air Force review,
the dispute may never be resolved.

By C.V. Glines

The mission of April 18, 1943, can be described in simple terms. A squadron of 16 Lockheed P-38 Lightnings took off from Guadalcanal and flew more than 400 miles to intercept two Japanese bombers and six fighters. The two bombers were shot down, but none of the escorting fighters was destroyed. One P-38 was lost.

The destruction of two Japanese bombers, and two more enemy fighters that had joined the fight from a nearby airfield, was not particularly significant as World War II aerial victories go. After all, there were more P-38s participating in the mission than enemy aircraft. What was significant was the identity of a passenger in one of those bombers. He was Isoroku Yamamoto, commander in chief of the Imperial Japanese Navy.

Out of this mission came a controversy that has not been resolved to everyone's satisfaction more than 50 years later, and may never be, as long as there remain proponents on both sides of a long-unresolved question: Who deserves the credit for shooting down the enemy's most brilliant naval strategist, the man who had planned the attack on Pearl Harbor in 1941?

The interception mission might be said to have begun months before, when U.S. Navy code-breakers succeeded in intercepting and breaking the Japanese navy's top-secret naval code, including the frequent changes that were made to protect its security. This knowledge enabled the U.S. Navy to know generally what Japanese

intentions were and to determine the disposition of most of the enemy's capital ships.

Before the war began, U.S. naval analysts had compiled dossiers on Japanese leaders, some of whom had served in assignments in the United States and attended American colleges. One of these was Yamamoto, who had attended Harvard University and had served as a naval attaché in the Japanese Embassy in Washington, D.C. When he ascended to the Japanese navy's top job, it was known that he was a complex, often contradictory character who had foreseen the future importance of the airplane for the navy. He was an inveterate gambler with a streak of superstition, a sometimes sentimental individual, but a tough leader when it came to discipline. He was also a realist and, although a tough adversary, did not believe that Japan could win a protracted war against the United States and Great Britain.

It was another of Yamamoto's personal traits that eventually contributed to his demise—he was punctual to a fault. He insisted on keeping schedules to the minute and was intolerant of lateness among his subordinates. Knowing his itineraries and putting to-

A Mitsubishi G4M2 bomber, transporting Admiral Isoroku Yamamoto to Bougainville, is intercepted by Lieutenant Rex Barber's Lockheed P-38G Lightning, in Yamamoto Shootdown, *by Jack Fellows.*

Admiral Isoroku Yamamoto (seated, fourth from left, aboard the battleship Musashi*) was a complex, flawed genius for whom punctuality became a fatal virtue.*

gether arrival and departure messages, U.S. Navy analysts could attest that he rarely, if ever, failed to make a precise schedule.

In the early hours of April 14, 1943, a Japanese coded message concerning Yamamoto's itinerary to visit units in southern Bougainville was intercepted. It stated that he would depart Rabaul on April 18 at 0600 (Tokyo time) to visit bases at Ballale, Shortland Island and Buin "in a medium attack plane escorted by six fighters." He would arrive at Ballale at 0800 and immediately board a submarine chaser to travel by water to Shortland Island. He would also visit the other units and return to Rabaul at 1540.

When this message was decoded by the cryptographers, it was passed on to Admiral Chester W. Nimitz, commander in chief of the U.S. Pacific Fleet at Pearl Harbor. Nimitz checked the distance between Guadalcanal, where there were Army and Navy fighters under Admiral William F. "Bull" Halsey's command, and Yamamoto's destinations on Bougainville. It would be the closest that Yamamoto had ever come to possible interception by U.S. fighters. Nimitz asked his chief intelligence officer, Commander Edward T. Layton, "Do we try to get him?" Layton thought it should be tried, and Nimitz agreed.

The decrypted message was sent to Halsey, who in turn sent it to his subordinate task force commanders in the Pacific, including Admiral Marc A. Mitscher, located on Guadalcanal. The message ended with a typical Halsey comment: "Tally ho. Let's get the bastard." Plans were begun immediately to see if Mitscher's fighters could carry out an intercept.

On April 17, concerned that the Japanese might learn that their code had been broken if an intercept was made, Nimitz approved a follow-up message to Halsey: "Believe specific effort worthwhile. Suggest pilots be told coastwatcher Rabaul area signalled our sub to effect unknown high ranking officer making trip to Ballale or some such source. Suggest every effort be made to make operation appear fortuitous. If forces you command have capability [to] shoot down Yamamoto and staff, you are hereby authorized [to] initiate preliminary planning. Our best wishes and high hopes go with those intercepting hunters." Nimitz added a personal note for Halsey: "Best of luck and good hunting."

It is at this point that controversy enters the scenario of the mission. It can be assumed but not proven that Nimitz kept his superior in Washington, Admiral Ernest J. King, commander in chief, U.S. Fleet, informed. It can also be assumed that information copies of message exchanges about the proposed Yamamoto interception between Nimitz and his subordinate commanders might be included. However, there is no indication that Admiral King, if informed, ever reacted to any of Nimitz's messages. It is considered by many that it was highly unlikely that Nimitz would have thought that he needed permission from his superior in Washington for a single mission such as this in his area of responsibility.

Some writers have said, without documentation, that the question of whether or not the enemy's top naval leader should be targeted in this manner was sent to Admiral King, who passed it on to Secretary of the Navy Frank Knox—who, in turn, forwarded it to President Franklin Roosevelt. One writer states that General Henry H. "Hap" Arnold, commander in chief of the U.S. Army Air Force (USAAF), was contacted and was enthusiastic. It has also been reported that Charles A. Lindbergh was asked if the USAAF fighters on Guadalcanal could fly such a mission; Lindbergh was said to have contacted Frank Meyer, a Lockheed aeronautical engineer, for advice. Still another writer says that Secretary Knox contacted the top Catholic clergy in the United States for counsel on the question of setting up an enemy commander for what some would call an assassination.

None of these stories has any basis in fact. Historians, analysts and this author have sought in vain for any scrap of evidence that anyone above Admiral Nimitz was ever contacted for "permission" or advice. One author confidently states that the messages between Nimitz, Knox and Roosevelt "were deliberately omitted from the record" but does not indicate how he knows this. He adds, "And yet, as a handful of men in Washington knew, several offices in the higher reaches of government were abuzz with plans to kill Yamamoto." Still, more than 50 years later, no evidence has been found to lay the decision at the feet of either Secretary Knox or President Roosevelt.

After the go-ahead for the mission was passed from Halsey to Mitscher on Guadalcanal, a number of questions were debated by Mitscher's staff. What type of aircraft could fly the distance from Guadalcanal to Bougainville, engage in a fight and return? How many aircraft would be needed? In what type of aircraft would Yamamoto be flying—the Mitsubishi G4M Navy medium bomber (called Betty by the Allies) or the older Ki.21 (Sally) used by the Japanese army? What about the nearly 100 enemy fighters located at Kahili? Would a number of them be sent up to escort their leader to Ballale in the same fashion as American fighters had flown out to escort Secretary Knox when he made an inspection visit to Guadalcanal shortly after it had been captured by the Americans?

Arguments ensued, and it soon became the consensus that the Navy fighters available did not have the range for such a mission. The U.S. Air Force P-38s of the 339th Fighter Squadron, based on the island's Fighter Two airstrip and under Mitscher's control, were the only ones that could make the intercept. But that was possible only if at least one large 310-gallon fuel tank could be installed under a wing of each aircraft to supplement one of the two smaller 165-gallon tanks usually carried.

Major John W. Mitchell, commander of the 339th Fighter Squadron, was resting on a cot in his squadron's headquarters tent. A veteran with eight kills to his credit, he had recently assumed command and was battling the heat, the insects and the dysentery like everyone else. As he dozed, Lt. Col. Henry Vicellio, commander of the 347th Fighter Group, poked his head in the tent. "Mitch," he said, "they want us over at the Fighter Command at

Henderson. They've got a mission for you."

En route, they picked up Major Louis Kittel and Captain Tom Lanphier. When they entered the dugout that served as operations center for Mitscher's staff, it was crowded with Army, Navy and Marine officers.

"When we got there," Mitchell recalled during an interview with this author, "everybody seemed to be talking at once. Major John F. Condon, a Marine officer, handed me a radio message from Admiral Halsey. The message said that Admiral Yamamoto was going to make a 315-mile trip from Rabaul to Bougainville, and gave the exact time of his expected landing at Ballale.

"There was a big discussion—a real hassle—as to how to get Yamamoto. The reason we were called in was because we were flying P-38s, the only fighters on the island that could make the trip. The Navy and Marine pilots would never have let us Army pilots in on a mission like that if any of their F4F [Wildcat] or F4U [Corsair] fighters could have flown the distance."

Mitchell could not get too many words into the discussion while the Navy and Marine pilots were arguing back and forth about how they thought Mitchell should fly the mission. The argument boiled down to two concepts: intercept Yamamoto's bomber in the air, or try to dive-bomb and strafe him on the submarine chaser en route to the Shortland Island outpost. Most thought Mitchell should try to get him after he boarded the sub chaser.

"Being an Air Force type," Mitchell recalled, "I didn't know one boat from another, a sub chaser from a sub. When I finally got a chance to put a word in, I told them that and added a second reason for not trying to get him on a boat. Even if we sank the boat, he might survive and take to a raft or swim to shore. Besides, the Japs had 75 fighters only about 20 miles from where Yamamoto was supposed to land. We would have to be over the target too long trying to get in trail to strafe a boat in the water. If they sent up fighters to escort the admiral, we'd be in a poor position to defend ourselves at such a low altitude and still get any hits on the target, assuming we could identify it in the first place.

"The debate went on for a long time and there was an obvious stalemate. Finally, Admiral Mitscher, who hadn't said much, shushed everybody up and said quietly, 'Since Mitchell's got to do the job, let's let him do it his way.' That ended the discussion."

Mitchell was told that the 310-gallon drop tanks were being flown in that night from Port Moresby, but there were only enough available to put one on each P-38 opposite the remaining smaller tank under each wing. Mitchell asked for a good Navy compass for the lead plane because the standard equipment compasses on the P-38s were not reliable. He was assured one would be provided.

He was then briefed on the expected weather and the anti-aircraft gun emplacements on Bougainville.

Delighted with the opportunity to tangle with what could be the greatest number of enemy aircraft he had ever engaged, Mitchell returned to Fighter Two and began planning the mission with enthusiasm. Joined by Lieutenant Joseph E. McGuigan, a Navy intelligence officer, and Captain William Morrison, McGuigan's Army counterpart, Mitchell laid out a map on the table. He had been given a small strip map with course lines drawn on it by Major Condon, but he did not trust the airspeed, distance and time figures. Condon did not fly Air Force P-38s and did not know at what airspeed Mitchell would set his throttles for a long-range cruise, nor at what altitude Mitchell would elect to fly.

By using Yamamoto's takeoff and arrival times, Mitchell approximated the airspeed of the bomber at 180 mph, or three miles per minute. "Strictly a guess," he remembered later, "because no one seemed to know for sure what kind of bomber he'd be in."

Mitchell figured the P-38's zero-wind ground speed using long-range cruise-control power settings at 200 mph. Based on a Navy forecast of visibility-limiting haze and a quartering 5-knot wind "off the port bow" on the first leg, Mitchell estimated his group would average 197 mph to the target area.

A direct flight to southern Bougainville would mean crossing or flying near several enemy-held islands. Mitchell plotted the course to circumvent the island chain to avoid detection. The scale of the small strip chart he had been given for the flight did not show many details of the land areas that might be used as checkpoints. Mitchell decided to fly at least 50 miles offshore, which meant dead reckoning over water all the way for more than 400 miles.

"At that time," Mitchell recalled, "I figured the odds were about a thousand to one of intercepting at that distance. Today, after

Captain Thomas G. Lanphier, Lieutenant Besby F. Holmes and Lieutenant Rex T. Barber pose before a P-38G of the 339th Squadron on April 19, 1943, the day after their special mission. The fourth member of their "killer" flight, Lieutenant Raymond K. Hine, did not return.

thinking about it for 50 years, I'd make that a million to one."

Taking the admiral's arrival time at Ballale, Mitchell worked backward with his figures to plan an intercept of the Yamamoto bomber at 0935. He divided his flight plan into five legs and figured takeoff should be at 0720 on the morning of the 18th. Allowing 15 minutes for formation join-up, the flight should depart the island area at 0735 Guadalcanal time.

There were to be 18 P-38s in commission for the mission, and although everyone volunteered, Mitchell, with Major Lou Kittel, chose the pilots. On the evening of April 17, Mitchell briefed the pilots, who were told that all 18 aircraft would fly 50 to 100 feet above the water. When they made landfall, a "killer" section of four aircraft would attack the bomber, which would be protected by the six Zeros. The other 14 planes would climb immediately to about 18,000-20,000 feet to provide top cover against the Zeros that were expected to come up from Kahili. Strict radio silence was

to be observed on the flight to the target area; Mitchell would use only hand signals to indicate when to spread out or close in.

"I really expected them to send up at least 50 fighters just as we had done for Secretary Knox when he visited previously," Mitchell said. "I anticipated a real turkey shoot, and I didn't want to miss it. I could have named myself to lead the killer flight, but I wanted to get after those Zeros. Besides, I didn't want all 18 ships going after those six Zero escorts and a lone bomber."

At daybreak the next day, the last large gas tank was being attached to the last plane. The Navy ship's compass that had been promised was installed in Mitchell's cockpit.

Mitchell took off at 0710, followed by the other Lightnings. Two of the four members of the "killer" flight, Captain Thomas G. Lanphier and Lieutenant Rex T. Barber, joined up, but Lieutenant James D. McLanahan blew a tire on takeoff and had to abort. Shortly afterward, while checking his wing tanks to be sure they would feed, Lieutenant Joseph F. Moore found that they would not. He signaled to Mitchell that he also was aborting. Mitchell signaled to Lieutenants Besby F. Holmes and his wingman Lieutenant Raymond K. Hine to fill in the attack flight's empty positions.

The Lightnings flew westward on schedule just a few feet above the water. There was nothing to disturb the scene—no ships, no land, no other planes, nothing. Mitchell recalled: "It was hot as hell in those cockpits and I dozed off a couple of times, but I got a light tap on the shoulder from the Man upstairs and caught myself."

One of the pilots got too low, and his propeller tips splashed seawater over his windshield. "I know damn well *that* woke him up," Mitchell said. "He admitted later that he didn't sleep or eat well for several nights after the mission."

Mitchell kept watching his compass and checked his watch frequently as he flew the planned legs toward Empress Augusta Bay off Bougainville. "We were about four minutes out and I was getting nervous then," he said. "It was hazy and the sun was directly in front of us. I couldn't see anything and wondered if I was near any land at all.

"Just as my time was up, I thought: I'd better do something now. I signaled for the formation to close up. Doug Canning, flying number three in my flight, suddenly broke radio silence and said, 'Bogeys! Eleven o'clock high!'"

I looked up and there they were, five miles away at about 4,500 feet [and] descending—two Betty bombers instead of the one we had been told to expect and six Zeros behind them about a thousand feet higher. I 'Rogered' and said, 'I have 'em.'"

Mitchell and the 11 top-cover pilots immediately started a full-throttle climb parallel to the bombers' route of flight. He radioed to the pilots to get rid of their external fuel tanks to avoid the chance of fire from enemy tracers and to improve maneuverability—and then told Lanphier, "He's your meat, Tom."

Lanphier and Barber jettisoned their tanks and started a slight climb toward the bombers, which were descending toward their destination at Buin. However, Holmes could not shed his tanks, and turned away from the action toward the water with Hine following. As he and Barber headed on an intercept path toward the two bombers, Lanphier sighted three of the Zeros bearing down on them from the left. He turned 90 degrees and climbed toward them.

It is at this point that the central controversy begins. Lanphier's story, published in *The New York Times* in September 1945, stated, "I saw the gray smoke from his wing guns and wondered with stupid detachment if the bullets would get me before I could work my guns into his face.

"He was a worse shot than I was, and he died. My machine guns and cannon ripped one of his wings away. He twisted under me, all flame and smoke. His two wingmen hurtled past and I wasted a few bursts between them.

"I kicked my ship over on its back and looked down for the lead Japanese bomber. It had dived inland. As I hung in the sky I got an impression, off to the east, of a swirl of aircraft against the blue—a single Lightning silhouetted against the light in a swarm of Zeros. That was Barber having himself a time.

"Excitement in a fight works wonders with a man's vision. In the same brief second that I saw Rex on my right, and saw the Zeros I had just overshot, I spotted a shadow moving across the treetops. It was Yamamoto's bomber. It was skimming the jungle, headed for Kahili.

"I dived toward him.

"I realized on the way down that I had picked up too much speed, that I might overshoot him. I cut back on my throttles. I crossed my controls and went into a skid to brake my dive.

"The two Zeros that had overshot me showed up again, diving toward Yamamoto's bomber from an angle slightly off to my right. They meant to get me before I got the bomber. It looked from where I sat as if the bomber, the Zeros, and I might all get to the same place at the same time.

"We very nearly did. The next three or four seconds spelled life or death. I remember getting suddenly very stubborn about

Rex Barber claims Mission Accomplished, *in a painting by Roy Grinnell. The Americans claimed three Betty bombers and three Zeros, but surviving Zero pilot Kenji Yanagiya (who was credited with downing Hine) later testified that only two bombers were lost.*

making the most of the one good shot I had coming up. I fired a long steady burst across the bomber's course of flight, from approximately right angles.

"The bomber's right engine, then its right wing, burst into flame....Just as I moved into range of Yamamoto's bomber and its [rear] cannon, the bomber's wing came off. The bomber plunged into the jungle. It exploded. That was the end of Admiral Isoroku Yamamoto."

Lanphier described how the pursuing Zeros continued to press

their attack but failed to hit him. He called for help. As he fled the area, he said he saw three columns of black smoke rising out of the jungle, behind which were "the burning bomber containing Yamamoto and two of his accompanying aircraft."

Rex Barber tells a different story: "Just before we would break right to fall in behind the Bettys, Lanphier suddenly broke about 90 degrees to the left and started a head-on pass up and into the oncoming Zeros to divert them. This was a wise maneuver on his part as it allowed me the opportunity to attack the bombers without the Zeros on my tail. I banked sharply right to fall in behind the Bettys and, in so doing, my left engine and wing briefly blocked out my view of both bombers. As I rolled back, there was only one Betty in front of me. I didn't know if it was the lead bomber or not.

"By this time, we were no more than 1,000 feet above the terrain, and the Betty again increased his dive in an evident attempt

Bullet holes in the wreckage of Admiral Isoroku Yamamoto's G4M2 indicate that the plane was attacked from the rear—as stated by Barber in his combat report.

to get to treetop level. My turn carried me slightly left of the Betty and about 50 yards behind. I opened fire, aiming over the fuselage at the right engine. I could see bits of engine cowling coming off. As I slid over to get directly behind the target, my line of fire passed through the vertical fin of the Betty. Some pieces of the rudder separated. As I moved right, I continued firing into the right engine. The engine began to emit heavy, black smoke from around the cowling. I moved my fire back along the wing root and into the fuselage, then on into the left engine.

"By this time I was probably no more than 100 feet behind the Betty and almost level with it. Suddenly, the Betty snapped left. As it rotated, I almost struck the right wing as the Betty slowed rapidly when it snapped. I looked over my left shoulder as I roared by and saw the bomber with its wing upended vertically and black smoke pouring from the right engine. I believe the Betty crashed into the jungle, although I did not see it crash."

Barber headed out to sea and ahead of him saw Holmes and Hine firing on a Betty. Holmes' shots walked up through the right engine, leaving a trail of white smoke. Hine's shots went into the water. The two P-38s then headed south. Barber, seeing his chance

to down the Betty, pulled in behind it, and the bomber exploded. As he flew through the smoke, a large chunk of the bomber hit his right wing, cutting out his turbo supercharger intercooler. Another piece hit the underside of his fuselage, making a large dent.

As Barber zoomed on by, he saw that Holmes and Hine had encountered Zeros that may have taken off from Kahili. Holmes shot one of them down. He saw Hine heading out to sea with smoke pouring from his right engine.

Barber, pursued by a Zero that scored some hits, saw a second Zero, which had broken off the engagement with Holmes, and shot it down. He looked for Holmes and Hine but saw neither of them again. Concerned about Hine, he looked for oil slicks and saw three—one where the Betty had gone in and two where the two Zeros had splashed. Now low on fuel, Barber headed for home.

Meanwhile, the top-cover aircraft did not see any of the action below. Several heard Lanphier call for help, so Mitchell started a dive, followed by his three section mates, Lieutenants Doug Canning, Jack Jacobson and Delton Goerke. Mitchell, going at top speed, came in behind a Zero and fired a few shots, but claimed no hits. He zoomed past his quarry and did not see it again. Jacobson also fired at the Zero without results.

The battle was over and 15 of the 16 Lightnings headed for Guadalcanal, some in loose formation, others singly. Holmes, short of fuel, landed on one of the Russell Islands. Lieutenant Ray Hine never returned.

Among the first to arrive at Fighter Two was Lanphier, who shouted on the radio as he approached, "I got Yamamoto!" When the others landed, Lanphier was riding up and down the flying line in a Jeep shouting that he had shot down Japan's top admiral.

When Barber landed with 104 bullet holes in his P-38, he was astonished to hear Lanphier's claim. He asked Lanphier how he knew which bomber the admiral was in. Lanphier became irate that his version of the action should be questioned, so Barber walked away shaking his head in disbelief.

Unfortunately, there was no formal debriefing of the mission and Lanphier, loud in his belief that he had shot the admiral down, seemed to carry the day. Barber quietly told his side of the story, confident only that he had shot down one Betty and finished the job of destroying the second one. When Holmes arrived after re-fueling, he claimed he had also shot a Betty down, despite the fact that no third Betty was ever seen.

In hindsight, Mitchell blames himself for not having insisted on a formal debriefing, especially of Lanphier, Barber and Holmes. Unfortunately, the P-38s had no gun cameras during this period at Guadalcanal.

The mission was considered top-secret, but word of it still spread rapidly all over Guadalcanal. Everyone seemed to accept Lanphier's word that he deserved the victory and that he had shot down two aircraft, bringing his claimed total to seven. He said that one of these—never substantiated—was when he manned a gun on a B-17 while flying as a passenger on a bombing mission.

After the first pilots had landed, the first of several top-secret messages was dispatched by Mitscher: "Pop goes the weasel. P-38s led by Major J. William Mitchell USAAF visited Kahili area. About 0930L [local time] shot down two bombers escorted by 6 Zeros flying close formation. 1 other bomber shot down believed on test flight. 3 Zeros added to the score sums total 6. 1 P-38 failed return. April 18 seems to be our day."

This final sentence referred to the launching of Jimmy Doolittle's 16 B-25s from the carrier *Hornet* on April 18 the year before. Mitscher had been in command of *Hornet,* while Halsey had been in command of the 16-ship task force on *Enterprise.* Halsey immediately sent a congratulatory message to Mitscher: "Congratulations to you and Major Mitchell. Sounds as though one of the ducks in their bag was a peacock."

Although the official score seemed to be three Betty bombers and three Zeros downed, none of the pilots could confirm one another's stories. All that Mitchell and the top-cover pilots ever saw was a single plume of black smoke coming up from the jungle. Since both bombers were shot down and Yamamoto was in one of them, "I didn't give a damn," Mitchell said. "We did what we were supposed to do. It didn't make any difference to me who shot the admiral down."

That night a mission report was prepared and signed by Captain William Morrison and Lieutenant Joseph McGuigan, the intelligence officers who had helped Mitchell when he was laying out the course. Neither Mitchell nor Barber was consulted during its preparation. Lt. Cmdr. William A. Read was instructed to prepare recommendations for Mitchell and the members of the attack flight to receive the Medal of Honor and spot promotions.

Barber and Lanphier were immediately sent on leave to New Zealand, where they met J. Norman Lodge, a wire service reporter who had heard about the mission. He questioned the two while playing golf with Brig. Gen. Dean C. Strother, then operations officer for the 13th Fighter Command. Lodge was able to confirm details of the mission from their answers to his questions. Later, Lanphier admitted to Barber that he (Lanphier) had written the mission report and also helped write the citations for the Medal of Honor.

Barber was stunned. He never saw the report until the late 1950s when it was declassified. Lodge, meanwhile, wrote his story, implying that either Lanphier or Barber had shot down Yamamoto and that both were recommended for the Medal of Honor. He noted that "intelligence had trailed Yamamoto for five days" and he gave details about the planning: "We had been tracking Yamamoto right into Truk and had known where he was every minute of those five days."

Lodge sent his account to Halsey's headquarters censors, who promptly denied approval. Such a news report would be a dead giveaway that the enemy's naval code had been broken. Naval code-breakers would be set back many months because the Japanese would change their code drastically. Halsey was furious and sent for Strother, Lanphier and Barber.

When they reported to Halsey, the hard-bitten admiral cut loose with a tirade of profanity about their violating security and accused the three of being traitors to their country and so stupid that they should not have the right to wear a uniform. He showed them five Medal of Honor recommendations lying on his desk for the four shooters and Mitchell. Halsey said they did not even deserve the Air Medal but that he was downgrading the recommendations to the Navy Cross.

When Nimitz and his intelligence staff learned about the Lodge story, they expected the worst. Nimitz radioed Halsey to "warn Lodge and all others having information on this matter to maintain complete silence." He ordered a complete investigation because it showed "widespread and flagrant disregard of security [for] Ultra [code breaking] information. Initiate immediate corrective measures and take disciplinary action as warranted."

It was a fruitless exercise. The mission and its outcome were general knowledge to everyone on Guadalcanal and the many who transferred to other units or back to the States, unaware that the story was considered top-secret. No one was ever disciplined. The 15 survivors of the mission received the Navy Cross as Halsey had indicated. Lanphier and Barber were transferred to Stateside assignments; Lanphier was assigned to the Pentagon, where his father was stationed as a colonel. Neither Lanphier nor Barber flew missions in the South Pacific again.

When the word was flashed to the world that Yamamoto had died, *Time* magazine put its staff to work. A story appeared on page 28 of the May 31, 1943, issue saying, "When the name of the man who killed Admiral Yamamoto is released, the U.S. will have a new hero." On page 66 of that same issue was a picture of Lanphier under the title "Heroes," and the caption told Lanphier's version of the mission without naming Yamamoto as the victim. The account ended with the statement, "The Squadron whisked back to the Solomons base, wondered if it had nailed some Jap bigwig in the bombers."

The services put a clamp on release of the details of the Yamamoto mission until September 11, 1945, when Lanphier's article, previously mentioned, appeared in *The New York Times*. It received wide coverage because it was also released by the North American Newspaper Alliance; the War Department also sent out a release giving Lanphier full credit for the shoot-down.

Barber, then stationed in California, was furious. Instead of going to the press, Barber tried to report his story through Air Force channels, but no one in his chain of command paid any attention to his request for a review of the mission. Neither John Mitchell nor any of the survivors of that mission, then or since, would support Lanphier's claim, since none saw the actual shoot-down.

Mitchell wrote to General Carl Spaatz, who had by then succeeded General Arnold as commanding general of the Army Air Forces, saying he considered it an injustice for Lanphier to receive full credit and asking that "some kind of public announcement be made to credit Barber with his share of this achievement." He received a noncommittal reply and no review was ever made.

Lanphier left the service, became active in the Air Force Association and was its first elected president. Everywhere he went to give speeches or meet the press, he was introduced as "the man who shot down Yamamoto."

Barber stayed in the service until retirement as a colonel.

In 1967, an unnamed Air Force officer investigated the original 1943 mission report signed by Morrison and McGuigan. He wrote: "The report is enough to make one weep. It reads like a fiction tale and the facts appear to be intertwined like Medusa's locks."

Six years later, two Air Force historians declared that Lanphier and Barber should receive equal credit. In May 1983, at a reunion of the American Fighter Aces Association, Lanphier apparently learned for the first time that he was sharing the credit with Barber and "came unglued," according to one witness. In April 1985, during a speech at the National Air & Space Museum, Lanphier retold his story, with added—but unsubstantiated—embellishments about President Roosevelt personally approving the shoot-down.

During a 1985 reunion, Mitchell, Barber, and several other former members of the 339th Fighter Squadron visited the Nimitz Museum in Fredericksburg, Texas, where there was an exhibit about the Yamamoto shoot-down. The visit was a turning point. Included in the exhibit was a filmed 1975 interview with Kenji Yanagiya, the only surviving pilot of the six Zeros that had escorted the admiral. He confirmed that there were only two Betty bombers, not three as Holmes had said. He also stated that after the first pass of the Zeros trying to ward off the attacking P-38s, he saw a P-38 "firing from *the rear of the lead bomber*"(emphasis added) into its tail. He saw it enveloped in flames and fall into the jungle. He saw no P-38 firing from the right side. Yanagiya also said none of the Zeros accompanying their leader was shot down.

"From that moment on, there was no doubt in my mind whatsoever," Mitchell said, "that Rex Barber deserves *full* credit for shooting down the lead bomber."

Although Lanphier had always claimed he shot down seven Zeros, the Air Force did not agree. He was credited with 5½ victories, including the one-half the Air Force decided that he shared with Barber. When Yanagiya revealed that none of the six escorting Zeros was shot down, the Air Force immediately reduced Lanphier's total to 4½. He died in 1988 not knowing that he no longer could claim the exalted title of "ace."

In the fall of 1988, George T. Chandler, an ace who had served on Guadalcanal, launched his own investigation and formed the Second Yamamoto Mission Association (SYMA) to organize an expedition to Bougainville, where the remains of the Betty bomber still exist. The objective was to obtain firm evidence that would support either one or both stories. Unfortunately, the visit to the wreckage could not be made because of unrest in the area.

However, since 1945, many Japanese, Australian and American visitors have traveled to the site. Several pilots and qualified accident investigators have inspected the wreckage closely, taken many photographs and measurements, and confirmed that there were no bullet holes in the fuselage that would indicate that shots were fired from right angles.

Chandler and the SYMA group felt that enough physical evidence existed and could be substantiated by those who had actually visited the scene to prove that Barber deserved full credit. Two witnesses testified about their visits to the wreckage, and the other evidence obtained was presented to an Air Force Victory Credit Review Board in October 1991. Mitchell and Barber repeated their respective stories. Although Lanphier had died, the board duly considered the articles he had written.

While the review board deliberated, the Veterans of Foreign Wars (VFW) also analyzed all the evidence and concluded that Rex Barber's story is true. In August 1992, the VFW presented Barber with the Commander in Chief's Gold Medal of Merit and Citation, thus giving him full credit for the shoot-down.

On January 13, 1993, after 15 months' deliberation, Secretary of the Air Force Donald B. Rice released the results of the review by the Air Force. Rice said he "was not convinced that the award of shared credit for the Yamamoto shootdown is either in error or unjust." However, two members of the board *did* find ample evidence in favor of Barber and reported that "the record...should be corrected." One member felt that, despite the fact that at least two men who visited the site testified that all bullet holes they found

An interior shot of a section of fuselage from Yamamoto's plane. Photographs and visitors to the site give no evidence of hits from the right, as Lanphier claimed he had inflicted on his victim.

came from the rear of the aircraft, what remains of the wreckage "has not been thoroughly examined for holes due to bullets coming from other than the approximately 6 o'clock position." The fourth member of the board merely sided with the third member, saying that he did not believe enough evidence had been provided to reverse the previous decision. The fifth member found that the Air Force historian's version of the attack was "suspect" and "fatally flawed" and that the Air Force should "cause a Victory Credit Review Board to be convened and render a final decision on this matter."

Since the board had not reached a majority decision, Rice said he denied the application for correction of the record because "there is substantial evidence that he (Lanphier) did fire upon and hit Yamamoto's aircraft." He did not explain what that "substantial evidence" was. He admitted, however, that "historians, fighter pilots, and all of us who have studied the record of this extraordinary mission will forever speculate as to the exact events of that day in 1943."

XV

RUHR DAM RAIDS

Guy Gibson and his 'Dambusters' flew deep into Germany to carry out
a dangerous mission—destroy three imposing dams.

By Daniel Wyatt

March 21, 1943. Early morning. One hundred forty-seven anxious officers and NCOs from 21 bomber crews jammed the briefing room at Scampton, Lincolnshire, a Royal Air Force (RAF) bomber base 150 miles north of London. They hailed from every corner of the Commonwealth. One officer was an American. There were pilots, navigators, bomb aimers, wireless operators, gunners and flight engineers.

They were veterans, hardened to aerial battle. Nearly all were 23 years old or younger. They were handpicked, the cream of the crop, the best of the RAF Bomber Command. Most crews had already completed a full combat tour, consisting of 30 operations. Some had even defied the odds by finishing two tours. Many of the airmen had already collected two Distinguished Flying Crosses (DFCs) for bravery, while others had at least one. Some had a Distinguished Service Order (DSO). Known simply as Squadron X for the time being, the squadron members all had one thing in common that day in March—none of them had willingly volunteered to be there.

After scanning the room, one Canadian tail gunner of the group uttered what was on his mind: "It looks like an NHL [National Hockey League] All-Star team."

At 9:30 a.m., a hush fell over the crowd as the commanding officer, Wing Commander Guy Gibson, a muscular, good-looking, 25-year-old Englishman, entered the room. His eyes fell upon the sea of faces, some not old enough to vote or shave. Only yesterday a handful of fliers had met with Gibson in the mess, under more lighthearted circumstances. Following him then was his lovable black Labrador retriever, the Squadron X mascot, who was noted in Gibson's previous squadron for his thirst for beer. While his master chatted and drank, the dog went about lapping beer from a pan placed on the floor.

But now Gibson was all business, a far cry from the day before. His speech that fateful morning was short and to the point: "You're here to do a special job. You're here as a crack squadron. You're here to carry out a raid on Germany which, I am told, will have startling results. Some say it may even cut short the duration of the war. What the target is I can't tell you. Nor can I tell you where it is. All I can tell you is that you will have to practice low flying all day and all night until you know how to do it with your eyes shut. If I tell you to fly to a tree in the middle of England, then I will want you to bomb that tree. If I tell you to fly through a hangar, then

Flight Lieutenant David Maltby launches his "bouncing bomb" at the Möhne Dam while the Avro Lancaster B.I. of Wing Commander Guy Gibson (foreground) overflies a German anti-aircraft position, in Breaching the Dam, *by Nicholas Trudgian.*

One of No. 617 Squadron's targets, the Möhne Dam. With a 112-foot-thick concrete and masonry base, it held back a lake 12 miles long, containing 140 million tons of water.

you will have to go through that hangar, even though your wingtips might hit either side. Discipline is absolutely essential.

"I needn't tell you that we are going to be talked about. It is very unusual to have such a crack crowd of boys in one squadron. There are going to be a lot of rumors—I have heard a few already. We've got to stop those rumors. We've got to say nothing. When you go into pubs at night, you've got to keep your mouths shut. When the other boys ask you what you're doing, just tell them to mind their own business, because of all things in this game, security is the greatest factor."

Once Gibson finished, each airmen, of course, attempted to picture in his mind what and where the target was. Was it *Tirpitz*, the menacing German battleship, or maybe submarine pens on the Continent? Nobody came close, including Gibson. In fact, all the wing commander himself knew was that he had been "volunteered" for a mission labeled Operation Downwood.

A few days after the Squadron X briefing, in a meeting with

British aeronautical engineer Barnes Wallis, Gibson sat in morbid silence and absorbed the proposed details of the operation. His role? Lead a squadron of planes deep into Germany to destroy three main hydroelectric dams feeding the Ruhr Valley: the Möhne, the Eder, and the Sorpe. The objective? Deny the Ruhr industries the power and the water they needed for their war production.

The dimensions of the dams astonished Gibson. The Gothic-styled Möhne was 2,500 feet long, 130 feet high, topped by a 25-foot-wide roadway, and had a concrete and masonry base 112 feet thick. It held back a lake 12 miles long that contained 140 million tons of water. A short distance south of the Möhne was the much smaller Sorpe. The two dams together controlled 75 percent of the total water available in the Ruhr Valley. Fifty miles to the east was the Eder, the big brother of the three, with a water capacity of 200 million tons.

The operation would require unconventional bombing means. The weapon used would be a powerful skipping bomb so gigantic in size that each aircraft would be capable of carrying only one. Resembling a depth charge or a huge oil drum, each bomb would carry 6,500 pounds of a high explosive named simply RDX. It would be fitted under the fuselage of an Avro Lancaster bomber and carried by two V-shaped legs with a mechanism that spun the bomb backward at 500 rpm by way of a belt drive from a motor inside the fuselage. Gibson said later that the above modifications made the bomber look like a "pregnant duck." Once a bomb was released toward the dam from upriver, the backspin was expected to not only allow the bomb to skip forward and over the dam's torpedo nets as it bounced along the water's surface but also hold the bomb against the wall of the dam as it sank. A depth-activated fuse would set off the explosion near the base of the dam, causing the wall to be breached. Wallis went on to say that the bomb had to be dropped precisely at a height of 150 feet, 425 yards from the dam, in the airspeed range of 230-240 mph—and under the cover of moonlit darkness.

Gibson was stunned. There was more. That same week he had another conference with Wallis at which the pilot learned that the best time to strike would be the middle of May, a full-moon period, when the water levels would be approximately 4 feet from the top of the dam as a result of the winter runoff and spring rains. Gibson was given less than two months to whip his forces into action.

Wing Commander Guy Penrose Gibson was already a legendary figure in the RAF. Born in Simla, India, and educated at Oxford, he had been an officer in the RAF since 1936 and had been fighting the war since its inception in 1939. He had just received a bar to his DSO. He had completed a combined total of 173 sorties in fighter and bomber commands, three full tours in bombers and one in fighters. He even had four enemy kills to his credit.

The commander in chief of Bomber Command, Air Chief Marshal Sir Arthur "Bomber" Harris, considered Gibson the right man for the mission and gave him a free hand in picking the crews.

During the next several weeks, the intense day-night training commenced, closely supervised by Gibson. In order to simulate nighttime flying in the daylight hours, light-blue screens were placed over the aircraft windows, and the crews donned yellow glasses. Low-level flying was no longer taboo, but a must—the more the better. Like schoolboys, the airmen were given the go-ahead to perfect normally forbidden flying practices. In Britain, no area between Cornwall and the Hebrides was off limits. The crews flew under bridges, skimmed wheat fields, brushed treetops, blew the soot from chimneys, and scattered herds of cattle and sheep—all in the name of practice makes perfect. All complaints from the outraged civilians were ignored.

There were, however, problems that could not be ignored. The operational height of 150 feet was a very serious factor. At that low altitude proper judgment of height over the water was difficult to make with the instruments in the Lancasters. That was until Gibson was approached by a technician who suggested placing two spotlights on the bomber—one in the nose, pointing straight down, the other just forward of the tail, pointing at an angle toward the first light and converging with it at 150 feet. When the lights merged into one on the water and formed a figure eight, they were at the proper height. Too high, and the "eight" would separate. Too low, and it looked like an "O." The lights were tested and worked, providing that it was the navigator who concentrated on the merging of the lights—Gibson decided that the pilot had enough to worry about.

Born in Simla, India, and educated at Oxford, Wing Commander Guy Penrose Gibson was already a legendary figure in the RAF.

Map-reading was exceptionally difficult for all navigators during the simulated operations. While they were flying at low levels, the ground whizzed by too quickly for the navigators to get a proper bearing with the large-scale maps they were using. To avoid constant flipping of the charts, homemade roller maps were introduced. It was also suggested that the bomb aimer be the key landmark-finder, letting the navigator stick to the charts. The flight engineer and mid-upper gunner could also help by keeping their eyes open. Altogether, eight pairs of eyes would watch for landmarks.

Normal bomb-aiming procedures, too, would not suffice. It was not until an expert with the Ministry of Aircraft Production sauntered into Gibson's office that the difficulties were resolved. "There are a couple of towers on top of the wall of each dam," the civilian informed the wing commander. "We've measured them from aerial photographs and they're 600 feet apart." He showed Gibson a small plywood triangle with a peephole at one corner and a nail sticking up at both the two other corners. The crude device would be their new bombsight, however unorthodox it first appeared. "When you look through the peephole, and the towers are in line with the nails, you are about 425 yards from the dam. You press the trigger and the bomb will then drop in the right spot," he explained.

In April, flying experiments were conducted at Parkstone, off England's south shore, under the careful watch of Barnes Wallis. In the aftermath of a number of these flights, the scientist discovered that the bomb's casing would break up at the prescribed height of 150 feet. After thoughtful consideration and precise calculations, Wallis had no choice but to insist upon a lower altitude.

When Gibson was informed less than two weeks before the attack that he had to go in on the bomb run at 60 feet, his first reaction was, "If 150 feet was too low, 60 feet was very low. At that height you would only have to hiccough and you would be in the drink."

At Scampton, tight security measures had been enforced since day one. Telephone wires were tapped. Guards were stationed around the compound. Policemen in plain clothes eavesdropped on the crews. All letters were censored. One incident arose that April when one of the airmen telephoned his girlfriend to tell her that he could not leave the base that night because he was going on a special operation. Gibson reamed the young flier out in the presence of the entire squadron and threatened to court-martial him or anybody else if that kind of talk occurred again. It didn't.

As testing at 60 feet was introduced, Gibson instituted more changes. He had all the Lancasters' radios equipped with the same VHF sets used in British fighters. As a precaution, he insisted on two sets in his own Lancaster, *G-George*. In addition, every pilot now had a second altimeter attached to the windshield for easy reference, saving him the trouble—and distraction—of looking down into the cockpit as the airplane neared the water. Also,

Gibson made the airplane roomier in the nose by asking the technicians to install stirrups for the mid-upper gunner (who had been moved up to the nose because of the placement of the bomb-spinning mechanism), thus preventing the gunner's feet from dangling in front of the bomb aimer's face.

Well into the first week in May, Gibson saw that the tension was high; the strain of the training was beginning to wear down the overtaxed aircrews. So he issued the entire squadron a three-day pass, with orders to keep their mouths shut. Gibson himself was becoming irritable and moody.

A few days later Gibson stood on the Parkstone shore and witnessed the first successful testing of Wallis' bomb. On May 15, Gibson briefed the pilots, navigators, bomb aimers and flight engineers of Squadron X (now tagged No. 617 Squadron) on the targets. The men were shown scale models of the Möhne, the Eder, and the Sorpe, complete with the surrounding terrain. Nothing was left out, including known flak positions.

One shocked airman blurted out, "At least it's not the *Tirpitz*." They all realized it would be one tough job. Gibson's final words were a bit tongue-in-cheek: "You'll all be given posthumous Victoria Crosses."

The next evening, 24 hours prior to takeoff, the gunners and wireless operators were briefed on the raid. After the meeting, Gibson received the sad news that his dog had been struck by a car and killed instantly. Too much was happening for Gibson to stop and mourn. He gave instructions to bury the dog at midnight. The following evening, at approximately the same time, the wing commander and his crews would be over the dams.

The next afternoon, Allied reconnaissance aircraft reported that the water was 4 feet from the tops of the three targeted dams. At 9 p.m., the seven-man crews boarded 19 Lancaster bombers, each with an all-up weight of 63,000 pounds.

Formation Two took off first, because its bombers had the longest distance to cover. The force consisted of five planes, piloted by Flight Lt. McCarthy, Sergeant Byers, Flight Lt. Barlow, Pilot Officer Rice and Flight Lt. Munro. Flying east across the North Sea, they were to turn south in order to fly between the German defenses, cross the Zuider Zee in Holland, and attack the Sorpe Dam from

One of the late-model Lancaster B.I. Specials used by No. 617 Squadron later in the war to carry the Grand Slam bomb.

the west. But trouble reared its ugly head before Formation Two left England. The leader, Brooklyn-born Joe McCarthy, quickly discovered a hydraulic leak in his Lancaster and had to return to base. He was finally airborne again 20 minutes late, having switched to a spare aircraft.

Gibson, leading Formation One, would take a more direct route into Holland. In this group were nine aircraft in three waves, which would leave England at 10-minute intervals. In the cockpits were Pilot Officer Knight, Squadron Leaders Young and Maudslay, and Flight Lts. Hopgood, Martin, Shannon, Astell and Maltby. The nine bombers were to attack the Möhne Dam first, breach it, and then head for the Eder Dam.

The five-ship Formation Three, consisting of Pilot Officers Ottley and Burpee and Flight Sgts. Townsend, Anderson and Brown, would take off last as the mobile reserve group, two hours after Formation Two.

As the sun disappeared and the moon rose, Gibson and his formation lifted their bombers off from the Lincolnshire countryside and set their course toward enemy territory. Over the North Sea they dropped down to 50 feet to avoid German radar.

It ultimately proved to be a bad night for Formation Two. Upon reaching the northern coast of Holland, Les Munro's aircraft, flying also at low level, was hit by flak badly enough to sever the inter-

com and radio lines. Munro cursed his bad luck and turned back to Scampton. Then, over the Zuider Zee, Geoff Rice slipped his bomber too low and struck the water. Although the pilot quickly pulled up, a hole was torn in the fuselage, and he had to return home. The German flak gunners were on the mark that night. Moments later the other two crews, piloted by Barlow and Byers, were shot down near the coast. Only McCarthy was left of the Sorpe team, and he was 60 miles behind Formation Two, which he was supposed to be leading.

Down as low as 40 feet over the Dutch countryside, Gibson, Martin and Hopgood flew tightly together, dodging telephone wires, houses and trees. The two other groups of Formation One were minutes behind Gibson's three-ship force. In the second group, Bill Astell's crew missed their turning point. Astell orbited away from the two other planes and was never seen again. Five aircraft were gone now.

Gibson, Martin and Hopgood reached the German border, where they met with some light flak. However, over the Rhine a line of tracers from a gun barge barely missed them. Two minutes later, three searchlights found *G-George*. Gibson's and Martin's forward gunners opened up. One light popped. The other two held and turned on Martin's bomber. Martin's gunners shot back. The searchlights quickly faded to the rear.

Gibson edged the team north on a course of 165 degrees magnetic, cutting between Soest and Werl. They were on the last leg. The moon, now at its highest and brightest, illuminated a set of hills looming ahead. They were at the target. Below was the mirror-like Möhne Lake leading up to the huge dam. The crews were awed at the size of the concrete structure and the expanse of water. Suddenly, the German flak, from as many as 10 guns, came at the bombers. Gibson began to circle the target with Hopgood and Martin, as he contacted the other aircraft in the formation. They all answered and flew into view except Astell.

"Well, boys, I suppose we'd better start the ball rolling," Gibson said calmly over his intercom.

As Gibson turned *G-George* around the eastern part of the lake, his bomb aimer, "Spam" Spafford, hit the switch to start the motor spinning the bomb at 500 rpm. Edging toward the surface at 240 miles per hour, Gibson eased the four-engine bomber down, then carefully began to level off over the smooth black sheet of mirroring water. The navigator flicked the spotlights on and watched for the figure eight to appear on the surface below.

Gibson held the bomber steady, aiming for the center point of the towers, seemingly oblivious to the fiery balls of flak closing in on him from the other side of the lake. His front gunner fired back. Spafford peered through the peephole of the aiming device, waiting for the towers to line up with the nails, while Gibson remained on course. There was no letup in the flak. Spafford saw the towers line up behind the nails and dropped the bomb.

Gibson roared over the dam, down into the valley, and banked back to take a look. The bomb exploded and a massive tower of water hung in the air at the wall. But when the spray subsided, the dam still held.

Hopgood made the second run of the night at Möhne Dam. But by now the German flak gunners had found the range and made several hits. Hopgood's wing began to burn before he reached the wall. His bomb aimer, presumed injured, dropped the bomb on the powerhouse on the other side of the dam. The plane's nose reached for the sky. It was apparent to all that Hopgood was trying to pull the damaged bomber up so that his crew could bail out. Moments later a bright flash lit the darkness. A wing separated, and the aircraft disintegrated into many flaming pieces three miles from the dam. Then the powerhouse went up in a huge explosion. Gibson waited for the billowing black smoke to clear, then called in Harold "Mickey" Martin...followed by Dinghy Young. Both runs were perfect, but neither crew breached the wall.

David Maltby went next, the fifth to try, and dumped his load on target. For a moment it looked as if he, too, had been unsuccessful until the radio transmitters in several bombers came to life. Pilots hooted and hollered. Below, a great flow of foaming water emerged from an enormous, 100-yard-long hole in the wall.

Gibson's excited wireless operator sent a prearranged signal back to Scampton to announce that the first objective had been destroyed. Gibson later related in his autobiography, *Enemy Coast Ahead*: "The whole valley was beginning to fill with fog from the steam of the gushing water, and down in the foggy valley we saw cars speeding along the roads in front of this great wave of water, which was chasing them and going faster than they could ever hope to go....The floods raced on, carrying everything with them as they went—viaducts, railways, bridges and everything that stood in their path. Three miles beyond the dam the remains of Hoppy's aircraft were still burning gently, a dull red glow on the ground. Hoppy had been avenged."

Gibson ordered Martin and Maltby to set course for Scampton. Then with Shannon, Maudslay, Knight and Young (who would assume command if Gibson was shot down) he flew east to the Eder Dam. The dam was difficult to find because of the surface fog that had rolled in. According to British sources, the Germans felt the Eder did not require gun protection because surrounding 1,000-foot-high hills provided a natural defense for the dam.

Ten days shy of his 21st birthday, David Shannon made five attempts at the enormous structure, but he was unable to line his bomber up on the run before he had to clear the hills with a steep climb. Impatient, Gibson ordered Maudslay to go in. On his third attempt, Maudslay erred. He was going too fast as he released the

bomb. It burst as soon as it hit the wall, catching his bomber above it. Another plane was lost in the night. Gibson ordered Shannon to try again. This time Shannon's timing was right, and he let the bomb go on target. The crews watched and waited. Following an explosive funnel of water, the Eder still stood defiantly.

The last hope now was Les Knight, an Australian. On his second run, his bomb aimer took aim and triggered the release of the deadly device on target. This time a massive wave soared into the air. The wall burst, and a flood rolled down the valley at 30 feet per second. Gibson's wireless operator sent his second coded message, indicating that the second objective had been destroyed. Gibson and the others in the formation headed for home.

The scene at the Sorpe Dam was similar to that at the Eder—fog, no guns, surrounded by hills. McCarthy, the sole survivor of Formation Two, found the dam, dropped his weapon after three tries,

In Raid on the Möhne Dam, *by Frank Wootton, Flight Lieutenant David Maltby's Lancaster clears its target while Wing Commander Guy Gibson's plane turns on its landing lights to draw German anti-aircraft fire away from the other attacking bombers.*

and then headed for Scampton, at the same time relaying the radio message that he had failed in his attempt.

The mobile reserve was now over Germany. Lewis Burpee was alerted to head for the Sorpe; he didn't answer. No one knew at that time that he had crashed near Hamm. Back in England his wife was about to have a baby. Canadian Ken Brown got the call next.

The Sorpe was the odd dam of the three, for it was earth-filled with a concrete wall to make it watertight. In order to bomb it, Brown had to drop his load parallel—not at a right angle—to the

An aerial photograph shows the breach in the Eder Dam on May 17, 1943. Between flooding and the loss of hydroelectric power to the Ruhr factories, the raid's results were devastating.

dam structure without any backspin at the mid-point of the upstream side of the dam. It was hoped that the bomb would roll down the sloping bank, away from the concrete section, and detonate at its predetermined depth. Wallis had decided that if the bomb was dropped at right angles to the structure, it would bounce over the sloping earth bank.

Locating the Sorpe was Brown's first problem. All low-lying reaches in the area were covered with fog, except for the steep hills. Unable to make a proper visual sighting, Brown flew to another area, believing that the first was not the proper location. Realizing his error, Brown returned to the original spot. The fog had cleared. Below was the Sorpe.

Brown tried eight runs. Each time, his Canadian bomb aimer, Sergeant Steve Oancia, could not judge his target in the mist with the wall and hills fast approaching. On the ninth attempt, Oancia

dropped a bundle of incendiaries in the trees near the approach to the dam. The next time Brown came around, Oancia saw the fire despite the mist, and he knew precisely where to drop the bomb. He let go and Brown thundered over the hills. The crew watched as a circular shock wave of air surrounded a towering blast of water. But when everything settled, the Sorpe remained unscathed.

Another flier, Ottley, set course for a secondary target, the Lister Dam, and never returned to base. With daylight fast approaching, the remaining bombers raced for England. They all made it, including Dinghy Young's crew, which had been hit by flak over Holland and had to settle for a ditching in the North Sea. It was Young's third sea rescue in his challenging RAF career. The nickname Dinghy was not without warrant.

The next day's photoreconnaissance pictures told only a part of the overwhelming cataclysm. The Eder and Möhne lakes were drained. Along a span of 50 miles, immense destruction had fallen upon the Ruhr region. Towns and cities were flooded. Roads, canals, bridges, power stations and railways were swept away. Power plants were destroyed. Factories were without electricity and water. Steel production had been halted. Livestock losses reached into the thousands.

The Germans sent hundreds of flak gunners to the remaining dams for protection against more attacks, and 20,000 workers from the coastal Atlantic wall were diverted to repair the Eder and Möhne dams before the autumn rains. They eventually accomplished the painstaking feat months later, using an enormous force of manpower that could have been employed elsewhere.

Along with all the industrial losses, 1,294 people drowned in the floods. More than half of these were from a Russian prisoner-of-war camp located below the Eder.

On the British side, 56 out of the 133 airmen in the raid were missing. Three had bailed out over enemy territory. It was a high price to pay for 617 Squadron, soon to be tagged in the media as "the Dambusters."

Decorations came through from Harris' headquarters, 34 in all, including a well-deserved Victoria Cross for Gibson.

Did Wing Commander Guy Gibson finally get the rest he had been seeking? Not immediately. He was ordered off "ops," though.

He sent his aircrew on a week's leave, his ground crew on three days' leave, then stayed on for two days at Scampton to write the mothers of the dead. He could have had his adjutant type up the usual appropriate form letters, but he insisted on notifying the mothers in his own handwriting. Then he proceeded to Cornwall to spend time with his wife. In the meantime, she was surprised to see her husband's picture across all the newspaper front pages, accompanied by accounts of the daring raid. All along, she had been under the impression that he was resting up at an RAF training school!

The King and Queen of England came to Scampton to inspect the squadron on May 27. Beforehand, Gibson let the King know that David Shannon was celebrating his twenty-first birthday. As the crews stood at attention in front of their bombers, the King stopped at Shannon and said, "You seem to be a very well preserved twenty-one, Shannon. You must have a party tonight."

In the thick of the ensuing nocturnal celebrations, a 617 Squadron officer turned to the birthday boy and said, "Shannon, I think you are drunk."

Flight Lieutenant Shannon was not at a loss for words. "If so, sir, it is by Royal Command."

Two months later, Gibson and England's Prime Minister Sir Winston Churchill left for America on a "show the flag tour." Back in England that year, Gibson wrote his autobiography, *Enemy Coast Ahead*. For a time he considered entering politics. But he rejected the idea and remained in the RAF at a desk job.

On July 11, 1944, Gibson was bitten by the flying bug again, when he saw his friend Mickey Martin put on an exhibition with a twin-engine Mosquito. "I'm fed up with sitting on my tail. I'm going back on ops," Gibson told Martin.

Gibson's superiors tried to talk him out of it. They wasted their time. In September, Gibson was in the pilot seat of a Mosquito, acting as Master Bomber for 5 Group on an RAF raid near the Rhur. When it was over, the pilots heard him say, "OK, chaps. That's fine. Now beat it home." On the way back, Gibson's plane was hit by flak and he crashed into a hillside in Holland. The Dutch buried him there, along with his navigator, Squadron Leader J.B. Warwick.

Interest in the famous raid on the dams continued after the war.

Six hours after the raid, water cascades into the Ruhr Valley through the 100-foot hole in the Möhne Dam.

A movie was produced in 1955 called *The Dambusters*, starring British actor Richard Todd as Gibson. But the legend of Gibson and the raid lives on from there. The operation is still talked about today. It's surprising how many school-aged youngsters are familiar with the story of Guy Gibson and the Dambusters.

The surviving aircrews of 617 Squadron have gotten together for the occasional reunion over the years, when stories of bravery over the Eder, the Möhne and the Sorpe are rehashed in fond tones over a drink or two. Perhaps the passage of years has stripped away some of the severity of those terrifying times and replaced it with memories of lighter moments, such as that evening in March, 1943, when an overworked, young Oxford-educated RAF wing commander entered the Scampton mess for the first time and asked the bartender for two beers—one for him and one for his faithful four-legged companion.

XVI

LUFTWAFFE'S INTRUDERS OF THE NIGHT

Just when the British airmen thought their bombers were home free,
Operation Gisela's night intruders unleashed an ambush.

By Timothy J. Kutta

The British tail gunner relaxed in his cramped turret. It had been a long night over Germany. The constant threat of German night fighters had kept him anxiously alert. As the bombers crossed over the white cliffs of Dover, however, he knew he was safe.

Suddenly the night exploded, as bright tracers arced across the sky toward the bomber. Cannon rounds slammed into the plexiglass turret and rear fuselage. The startled gunner died before he realized that German night-intruder aircraft had crossed the English Channel and were now attacking the returning British bombers over their home ground.

Operation Gisela had begun.

Within the first two years of World War II, both Britain and Germany had launched concentrated night-bombing campaigns against one another's cities—and both in turn had created specialized night-fighting organizations to protect themselves. The British modified the Bristol Beaufighter and the de Havilland Mosquito to operate as night fighters. The Germans took the Messerschmitt Me-110, the Junkers Ju-88 and the Dornier Do-17 and turned them into night fighters. In addition, both countries set up defensive systems that placed listening posts, searchlights and anti-aircraft batteries along the most likely routes night bombers would use. A sophisticated system of control was established to allow the night fighters to operate without fear of being shot down by their own forces.

By 1943, German night bombing of England had been reduced to a few occasional raids. The number of British raids against the Reich, however, had grown substantially. In October 1941, the British had flown 2,051 sorties against the Germans; the number increased to almost 8,000 sorties during 1943. In addition, the British had developed new and bigger bombers such as the Avro Lancaster. Each sortie now dropped three times the bomb weight of a 1941 sortie.

The Germans, in turn, increased their night-fighter force while trying new tactics. In addition to inter-

Searchlights from a German city probe the night for attacking Avro Lancasters of Royal Air Force Bomber Command, in Night Raiders, *by Stan Stokes.*

A German Nachtjäger *crew plays chess between missions. At night, they played a deadlier game, using radar and cannon as they matched wits with their RAF counterparts.*

cepting the British bombers as they flew over Germany, they began flying intruder missions. Intruders were highly specialized night fighters, with specially trained crews. They did not intercept enemy bombers over the Reich but rather flew deep into Britain and circled enemy airfields, waiting to attack the bombers as they began their landing approach.

Bomber pilots returning to base after a mission were tired; all their concentration was required just to get the airplane on the ground. It was customary for the bombers to turn on their navigation lights when they were close to their base in order to avoid collisions with other returning aircraft. Friendly airfields also turned on the runway lights when the bombers neared. All of those factors made attacking bombers over their own airfields much more profitable than hunting them over their targets.

The psychological impact of the German intruders far outweighed the few bombers they would actually destroy. Tired bomber crews were forced to take evasive action in an area congested with other aircraft. In addition, the British bombers were

flying at a low altitude when they encountered intruders, and many of them, in an attempt to get away, flew into the ground or other nearby obstacles. Also, when an attack started, the British airfields turned out the lights and activated their defenses. No aircraft were allowed to land. Many bombers that were low on fuel, or had suffered battle damage, crashed as they attempted to reach auxiliary airfields.

The Germans first used intruders in 1940. Intruder missions were only flown by the most experienced night-fighter crews. Because there were only a few such crews, the number of kills attributed to intruders grew slowly. The British lost only five aircraft to intruder attacks in 1940.

In 1941, German intruders shot down 85 British aircraft, but in early 1942, Adolf Hitler ordered the intruders to cease operations over England. The British night attacks were growing in intensity, and the *Führer* wanted the German people to see British bombers being shot down over the Reich. An enemy bomber shot down over England did not have the same immediate psychological effect on German resolve as one shot down over Düsseldorf.

By August 1943, the night-bombing raids over Germany were getting worse. *Generalmajor* Josef Schmid, who took over as the head of Germany's night fighters in the summer of 1943, decided that the best way to stop the British night bombing was to launch a massive intruder raid on their airfields. Regular German night fighters would attack the bombers as they penetrated the Reich. When the bombers turned for home, Schmid would launch all his intruders. They would follow the bombers back to their airfields and destroy them when they tried to land.

The German plan included four waves of night fighters. The first wave would consist of Messerschmitt Me-110s that would pursue the bombers over Germany to keep them under attack and observation for as long as possible.

The second wave would include Messerschmitt Me-410A-1s that would take off from northern France. Their mission: saturate British night-fighter defenses and lure the British night-fighter force away from the rest of the German planes.

The third wave would consist of Junkers Ju-88 intruders that would attack the bombers as they tried to land, as well as sow airfields with iron spikes designed to puncture the tires of British planes as they landed. Some of the planes would also carry small bombloads to attack the airfield facilities.

The fourth wave would also be composed of Junkers Ju-88s, which would leave about an hour after the third wave. Their mission was to reinforce the initial intruders and to attack the alternate airfields used by the bombers.

Schmid planned to use all 700 aircraft of his night-fighter force in the attack. He would issue the plan to his units and wait for the British to launch a big raid. Once one was detected, he would issue a simple code word to his units that would signal them to execute the raid. The Germans estimated that they would destroy 300 bombers in the raid. Losses of that magnitude were certain to stop Britain's night-bombing campaign for a few months. The respite would allow the Germans to regroup and rebuild. The plan was brilliant, simple, and had the potential to reap great rewards. However, it was not accepted by the high command.

Although Schmid's domain was the night sky over the Reich, cross-Channel attacks were the responsibility of *Generalmajor* Dietrich Peltz. Neither Peltz nor any of the other Nazi high officials was particularly enamored with the intruder plan. The thought of a large portion of the German night-fighter force over England for several hours was not a pleasant prospect for those officials. If a substantial number of intruders were shot down, the German night-fighter force would suffer. The plan was shelved despite Schmid's repeated attempts to get it approved.

Thousand-plane British raids against German cities became more and more frequent. German night-fighter losses were also rising, as new models of British de Havilland Mosquito night fighters were having a telling effect on the German night-fighter force. In addition, British intruders began flying patrols around the German night-fighter bases. Increasingly, German night fighters were being shot down as they tried to take off or land. The *Luftwaffe* would have to do something drastic to redress its losses. When General Schmid resubmitted his plan for the massive intruder raid in October 1944, the high command had come to appreciate the value of a massive strike against the British night-bombing force. Schmid was given the go-ahead and told to launch the raid at the earliest

moment. He spent two weeks redesigning the plan to accommodate the new aircraft and weapons now in the inventory.

One of the new aircraft was the Junkers Ju-88G-6c, a twin-engine medium bomber, heavily modified for its role as a night fighter. It was equipped with two new 1,750-hp Junkers Jumo 213A in-line, liquid-cooled engines. The plane had a maximum speed of 360 mph while carrying a crew of three. It was armed with four 20mm cannons in a gun pack under the fuselage, and many of the aircraft also carried two 20mm cannons atop the fuselage behind the cockpit, pointed forward and upward at a 20-degree angle. The arrangement was called *Schräge Musik* ("jazz music"). It allowed the night fighter to shoot the bomber from below and slightly behind, where British aircraft designers had left a conspicuous blind spot in the crew positions.

The night fighters were also equipped with the latest airborne interception radar, which could pick up targets as close as 660 feet and as far away as three miles. They were equipped, as well, with a tail warning system that alerted the crew if enemy radar had detected their plane.

The crews of the night-fighting force received their briefing on the new raid on December 1, 1944. A total of 150 Junkers Ju-88G intruders from I, II and III *Gruppen* of *Nachtjagdgeschwader*-2 (NJG-2), III and IV *Gruppen* of NJG-3, III *Gruppe* of NJG-4 and III *Gruppe* of NJG-5 were earmarked for the raid.

The intruders would cross the coast at low level, below British radar, in order to avoid detection. Crews were briefed on British airfield lighting, night-landing procedures and night-fighter warning procedures. The operation would be activated with two code words. "Zeppelin" would tell the night fighters that a massive British raid appeared to be forming. "Gisela" would send the intruders to England.

The crews were briefed and the operation was ready for launch by mid-December. Until it was activated, the night-fighter crews would continue to intercept British bombers flying over the Reich. There would be no lull in operations to alert the British.

Britain's aerial defenses had lapsed substantially by December 1944. The *Luftwaffe* had stopped its night bombing many months before, and the RAF had only three night-fighter squadrons guard-

The versatile Junkers Ju-88 bomber was pressed into service as a night fighter to counter the British threat. This 1943 version, a Ju-88C-6b, carries a FuG 202 Lichtenstein BC radar array. Later types carried progressively more sophisticated radar and armament.

ing the coast. There was still a substantial number of anti-aircraft guns and searchlights guarding the approaches to the British Isles, but the efficiency of their crews had dropped.

On January 1, 1945, one of the night-fighter crews that was to take part in the intruder raid was forced down behind Allied lines in France. Under interrogation, one of the crew revealed that the Germans were planning a massive night-intruder mission. That information, coming on the heels of Operation Bodenplatte, a huge low-level *Luftwaffe* raid on Allied airfields in Belgium and Holland, was taken quite seriously. The RAF immediately revised its intruder warning system. Night-fighter units were alerted; Bomber Command and its airfields were briefed. Anti-aircraft guns were also given greater freedom to shoot at unidentified planes after dark.

The RAF launched 817 bombers against targets in the Münster area on March 3, 1945. The *Luftwaffe* monitored the volume of air traffic as the bombers took off from their various bases in England and determined that this was the day to launch Operation Gisela. Crews were briefed on last-minute details of the raid and moved to their waiting airplanes.

The first wave of night intruders left their airfields for England at 11 p.m. Shortly after midnight, a Ju-88 caught up with a Boeing Flying Fortress operated by a British crew over the coast of England. In a short engagement the Fortress was damaged and the intruder disappeared into the evening sky. The bomber crew, however, alerted its base, which passed on the chilling news: German intruders were back over England.

The commander of Oulton Airfield, near Norwich, reported an "unknown" airplane flying over his airfield. Shortly thereafter, a Mosquito of No. 100 Squadron was shot down. Six minutes after midnight a Fortress from No. 214 squadron was shot down as it tried to land at Oulton. Another Fortress was also attacked but escaped with only minor damage.

The reports alerted Bomber Command, which realized that Operation Gisela was underway. Intruder alerts were issued to all units and airfields. British bombers immediately began to divert to airfields in the far west of England, out of the range of the early wave of intruders.

Unfortunately, many of the diverted bombers were shot down by intruders of the fourth wave, which had taken off later than the earlier waves and were able to reach the outlying RAF bases. Along the way the Ju-88Gs also caught up with many bombers on training missions. Those, too, were quickly shot down. Other British bombers returning from the Münster raid could not divert to other airfields. Bombers that had suffered battle damage, were low on fuel, or had wounded crewmen on board needed to land immediately.

Although the pilots and crewmen of returning British bombers had been alerted to the presence of intruders, avoiding them was still a difficult matter. The typical defense for a bomber pilot against an intruder attack was to throw his plane into a violent diving turn called a corkscrew maneuver, designed to throw off both the radar and the aim of the German intruders. Although the maneuver was quite effective, it required several thousand feet of altitude to accomplish successfully. Several bombers attempting the corkscrew forgot that they were already at a low altitude. One Lancaster, trying to avoid a night intruder, dove into the ground at its home airfield. The biggest piece of the bomber that was recovered was 4 feet long.

Operation Gisela would continue until 2:15 a.m.; by then, most of the bombers, including the stragglers, had returned to their bases or had landed at alternate airfields. The last bomber attacked was a Lancaster, which managed to avoid damage by eluding its attacker. With that, the intruders dropped from British radar as they flew low across England and returned to their bases in Germany. The last of the night fighters landed at their bases just before dawn.

The British still continued to lose airplanes even after the Germans were gone. The British anti-intruder night fighters were still airborne, chasing the last Ju-88s and patrolling the coast in search of others. Several were damaged or destroyed as they tried to land in the early morning darkness.

A Mosquito of No. 68 Squadron was the last official casualty

All in vain: Grounded by shortages of fuel and spare parts, Ju-88Gs await disposal on a German airfield following the Nazi surrender on May 8, 1945.

of the operation. The aircraft's landing gear would not come down, and an engine failed. Although those were usually minor emergencies for a combat pilot, they were too much for the exhausted Mosquito crew. The airplane crashed and burned at Coltishall Airfield.

The results of the intruder raid were less than satisfactory for the Germans. The night intruders could definitely claim 16 bombers destroyed during the operation. They could not count the ones damaged, the ones that flew into the ground or the ones that crashed while trying to land. In return, the Germans lost five Ju-88s over England, with eight crews missing and presumed dead after crashing in the North Sea on the return flight. Three intruders crashed during takeoff; six sustained major damage during the operation, but the crews bailed out over Germany; and 11 other aircraft received some damage but made it back to friendly airfields.

A check of RAF records shows that 34 bombers were destroyed

or damaged beyond repair on the night of the raid. In addition, the Germans had managed to throw Bomber Command into confusion. British bombers had been forced to land at alternate airfields all over England. It would be several days before the various squadrons could reunite their crews and airplanes at their respective airfields.

Many of the damaged bombers had landed at airfields that did not have the facilities to repair them. It would take about a week to get the necessary ground crews and repair parts to those airfields, fix the bombers, then return them to the proper airfields.

The chaos, confusion and losses caused by Operation Gisela motivated the British authorities to beef up both the ground and night-fighter defenses around England. The redistribution of forces allowed the Germans about one week of respite from Bomber Command and British night-intruder missions.

At that point in the war, 150 night fighters were not going to destroy Bomber Command. But if the German raid had been repeated, there is no doubt that the British would have had to react more extensively. In order to get the intruders out of Britain, they would have had to pull all their night fighters, plus those of the Americans, back to England. That action would have returned the night air initiative to the German night fighters.

All in all, the raid gave the German night-fighter force one last chance to slow or stop the British night bombing of the Reich. By March 1945, however, it was a case of too little, too late. The Reich was collapsing under the day and night bombing, and victorious Allied armies were pressing the borders of the Reich from the east and west. It was only a matter of weeks before the "1,000-year Reich" would come crashing down, and with it any hope of last-ditch measures like Operation Gisela.

XVII

THE SURRENDER FLIGHT THAT ALMOST FAILED

Aircraft provided the fastest means of transporting Japanese delegates to and from the surrender talks—but their trip was plagued by tricky timing and airplane problems.

By Robert C. Mikesh

"The cabin was dark, with only the lights seen ahead from the cockpit," recalled a former Imperial Japanese Army lieutenant. "The droning noise from the engines had a soothing sound, which put most of us to sleep, exhausted from our mission to General [Douglas] MacArthur's headquarters in Manila. I tried to sleep, but my mind kept racing over the events of the past 36 hours—first, our flight from Tokyo to Manila, and then meeting with MacArthur's staff to discuss the surrender of our country. Finally, there were the tiring hours that followed, as I meticulously translated into Japanese the documents that would finalize surrender arrangements.

"A shift of my left foot confirmed for me that my briefcase was still safely at my side on the cabin floor. Inside were the important documents we were carrying to our emperor that contained the American demands for assuring a safe and effective surrender of our country to Allied forces."

The experience about to unfold, as told by Harumi Takeuchi, left an indelible memory in his mind. He was one of two interpreters and translators in a group of 16 Japanese officers sent to Manila by Emperor Hirohito in August 1945 to assist Allied forces with the surrender and occupation of Japan. Negotiations had gone smoothly, but an event was about to take place that could result in grave mistrust between Japan and the United States.

Takeuchi continued: "I must have dozed, for I was startled when I felt a hand firmly shaking my shoulder. In the dim glow of the cabin, I recognized one of the pilots as he shouted to us, 'We're going to ditch! Everyone, life jackets on!'

"The engines sounded as though they were running smoothly. But I hastily donned my life preserver as I was told to do and, after further instructions, covered my head with my hands to prepare for a crash

In Michael P. Hagel's painting, two North American B-25s of the 345th Bomb Group escort two specially marked Japanese Mitsubishi G4M1s as they fly to Ie Shima to Surrender.

The first G4M1 comes in for a landing at Birch Airstrip on Ie Shima.

landing. I was totally confused as to what was taking place.

"I pressed the leather briefcase between my chest and lap. My mind was filled not only with thoughts of my own danger, but also with the consequences of losing those surrender instructions. Would the tedious hours of conferences in Manila—the product of which I was clutching—disappear with me into the inky water below? But incomparably more important would be the reactions from both opposing forces when it became known that the Japanese delegations and the surrender arrangement plans had not reached Tokyo. Would either side—or both—believe that the other had perpetrated an act of deception, and so continue the fighting, with the loss of many more lives?"

The roar of the engines diminished, followed by a terrifying shudder and a scraping sound as the plane hit the first wave. Then, after what seemed like an eternity of silence and being motionless

in space, came the agonizing impact as the plane bellied into the black water.

In Tokyo, lights burned all that night in the quarters of the newly appointed Japanese prime minister, Prince Naruhiko Higashi-Kuni, uncle-in-law of the emperor. Troubling thoughts filled his mind— it was well past the time of the delegation's expected return. Had Japan's *Tokko Tai* (air attack units) made good their threat to shoot down the surrender delegation, thus refusing to allow their country to surrender? Or could this be an American trick? Had they made prisoners of the envoys for some unknown reason while the envoys were in Manila?

The emperor was also vitally concerned. Although 3 to 4 million Japanese soldiers were still poised against an invasion, the emperor had responded in good faith to the demands of the supreme commander of the Allied powers once the surrender decision had been reached.

Chaos and confusion had reigned throughout Japan following the emperor's announcement of surrender—the first such announcement in the nation's history. Three hours after the emperor had spoken, Japan's cabinet, led by Prime Minister Kantaro Suzuki, had offered to resign. But the emperor ordered them to function until a new cabinet could be formed by Suzuki's successor, Prince Higashi-Kuni.

Japan's situation was entirely different from Germany's situation a few months earlier. The Japanese government was intact, and the military services were still organized. Imperial General Headquarters, within the limits of its communications, still exercised control over the armed forces. It was through the military that initial surrender and occupation arrangements with the Allied forces would be made. General MacArthur, supreme commander of the Allied forces, conducted most of his communications through the Imperial General Headquarters.

The language barrier was formidable. At headquarters, Lieutenant Takeuchi and his colleague Lieutenant Sadao Otake were made responsible for translations. Otake, who was assigned to the intelligence branch of Imperial General Headquarters, recalled that "after the emperor's surrender announcement at noon on August 15, 1945, the directives from General MacArthur's headquarters

A color photograph of one of the arriving G4M1s shows how effective the white finish and green crosses were in setting the planes apart; the special markings contrasted conspicuously with the green camouflage and red hinomaru *insignias of a wartime Betty bomber.*

mounted and had to be handled most delicately." One of the messages read, in part: "Send emissaries [to Manila] at once to the Supreme Commander for the Allied Powers with information of the disposition of the Japanese forces and commanders, and fully empowered to make any arrangements directed by the Supreme Commander for the Allied Powers to enable him to receive the formal surrender."

Some ranking Japanese officers at headquarters thought the delegation would be responsible for signing the surrender agreements; others believed differently.

Otake boldly suggested, "Let's ask!" Educated in the United States, he had learned the direct approach, quite the opposite of typical Japanese methods. Thus, on August 16, a message was sent asking for clarification of a phrase, "certain requirements for carrying into effect the terms of surrender."

General MacArthur, with a good grasp of the Japanese mind, fully understood the nature of the question. He replied that signing the surrender terms would not be among the tasks of the Japanese representatives in Manila.

The day before the envoys' departure, Otake and Takeuchi were told they would be interpreters for the delegation headed by Lt. Gen. Torashiro Kawabe, deputy chief of the army general staff. "The thought of being confronted by the Americans under these circumstances did not bother me as one might suspect," Otake recalled, "but this was not so with others in our group. Though it was a distasteful task, it was the emperor's wish, and all of us prepared for our respective areas of responsibility."

At daybreak on August 19, members of the delegation met at Haneda Airport on the edge of Tokyo Bay. The airplane waiting for them was a Japanese version of the Douglas C-47 (DC-3), painted white and marked with green crosses as MacArthur had directed. They took off from Haneda at 0611 hours, and landed at Kisarazu Airfield on the east side of the bay 14 minutes later. There, the delegates were divided into two groups of eight each, then hustled aboard two twin-engine bombers. Both of those airplanes also were painted white and marked with green crosses, just as the transport had been. Both bombers were airborne by 0707, heading for Allied territory.

Otake continued: "I had heard of the many threats by resistance groups to prevent our departure for these surrender negotiations. However, there had been no signs of resistance along the road or even from onlookers at the airfields. The original instruction received from the Americans was to depart on the 17th. We found it impossible to make all the safety precautions for the flight by that time, mainly due to the reorganization of our government. We asked for various changes. In reply we were advised that the intended measures were satisfactory and were promised every precaution to ensure the safety of the emperor's representatives.

"It was learned that Captain Yasuna Ozono, the commander of the 302nd *Kokutai* (naval air group) at Atsugi Airfield near Tokyo, had pledged his forces to intercept and destroy the transport planes before they could reach American-controlled airspace. I did not hear until later that he had committed *hara-kiri* the night before our departure when he learned that he was not fully supported by his officers.

"Our aircraft was a similar version of the Mitsubishi Navy Type 1 land attack bomber, one that had been converted to transport duties [and was] known as a G4M1-L2. All of this type had the Allied nickname of 'Betty.' There were bucket seats along each side for 20 passengers, which proved most uncomfortable through the many hours of sitting. [The second airplane was a G4M1 of the same basic bomber type, but field-modified for transport duties.]

"For no apparent reason, I remember most vividly an empty gasoline can that rolled on the floor as our cigar-shaped bomber wallowed through the air. As none of us were 'men of the air,' we were somewhat timid to assert ourselves about anything to do with the craft. But after several hours of the can's annoying rolling, we finally took it upon ourselves to set it upright on the floor.

"We approached the southern tip of Kyushu at 1115, and soon afterwards, I could see that we were being escorted by 12 American P-38s, weaving back and forth overhead. Soon we were joined by two North American B-25s, and I was summoned into the cockpit, as our pilots were unable to converse on the radio with the Americans. The B-25s merely wanted to confirm our identity and find out who was on board. They advised us to follow their escort to the prearranged landing field on Ie Shima island." For this journey into Allied airspace the two aircraft were to use the identifying call signs of Bataan 1 and Bataan 2. However, the significance of this irony was not fully understood by the Japanese aircrews.

The escorting Lockheed P-38 Lightnings were from the 49th Fighter Group. The group was worthy of this mission, for it had more confirmed air victories than any other group in the Far East. While providing top cover for the Bettys, the B-25s from the 345th Bomb Group "Air Apaches" moved in as escorts. Six planes, in flights of two, had been dispatched to escort the Japanese to their home base at Birch Airstrip, Ie Shima, an island a few miles northwest of Okinawa.

The lucky pair of B-25s to first spot the Bettys were Mitchells from the 498th and 499th bomb squadrons, piloted by Majors Jack McClure and Wendall Decker, respectively. They closed in on the formation, McClure taking the lead and Decker closing the formation so that no other aircraft would cut in and "spoil their show." As the formation came in for landing, however, a stray Mitchell cut into the pattern, causing the first Betty to go around for another attempt.

At 1240, the first of the two planes landed on the coral airstrip at Ie Shima. There, four months earlier, Ernie Pyle, the Pulitzer Prize–winning war correspondent, had been killed during the invasion of the island. To onlooking American GIs, the landing aircraft meant the realization of what they had been fighting for from one island to another. The Japanese inside the aircraft were well aware of those feelings. Lieutenant Takeuchi recalled: "As our plane approached the runway, we saw what seemed to be thousands of American soldiers forming a solid ring around the field. It was obvious that this was not security, but merely curiosity. But so many!

"A sudden jolt; our plane contacted the runway firmly, only to become airborne again for a few moments. I learned later that our pilot was also so impressed by the crowds of Americans that he neglected to lower the landing flaps, causing a higher sink rate than expected.

"The moment of being confronted by our former enemy had arrived. After a pause, General Kawabe rose firmly to his feet and strode to the door. My own fears and uneasiness were put aside with the thought of the heavy burden placed upon this man and the personal anxiety he must be undergoing."

Heat and a bright glare from the sunbaked coral surged into the aircraft as the door was opened. General Kawabe stepped out, with hundreds of eyes upon him. His officers followed by rank. The second aircraft was parked immediately behind the first and its passengers deplaned. News photographers were everywhere.

The Japanese moved toward the small delegation of waiting Americans. No salutes or any form of greeting were exchanged. Kawabe stepped forward to the senior American officer and handed him his credentials. Then the group was motioned into the shade of an American Douglas C-54 four-engine transport that would take them the rest of the way to Manila.

Lieutenant Otake continued: "Standing beside the senior American officer was a darker-skinned American acting as interpreter. Very formally, instructions were passed to him with the intention of their being relayed to us in Japanese. It was here that I would have broken out in uncontrolled laughter had the tenseness of the situation not prevented it. I could not hear the words in English, but only a few words the 'interpreter' relayed to us sounded anything at all like Japanese.

"When this gibberish ended, we were motioned to board the American craft that was to take us to Manila. We left with the feeling that the Americans were fully satisfied they had flawlessly conveyed their message to us, yet I had no idea of one word that was said."

Japanese and American delegates conduct surrender negotiations at General Douglas MacArthur's headquarters in Manila on the Philippine island of Luzon, on August 20, 1945.

After the C-54 took off, it stayed beneath the scattered clouds as it passed over nearby Okinawa. Here, the Japanese could see the military might being amassed below for Operation Olympic, the planned invasion of Japan. The magnitude was beyond anything the Japanese could have imagined.

En route to Manila, the Japanese were served American box lunches, pineapple juice, and coffee with plenty of sugar, a commodity that had been scarce in Japan for many years. In return, they offered the Americans Japanese cigarettes and tips in U.S. currency, but both were politely refused.

The C-54 landed at Manila's Nichols Field at 1800. The Japanese envoys were received correctly but coolly. To meet the Japanese, who were small in stature, MacArthur had deliberately selected one of his tallest officers, Maj. Gen. Charles A. Willoughby, his chief of intelligence.

United States Army and Navy personnel stationed at Ie Shima congregate atop one of the unique-looking Japanese surrender aircraft to commemorate the occasion.

Otake recalled: "We left Nichols Field in a parade of staff cars. As we drove down Dewey Boulevard [later Roxas Boulevard], Filipinos along the way paused to stare. Seeing Japanese inside the cars, many onlookers sneered and loudly shouted the Japanese words '*Baka Yaro*' at us [English equivalent: SOB]. I could not help but jokingly remark, 'Is that all we were able to teach these people while we occupied the Philippines?'"

The motorcade proceeded to Rosario Manor, where the delegation was to be billeted. Few other buildings remained standing in the area. To the delight of the Japanese envoys, a complete turkey dinner was waiting for them. Because of the acute food shortage in Japan, many of them had not tasted meat for years. "I felt I was partaking once again of an American Thanksgiving dinner," Otake remarked.

"We had no sooner finished dinner," he continued, "than an American colonel stood before us. It was time for the conference to begin. The colonel requested that the Japanese officers leave their swords behind. I sensed a tenseness throughout our delegation, and our eyes all turned toward our general, wondering what his reply would be.

"With little hesitation, Kawabe's words to be passed on to the colonel were, 'Sir, our swords are part of our uniform. We would like to be permitted to wear them, but we will leave them outside the conference room with our hats, if you desire.' The colonel nodded, and the procedure was followed."

It was almost 2100 when the Japanese arrived at city hall. In the conference room, the Japanese and American officials sat on opposite sides of the table, with counterparts facing each other. Each side was represented by specialists in such areas as supply, engineering and power facilities. Of special interest to the Americans were the harbor facilities at Yokohama and the landing field at Atsugi, which were to be the first staging bases for the occupation, then set to begin on August 25.

"Later, after some of us returned to Rosario Manor," Otake said, "there was much discussion of this early occupation date. Because of the unpredictable reactions of both the Japanese civilian and military elements, an attempted occupation at this early date might have its misfortunes.

"I brought this point up with an American lieutenant colonel who was assisting in translations. The question was whether or not we should attempt to have the date postponed. He said there was no harm in trying, which to me was a typical American attitude that I admired. Consequently, at the second conference, Kawabe again explained the problem.

"With little hesitation, Lt. Gen. Richard Sutherland, MacArthur's chief of staff, granted a three-day extension. This to us was but one example of the fairness with which the Americans handled many problems that arose. It was far different from the treatment we had expected, but this approach probably prevented consequences that the Japanese might not have been able to control."

The meetings continued through the night of August 19 and into the early morning hours of the 20th. As General Sutherland led the discussions, linguists translated, and photostats were made of the various reports, maps and charts the Japanese had brought

Standing in front of a delegation of Allied senior officers, General MacArthur presides over the final surrender ceremony aboard the battleship Missouri *on September 2, 1945.*

with them. Translators worked all night to put MacArthur's requirements into accurate Japanese.

It was vitally important that all documents be correctly translated so that surrender arrangements could be completed with min-

imum misunderstanding and maximum speed. Kawabe was handed the "Requirement of the Supreme Commander of Allied Powers." These directives set down demands concerning the arrival of the first Allied forces in Japan, the formal surrender ceremony aboard the battleship *Missouri*, plus the subsequent reception of the occupation forces.

The Manila conference was over. The Japanese had not once seen General MacArthur. His absence added great impact to his new position as Japan's military governor.

By early morning on August 20, the Japanese prepared to leave their billets. Hard candies, packed in tins, had been at their disposal. It had been so long since the men had had any sweets that several asked if they might take some to Japan. All received fresh cans of candy for the journey home.

Hospitality at the manor had been most gracious. Lieutenant Takeuchi was the keeper of the money purse for the group, but there had been no expenses. To express his group's appreciation, Takeuchi left a tip for the manor's employees. (The building had served as the Japanese Embassy during the occupation, and as the American Embassy after the American liberation. It later became known as the Rosario Apartments, and in that capacity few occupants or staff were aware of its wartime history.)

At Nichols Field, the Japanese again boarded the C-54 and were on their way to Ie Shima by 1300. Otake and Takeuchi were kept busy with further clarifications and translations of the vital documents that were divided between their two briefcases.

At Ie Shima, the group was informed that one of its aircraft had mechanical problems and could not be repaired until the following morning. Not all the Japanese could be transported in one aircraft. The group and the documents were purposely divided so that if one plane should have trouble, all would not be lost.

Kawabe asked for volunteers to remain behind until the airplane was fixed. Since living among Americans was not foreign to Otake, he volunteered, along with four others. They were assigned billets with American officers of equivalent rank.

Otake moved in with a nisei lieutenant, and they got along famously. Bottles of sake were opened while they stayed up most of the night discussing things they had in common—mostly the war.

The first of the two white Bettys had left Ie Shima late that afternoon at 1840. With the group aboard this transport was Lieutenant Takeuchi, in whose care were placed the conference documents. The aircraft had no inside lighting, and about an hour of daylight remained in which he could continue putting the documents in workable order for immediate use upon arriving in Japan.

"I did the best I could with the remaining daylight, and then packed the papers carefully into my briefcase," Takeuchi recalled. "Now that it was dark, the P-38s discontinued their escort and the tensions that we had felt for so many hours began to ease. A bottle of whiskey was passed around, and I began to relax."

The converted bomber droned toward Tokyo. It was almost midnight when the shocking command was given to prepare for a crash landing. Soon came the sickening sound of impact with the water. Then, "as I became aware of the lapping sound of the water around me," Takeuchi said, "I had the surprising awareness that I was still alive. The pilots stumbled from their compartment, one stopping to check on his passengers, the other moving directly to the rear door. As he opened it, water gushed in at a very great rate. I started moving toward the door, prepared to swim, briefcase and all. I saw the pilot step out, and expected to see him disappear beneath the inky water. To my surprise, the water came only to his knees, and the two pilots began carrying us on their shoulders to the beach. Miraculously, no one was seriously injured.

"The pilots had landed in the surf along a wide beach near Hamamatsu, about 130 miles short of Tokyo. I never did probe completely into the reason for the forced landing, but some thought that because of the language barrier a few of the fuel tanks were not serviced at Ie Shima, and enough fuel was not on board to reach Tokyo.

"Our plane had come down at 2345, and there was not a light to be seen. Shortly, a figure cautiously came from the shadows. After his request to identify ourselves, we found that he was a fisherman.

"He led us some distance to a telephone, and we called the nearby Hamamatsu Air Base to explain our predicament. They sent transportation for us, and by 0330 that morning we arrived at the base."

At 0700 on the 21st, Kawabe, Takeuchi and the other envoys left Hamamatsu with the surrender documents in an army heavy bomber. They arrived an hour later at Chofu Airfield on the west side of Tokyo. That same morning, Otake and his four associates left Ie Shima with their repaired aircraft for an uneventful flight to Kisarazu.

Prime Minister Higashi-Kuni promptly took Kawabe to the palace for a detailed report. He was glad to hear that both groups of the party were safe, but was far happier to learn that General MacArthur's terms for his nation were not as severe as he had feared. According to Higashi-Kuni: "The emperor was quite relieved. He was thankful not only for the safe return of all his envoys, but that the dark days of the war had now ended."

Photo and Art Credits

COVER: Robert Taylor, Courtesy of The Military Gallery, Ojai, California

Acknowledgments:
p. 2 Canadian Forces Photographic Unit

THE MEN
pp. 8-9 William B. Allmon Collection

I. Guts and Glory in the RAF
p. 11 Charles J. Thompson
pp. 13 & 14 William B. Allmon Collection
p. 15 Robert Taylor, Courtesy of The Military Gallery, Ojai, California
p. 17 William B. Allmon Collection

II. Flying Circus Over the Pacific
p. 19 Jack Fellows, ASAA, Cactus Air Force Art Project
pp. 21 & 23 Cactus Air Force Art Project
p. 24 John Stanaway Collection
p. 25 Cactus Air Force Art Project
p. 26 John Stanaway Collection

III. Air War's Top Ace
p. 29 Jerry Crandall, Eagle Editions Ltd.
pp. 31-35 Jerry Crandall Collection
p. 36 Harley Copic

IV. Butch O'Hare: "Friendly Fire" Victim?
p. 39 Michael P. Hagel, Hailstone Graphics
p. 41 National Archives
pp. 42-44 U.S. Naval Historical Center
p. 45 Hugh Polder, Hugh's Aviation Prints

V. Wolfpack at War
pp. 46-47 Jim Laurier
p. 48 William S. Phillips ©1990, Courtesy of
The Greenwich Workshop, Inc., Shelton, Connecticut
pp. 49-53 Jeffrey L. Ethell

VI. Battling the Zeros Over New Guinea
p. 57 Jack Fellows, ASAA, Cactus Air Force Art Project
p. 59 Richard J. Vodra
p. 61 National Archives
p. 63 Richard J. Vodra

THE MACHINES
pp. 66-67 Jerry Scutts Collection

VII. Zero: Flimsy Killer
p. 69 Tony Weddel, Glenn Illustrators
p. 70 National Archives
p. 71 Lance Kitchens, Squadron Ace Studios
pp. 72-73 National Archives

VIII. Eagle Flies a Mustang
pp. 74-75 Harley Copic
p. 76 Jeffrey L. Ethell
p. 77 George D. Guzzi, Jr., U.S. Air Force Art Collection
pp. 79-81 Jeffrey L. Ethell

IX. Avenger!
pp. 82-83 Robert Watts
p. 85 Jack Fellows, ASAA, Cactus Air Force Art Project
pp. 87-91 Jerry Scutts Collection

X. Buzz Bomb Blasts Britain
p. 95 Ronald Wong
pp. 96-102 Imperial War Museum

XI. The Bomb That Ended World War II
p. 105 Randy Green, The Aviation Art of Randy Green
p. 106 U.S. Air Force
p. 107 Craig Kodera ©1995, Courtesy of
The Greenwich Workshop, Inc., Shelton, Connecticut
p. 109 U.S. Naval Historical Center
p. 111 U.S. Air Force

THE MISSIONS
pp. 114-115 Canadian Forces Photographic Unit

XII. First Strike Against Japan
pp. 116-117 John D. Shaw, Liberty Studios, Clovis, California
p. 119 Jeffrey L. Ethell
p. 120 William S. Phillips ©1992, Courtesy of
The Greenwich Workshop, Inc., Shelton, Connecticut
p. 121 U.S. Air Force
p. 123 Craig Kodera ©1992, Courtesy of
The Greenwich Workshop, Inc., Shelton, CT

XIII. The Cactus Air Force: A Thorn in Japan's Side
p. 127 Robert Taylor, Courtesy of The Military Gallery, Ojai, California
pp. 128-130 National Archives via Cactus Air Force Art Project
p. 131 William S. Phillips ©1991, Courtesy of
The Greenwich Workshop, Inc., Shelton, Connecticut
pp. 132-134 National Archives via Cactus Air Force Art Project

XIV. Whose Kill Was It?
p. 137 Jack Fellows, ASAA, Cactus Air Force Art Project
pp 138-141 C.V. Glines
p. 143 Roy Grinnell, American Fighter Aces Association
pp. 144-147 C.V. Glines

XV. Ruhr Dam Raids
pp. 148-149 Nicholas Trudgian, Courtesy of The Military Gallery, Ojai, California
pp. 150-153 Canadian Forces Photographic Unit
p. 155 Frank Wootton
pp. 156-157 Canadian Forces Photographic Unit

XVI. Luftwaffe's Intruders of the Night
pp. 158-159 Stan Stokes, The Stokes Collection
p. 160 Cowles Photo Archive
pp. 162-163 Imperial War Museum

XVII. The Surrender Flight That Almost Failed
pp. 166-167 Michael P. Hagel, Hailstone Graphics
p. 168 National Archives via Robert C. Mikesh
p. 169 F. Hill via Jeffrey L. Ethell
pp. 171-172 National Archives via Robert C. Mikesh
p. 173 Jeffrey L. Ethell